# The Official Guide to
## THE
# Print Shop Ensemble III

# The Official Guide to

## THE

# Print Shop® Ensemble™ III

---

### SECOND EDITION

## James R. Caruso and Mavis E. Arthur

### SYBEX

San Francisco • Paris • Düsseldorf • Soest

Acquisitions Manager: Kristine Plachy
Developmental Editor: Dan Brodnitz
Editor: Ben Miller
Technical Editor: Tanya Strub
Electronic Publishing Specialist: Dina F Quan
Production Coordinator: Anton Reut
Book Designer: Catalin Dulfu
Technical Artist: Catalin Dulfu
Indexer: Matthew Spence
Cover Designer: Lynx Graphic Design

Library of Congress Card Number: 96-70210
ISBN: 0-7821-1992-1

Manufactured in the United States of America

10 9 8 7 6 5 4 3 2 1

*We'd like to dedicate this book to the developers of this incredibly versatile and imaginative program that makes artists of us all—the Brøderbund team. The next time you're in the Main Project Window, select Help menu ➤ About ➤ Credits to see a list of this great team.*

# Acknowledgments

This book was written with the assistance of a really super team in the marketing, public relations, customer service, and product management departments at Brøderbund Software, Inc. They not only provided us with anything we needed to make a great book but also assisted in making this the *official* book on the Print Shop Ensemble III. For all their help and confidence, we are grateful.

We'd also like to thank the team at Sybex who helped us to pull it all together and make it work, including Dan Brodnitz, developmental editor; Ben Miller, editor; Tanya Strub, technical editor; Dina Quan, electronic publishing specialist; Anton Reut, production coordinator; Catalin Dulfu, technical artist; and Matthew Spence, indexer.

# Contents at a Glance

| | Introduction | xxi |
|---|---|---|
| **Part One:** | **Getting Started** | **1** |
| 1 | **Creating Your First Project** | **3** |
| 2 | **Discovering Tools** | **29** |
| 3 | **Mastering Menus** | **55** |
| 4 | **Getting Help** | **95** |
| 5 | **Understanding Print Shop Projects** | **107** |
| 6 | **Creating Online Greetings** | **135** |
| **Part Two:** | **Managing Graphics** | **147** |
| 7 | **Working with Graphics Libraries** | **149** |
| 8 | **Creating Special Graphics** | **169** |
| 9 | **Importing Images** | **193** |
| 10 | **Exporting Graphics** | **203** |
| **Part Three:** | **Finishing Touches** | **213** |
| 11 | **Working with Text and Headlines** | **215** |
| 12 | **Creating and Merging Lists** | **245** |
| 13 | **Using the Idea Guide** | **263** |
| 14 | **Printing Made Easy** | **289** |
| **Appendices** | | **297** |
| A | **Installing and Uninstalling The Print Shop Ensemble III** | **299** |
| B | **Specialized Paper Sources** | **305** |
| | Index | 309 |

# Table of Contents

**Introduction**

**xxi**

## Part One: Getting Started
## 1

◆

### Chapter 1:
## Creating Your First Project

**3**

| | |
|---|---|
| Making a Project Decision | 4 |
| Starting a Project | 4 |
| Choosing a Method | 5 |
| Choosing a Size | 6 |
| Choosing an Orientation | 6 |
| Designing the Front of the Card | 8 |
| Selecting a Backdrop | 8 |
| Selecting a Layout | 12 |
| Creating a Headline | 14 |
| Editing Text | 17 |
| Moving Objects | 19 |
| Adding a Graphic | 20 |
| Designing the Inside of the Card | 22 |
| Selecting a Backdrop | 22 |
| Selecting a Layout | 23 |
| Adding Text | 24 |

Designing the Back of the Card    25

    Selecting a Graphic    26

    Putting a Frame around the Text Box    26

Endnotes    27

## Chapter 2:
## Discovering Tools

### 29

Starting the Project    30

Getting Acquainted with the Toolbar    32

Moving and Resizing Objects    34

    Moving a Single Object    34

    Moving Multiple Objects Together    35

    Resizing Graphics    35

    Resizing Headline or Text Blocks    37

Rotating Objects    38

    Rotating a Single Object    38

    Rotating Multiple Objects Together    39

Moving around in the Document    40

Adding Objects    41

    Understanding Placeholders    42

    Adding Objects with Placeholders    44

    Customizing Placeholders    45

    Changing the View    46

    Deleting Objects    46

    Flipping Objects    48

    Framing Objects    48

Undoing or Redoing Your Last Action    50

    Undoing Your Last Action    50

    Redoing Your Last Action    50

Coloring and Shading an Area    51

Endnotes    54

## Chapter 3:
# Mastering Menus

### 55

Using the File Menu                                          56
    Starting a New Project                                   57
    Opening an Existing File                                 57
    Saving a File                                            61
    Saving As                                                63
    Reverting to a Previously Saved Version                  63
    Choosing Preferences                                     64
    Printing a Project                                       66
    Setting Up Your Printer                                  69
    Previewing a Project                                     69
    Exiting the Program                                      70
Using the Edit Menu                                          70
    Undoing an Action                                        70
    Cutting Objects                                          71
    Copying Objects                                          72
    Pasting Objects                                          72
    Deleting Objects                                         73
    Duplicating Objects                                      73
    Selecting All                                            74
Using the Object Menu                                        75
    Adding Objects                                           75
    Editing Objects                                          76
    Adding Shadows to Objects                                79
    Framing an Object                                        80
    Putting Objects in Order                                 80
    Scaling an Object                                        81
    Rotating an Object                                       82
    Flipping Objects                                         83
    Locking and Unlocking Objects                            83
    Aligning Objects                                         83

Using the Project Menu    84
   Changing the Backdrop    85
   Changing the Layout    86
   Changing the Banner Length    86
   Blending the Colors on a Page    88
   Choosing Other Project Commands    90
Using the View Menu    90
Using the Extras Menu    91
   Using Smart Graphics    91
   Customizing Libraries    92
   Accessing Lists    92
   Exporting Graphics    92
   Connecting with the Internet    92
Using the Help Menu    92
Endnotes    93

## Chapter 4:
# Getting Help

## 95

Using the Main Help Screen    96
   Using Links    97
   Using the Help Chapters    98
Setting Up Help    99
Searching Help    100
Using the Help Menu Bar    102
   Using the File Menu    102
   Using the Edit Menu    102
   Using the Bookmark Menu    103
   Using the Options Menu    104
   Using the Help Menu    105
Finding Help in Dialog Boxes    105
Endnotes    105

## Chapter 5:
# Understanding Print Shop Projects
### 107

Common Design Elements                         108
  Selecting a Path                             108
  Choosing an Orientation                      110
  Browsing for a Backdrop                      111
  Selecting a Layout                           111
Project-Specific Design Elements               113
  Designing Greeting Cards                     113
  Designing Signs and Posters                  116
  Designing Banners                            118
  Designing Certificates                       120
  Designing Stationery                         121
  Designing Calendars                          123
  Designing Labels                             127
  Designing Photo Projects                     129
One Last Tip                                   131
Endnotes                                       132

## Chapter 6:
# Creating Online Greetings
### 135

Creating an Online Greeting                    136
Sending an Online Greeting                     136
  Setting Up Your Internet Connection          138
  Sending the Greeting inside Print Shop       140
  Sending as an Attachment                     142
Viewing an Online Greeting                     143
Accessing the Print Shop Connection            144
Endnotes                                       144

# Part Two: Managing Graphics
## 147

◆

## Chapter 7:
# Working with Graphics Libraries

### 149

| | |
|---|---|
| Types of Graphics | 150 |
| The Libraries | 151 |
| Navigating the Graphics Browser | 153 |
| Starting a Project | 154 |
| Broadening the Search Options | 155 |
| Searching by Category | 157 |
| Searching by Multiple Keywords | 157 |
| Searching with Project Text | 159 |
| Merging Graphics Libraries | 160 |
| Preparing to Merge Libraries | 161 |
| Starting the Merge | 163 |
| Modifying Graphics Libraries | 164 |
| Preparing to Modify a Library | 164 |
| Modifying a Library | 165 |
| Endnotes | 167 |

## Chapter 8:
# Creating Special Graphics

### 169

| | |
|---|---|
| Customizing Smart Graphics | 170 |
| Designing an Initial Cap | 171 |
| Designing a Number | 176 |
| Selecting a Timepiece | 178 |
| Naming Smart Graphics | 180 |
| Customizing Borders | 180 |
| Arranging a Border | 181 |

Choosing Border Graphics                      183
Saving a Custom Border                        186
Adding a Custom Border to a Project           186
Designing a Seal                              187
Adding a Graphic                              187
Adding Text                                   189
Saving a Customized Seal                      190
Endnotes                                      191

## Chapter 9:
# Importing Images

### 193

Importing Graphics                            194
Looking at Available Files                    195
An Importing Tip                              196
Importing Photos                              197
Cropping and Adjusting Photos                 199
Resizing and Adding Accessories               200
Endnotes                                      201

## Chapter 10:
# Exporting Graphics

### 203

Opening the Graphics Exporter                 204
Choosing a Graphic                            205
Exporting a Graphic                           206
Designating a File Type                       206
Choosing a Destination                        208
Exporting a Library                           209
Printing a Catalog                            209
Printing to File                              210
Exiting the Graphics Exporter                 211
Endnotes                                      211

# Part Three: Finishing Touches
## 213

◆

## Chapter 11:
# Working with Text and Headlines
### 215

Using Spell Check and Thesaurus 216
Checking Your Spelling 217
Choosing Your Words 218
Editing Text Blocks 221
Choosing Text Attributes 222
Using the Text Toolbar 224
Working with Headlines 226
Changing Headline Text Attributes 228
Choosing a Headline Shape 229
Customizing Headline Text 230
Working with Title Blocks 232
Choosing Type Styles for Title Blocks 232
Customizing a Title 233
Adding a Signature Block 234
Selecting a Block Type 234
Choosing Text Attributes for Signature Lines 235
Adding Text to Signature Blocks 236
Inserting Autographs 236
Adding a Word Balloon 238
Exploring Quotes and Verses 241
Endnotes 244

## Chapter 12:
# Creating and Merging Lists
### 245

| | |
|---|---|
| Creating Lists | 246 |
| Making an Address List | 246 |
| Making a Custom List | 250 |
| Modifying Lists | 253 |
| Merging Lists | 254 |
| Merging a List into a Project | 254 |
| Choosing a List to Merge | 256 |
| Selecting Merge Fields | 256 |
| Printing a List | 258 |
| Importing Lists | 260 |
| Exporting Lists | 261 |
| Endnotes | 262 |

## Chapter 13:
# Using the Idea Guide
### 263

| | |
|---|---|
| Party Ideas | 265 |
| Start with the Invitation | 265 |
| Make a Table Runner | 266 |
| Create a Place Card | 267 |
| Play a Game | 268 |
| More Party Ideas | 270 |
| Gift ideas | 271 |
| Making a Gift Label | 272 |
| Giving a Gift Certificate | 272 |
| Creating Money Envelopes | 274 |
| Sharing a Recipe | 276 |
| More Gift Ideas | 277 |

Holiday Ideas                                       278
    Creating a 3-D Card                         278
    Creating Personalized Ornaments             279
    Choosing Paper Chains                       280
    Counting Down the Days                      282
    More Holiday Ideas                          283
Building on an Idea                                 285
Endnotes                                            287

## Chapter 14:
# Printing Made Easy

### 289

Printing Specific Projects                          290
    Printing Banners                            290
    Printing Name Lists                         291
    Printing Labels                             291
    Printing Business Cards                     292
    Printing Envelopes                          293
    Printing Transfer Designs                   294
Troubleshooting Print Problems                      294
    Dealing with Partial Printouts              295
    Printing Imported Bitmaps                   295
    Slow Printing                               295
Endnotes                                            296

# Appendices
## 297

◆

### Appendix A:
# Installing and Uninstalling
# The Print Shop Ensemble III

## 299

Requirements                                    299
Installation Options                            300
   Options for Typical Installation          300
   Options for Full Installation              301
   Options for Custom Installation            302
Electronic Registration                         303
Uninstalling the Program                        304

### Appendix B:
# Specialized Paper Sources

## 305

Avery®                                          305
Beaver Prints™                                  306
Idea Art                                        306
Paper Access                                    306
Paper Direct®                                   306
Queblo®                                         307

### Index
## 309

# Introduction

You are in for a treat. You now own the latest version of the number one personal publishing software. With more than ten million copies sold, Brøderbund's Print Shop is without question the standard for graphics programs, letting you create a variety of projects with ease. Not only that, it's fun.

This newest version, called The Print Shop Ensemble III, is a 32-bit Microsoft Windows 95 application. It takes giant steps in making it even easier to create striking projects (a version for Windows 3.1 will be available soon). It keeps all the exciting features of past programs and adds:

- Half-fold greeting cards
- Approximately 500 more ready-to-print designs
- Approximately 700 more pre-written greetings, quotes, and verses
- Over 100 professionally photographed, scanned, and cleaned photo images
- Photo Accessories to add frames or graphics to your projects
- More than 5,500 graphics
- The ability to flip headline text blocks
- The ability to drag and drop to open, print, delete, and mail a project (through the Microsoft Exchange mailbox)
- More than 100 True Type fonts
- The Print Shop Idea Guide to get you thinking about creative ways to use the program
- Thesaurus
- Spell Checker

In other words, you have nearly unlimited creative possibilities.

What was great just got better with the release of The Print Shop Ensemble III.

Your mission is to learn how to make use of every feature. This book endeavors to help you accomplish your mission and push this program to its limits.

# Features of the Book

This book is designed as both a reference tool and as a hands-on guide, taking you step by step through the process of creating projects with The Print Shop Ensemble III, using the following features:

**Mission** Every chapter begins with a mission, an objective for that particular chapter to keep you motivated and informed about what lies ahead.

**Visuals** This book is full of illustrations, designed to make the reading simpler and the understanding more comprehensive. Print Shop is a graphics-intensive program. You'll see the creative use of a great many Print Shop graphics within the pages of this book.

**Hands-On Exercises** Chapter 1 sets the tone for the book by jump-starting you right into a project, involving you from the very beginning in the creative process with this versatile and interesting program. As you move from chapter to chapter, you'll work with the features that make this program truly outstanding as a creative tool. Every chapter will involve you in the intricacies and nuances of the program while putting you in control of the learning process.

**Special Projects** You'll have the chance to work creatively with ready-made projects as well as design a few new ones. You'll be encouraged to strike out on your own, to infuse your own ingenuity into the projects that fill these pages.

 Special notes call your attention to tips that might be helpful or to information that will save you time and frustration in the creative process.

**Endnotes** Every chapter ends with a wrap-up of what was covered in the chapter, followed by a preview of what lies ahead in the next chapter.

# Structure of the Book

This book is divided into three parts:

**Part One: Getting Started**  This part of the book gets you started on your first project and introduces you to the basics of the toolbar, the main menu, and the Help system. Finally, it takes you on a tour of the individual Print Shop projects, including creating online greetings.

**Part Two: Managing Graphics**  Your Print Shop graphics library has more than 5,500 graphics—and that's before you add your own. That's great, but with so many, how do you remember what's there, and how do you find them when you want to use them? This part of the book will give you tips on searching graphic libraries and suggest ways to analyze the structure and content of the graphics libraries so that you can customize them to suit your own areas of interest.

**Part Three: Finishing Touches**  Now that you know your way around Print Shop and you can manage all the graphics you'll ever need, this part of the book covers the final details of creating a project, such as working with text, creating and merging lists, and solving printing problems. (The importance of this last topic can't be overestimated: you may have the greatest project in the world, but if you can't print it out, who will know?) Also, we'll take you for a brief preview of the Idea Guide with some creative suggestions of our own.

Additionally, there are two appendices in this book. Appendix A tells you how to install, uninstall, and register The Print Shop Ensemble III. Appendix B tells you where to find special paper on which to print your perfect project.

In short, this book is designed to be not only instructive but also fun. We had fun writing it. We hope you'll have as much fun using it to learn everything there is to know about The Print Shop Ensemble III.

# Off You Go

While it is true that you will be able to create a good project without learning the finer points of Print Shop, it's equally true that you will be able to create a really terrific project if you take the extra time to learn what the program can do and how far you can push it with your creativity. The frustration factor will be much lower if you spend the time now to run through the basics of how the program operates, what it has to offer, and how you can make all this work for you and your projects.

You're about to take a journey through a truly exciting program. Enjoy the ride!

# Part One:

## Getting Started

# Creating Your First Project

## Your mission: to create a Print Shop project

◆

Being creative with Print Shop Ensemble III is, as they say, a piece of cake. The program gives you a multitude of choices each step of the way. No matter what the project—greeting card, sign, poster, banner, letterhead, calendar, label, certificate, business card, envelope, postcard, or an online greeting—your final product will truly be your own.

In this chapter, we'll go step-by-step through the process of creating a project with Print Shop. When you finish, you'll know the basics of working with Print Shop, enough to convince you of its versatility and your own ability to create unique projects. So let's make Print Shop do something that we can see and feel, and let's do it in a matter of minutes.

# ◆ Making a Project Decision

First, we need to decide what kind of project we want to create. For our purposes, let's say we're going on a cruise, and we're inviting our friends to join us for a shipboard party—a Bon Voyage party—right before we depart. So we need an invitation to the party.

With the help of our computer, Print Shop, and you, we are going to make an original invitation, one that will not only please us but tell our friends all about the party. We'll want to include the following information:

◆ When the party will be

◆ Where the party will be

◆ What kind of party it will be

◆ In Print Shop, we'll create an invitation using a greeting card project.

# ◆ Starting a Project

With all that in mind, let's start.

**1.** If you haven't started the program yet, click Start and select Programs, The Print Shop, and click on The Print Shop Ensemble III to open the program.

 The first time you open The Print Shop Ensemble III you will be asked to Please Personalize Your Product by typing in your name. Your name will become a part of the Print Shop program title screen. Every time you open the program it will say, "This copy belongs to (your name)" across the bottom of the screen.

The first screen that you see is the program title, followed quickly by the Select a Project dialog box. As you can see in Figure 1.1, your project choices are Greeting Cards, Signs & Posters, Banners, Certificates, Stationery, Calendars, Labels, Extras, and Online Greetings.

**2.** Click on Greeting Cards.

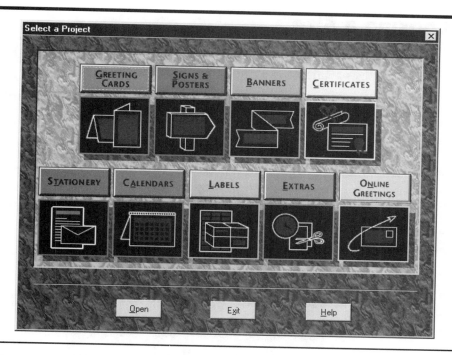

**Figure 1.1:** Print Shop's Select a Project dialog box

# Choosing a Method

The Select a Path dialog box appears. Here you can choose between customizing a ready-made card or starting from scratch. Ready-made cards are just that, cards that are ready to print or customize. They can be useful, but for this project we want to design our own.

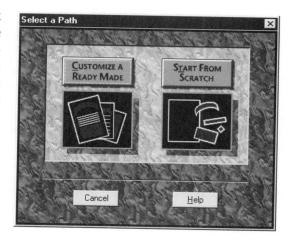

**3.** Click on Start From Scratch.

## Choosing a Size

Next you're asked to choose a greeting card size. Figure 1.2 shows the two different sizes available in Print Shop: Half Page and Quarter Page.

For our invitation, we'll choose Quarter Page, which means our card will be folded twice to a quarter-page size.

**4.** Click on Quarter Page.

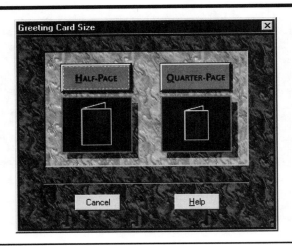

**Figure 1.2:** Choose a greeting card size.

## Choosing an Orientation

Here you're asked to choose a greeting card orientation. Figure 1.3 shows the four different ways to lay out a greeting card in Print Shop: Side Fold, Side Fold Spread, Top Fold, and Top Fold Spread.

For our invitation, we'll choose Side Fold Spread, which gives us a front and back page area of 5½" high by 4¼" wide. The inside panel of the card is 5½" high by 8½" wide.

**5.** Click on Side Fold Spread to select it.

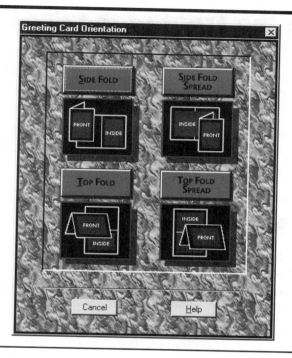

**Figure 1.3:** Choose a greeting card orientation.

 All Greeting Card layouts work with one sheet of 8½" by 11" paper, folded to fit the specific card orientation. With quarter page cards, the Side Fold selection gives you four panels 5½" high by 4¼" wide, the Top Fold selection gives you four panels 4¼" high by 5½" wide, and the Top Fold Spread gives you a front and back panel 5½" wide by 4¼" high with the inside panel 5½" wide by 8½" high. With half page cards, the Side Fold selection gives you four panels 8½" high by 5½" wide, the Top Fold selection gives you four panels 5½" high by 8½" wide, and the Top Fold Spread gives you a front and back panel 5½" high by 8½" wide with an inside panel 11" high by 8½" wide. (The actual printable area for each spread is somewhat smaller.)

# ◆ Designing the Front of the Card

Once you've chosen the orientation, Print Shop assumes you want to start working on the front of the card right away. The first screen you see is the Backdrops Browser.

The first thing you'll be asked to design is the front of the greeting card. You'll design the inside and back of the greeting card after you reach the main project window.

## Selecting a Backdrop

The Backdrops Browser offers many graphics choices listed by descriptive names. Note that the default library is PS (Print Shop) Backdrops; in this library, you can select from 126 different graphics. The choices offered are names that briefly describe the backdrops.

**1.** To see what each one looks like, click on the file name once to highlight it, and it will show up in the preview box, as shown in Figure 1.4.

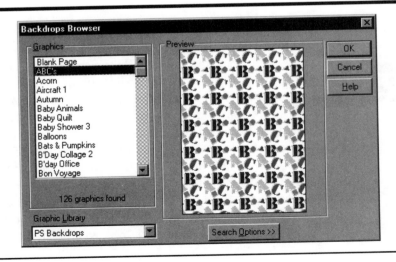

**Figure 1.4:**  You can preview available backdrops in the Backdrops Browser dialog box.

Take some time here to preview some of the fabulous backdrops Print Shop makes available.

## Accessing Other Graphics Libraries

Next we'll look at the other graphics libraries.

**2.** Click on the arrow that appears next to the Graphic Library box in the lower-left corner (it now says PS Backdrops). Note that you have other libraries available. You can select one of these, or you can select All Libraries and all the graphics will be available.

**3.** Select All Libraries.

## Using Search Options

We now have 176 graphics from which to choose our backdrop. Let's narrow the search a bit.

**4.** Click on Search Options. The Backdrops Browser dialog box expands and offers options to help you locate a graphic that's perfect for your project (see Figure 1.5).

**5.** Click on Category Keywords. The Select Category Key-words dialog box appears, from which you can choose one or more of 18 different categories.

**6.** Since we're having a party prior to departing on a trip, select Travel, then OK. You return to the Backdrops Browser with Travel appearing in the Keywords text box.

| Select Category Keywords | ✕ |
|---|---|
| ☐ Animals | ☐ Holidays |
| ☐ Birthday | ☐ Home |
| ☐ Celebration | ☐ Nature |
| ☐ Children | ☐ People |
| ☐ Education | ☐ Religion |
| ☐ Entertainment | ☐ Sports |
| ☐ Food | ☐ Technology |
| ☐ Geography | ☐ Travel |
| ☐ Matching Sets | ☐ Photo Accessories |

| OK | Cancel | Help |
|---|---|---|

**7.** Click the Search button to see what backdrops are available with a travel theme. Twelve backdrop names appear in the graphics list.

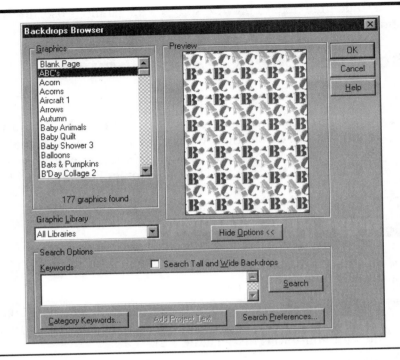

**Figure 1.5:** When you click on Search Options, the Backdrops Browser box expands to include an area where you can specify search criteria.

8. Click on Hide Options to hide the search options. We will take a closer look at search options in Chapter 7, "Working with Graphics Libraries."

## Previewing the Backdrops

The decision of which backdrop to use will depend on your interpretation of the party theme. Let's take a look at a few.

**9.** Click on Bon Voyage. It seems an obvious choice for our Bon Voyage party, but let's take a look at some others before we make a decision.

**10.** Click on Coastal Scene. If we selected it, it could indicate that we're planning to spend considerable time on a beach on some remote island. That's a nice idea.

**11.** Click on Travel, and there we are lounging on the beach with a cruise ship at anchor waiting for our return. We could live with that scenario.

**12.** Click on Ocean & Jungle for a totally different theme.

**13.** Click on Picture Postcard and a beach chair awaits our ship's arrival.

As you can see, there are plenty of choices for the backdrop that expresses diverse party themes and still allows plenty of room for individual creativity. If none of these fit the project, you can choose Blank Page and design your own or import a totally different graphic, as you'll discover in Chapter 9, "Importing Images."

**14.** For now, let's select the Bon Voyage backdrop. Click on it, then click OK.

# Selecting a Layout

The next screen is the Select a Layout dialog box (see Figure 1.6), which offers a selection of layout designs. These are designed to help determine where to put the text and graphic elements.

If you choose No Layout, the Bon Voyage graphic will remain as it is. Once you're in the main project window, you can add your own layout elements.

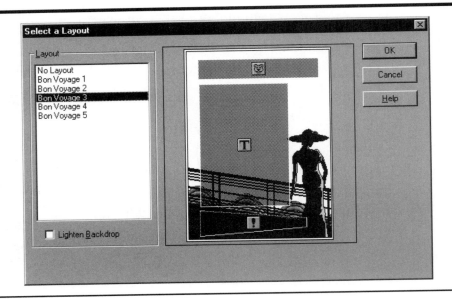

**Figure 1.6:** Select a Layout offers a selection of layout designs.

Let's see what the stock layouts look like:

**1.** Highlight one and then another. Each layout selected is previewed over the backdrop.

The shaded boxes on the layouts are called *placeholders*. They hold a place for type or headlines or graphics. Headline placeholders have an exclamation point (!) on them, text placeholders have a *T*, and graphics placeholders have Print Shop's Smiley Bear icon.

In the lower left corner of the Select a Layout dialog box you will see a box titled Lighten Backdrop. If you click on this box, the backdrop will fade to 40% of its original tint. This lightened backdrop is less dominant and will allow you to choose from a larger selection of layouts. More on this in Chapter 5, "Understanding Print Shop Projects."

**2.** For this project, click on Bon Voyage 2, then click OK. You move directly to the main project window with the basics of the invitation in place, as shown in Figure 1.7.

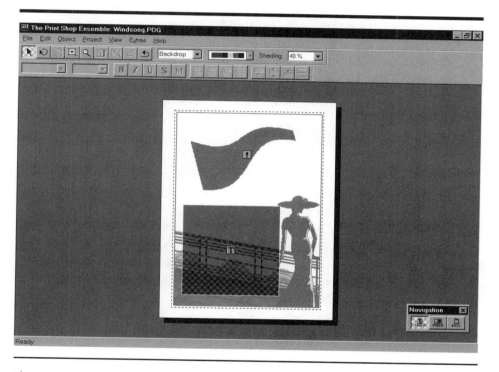

**Figure 1.7:** Once you've selected the backdrop and layout for your card, you jump to the main project window, where you can continue designing the project.

## Creating a Headline

Now we need to fill in the headline placeholder.

**1.** Double-click on the exclamation point. You go directly to the Headline dialog box, shown here.

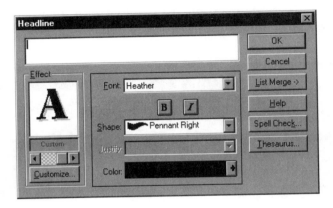

**2.** The cursor is parked in a blank rectangle in this headline composition screen. Type your title here. In this case, type WIND SONG, the name of our cruise ship.

 Headline text sizes itself to fit the headline placeholder box. If you want a smaller or larger text type, resize the headline box, and the text will automatically resize to fit the new box.

## Changing the Font

Below and to the left of this rectangle is an area labeled Effect. In this area is a capital letter *A* in the selected font style (indicated to the right in a box labeled Font). The font can be changed easily by clicking on the Font box and choosing from the selections offered.

**3.** Select the font Moderne by highlighting it; the *A* changes to this new type style. This way you can check to see if it's the style you want.

**4.** The font selection box has two buttons: one labeled B, to boldface type, and one labeled I, to italicize type. (Note that not all fonts can be made bold or italicized.) Select bold to make the headline stand out more.

## Customizing the Text

Next let's look at customizing the headline text. You can customize this text by adding shadow to the letters, outlining them, or filling them with color in a variety of ways. The Print Shop program has already created 25 different combinations of these effects. You can scroll through these by clicking on the Custom Effect slider box under the letter *A*. As you scroll through, you'll note that the effect title changes from Effect 25 to Effect 24 to Effect 23 and so on. The 26th effect is labeled Custom Effect and represents the current effect.

You can create your own custom effect by clicking on the button labeled Customize. The Custom Effect dialog box pops up. Here you an select a text effect, a shadow effect, and the color of your elements.

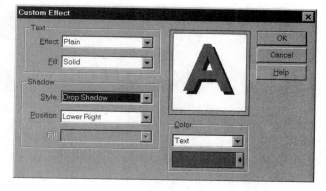

From Text Effect, choose from Plain, Thin Outline, Thick Outline, and Highlighted. From Text Fill, choose from Solid, Blend Across, Blend Down, Radiant, and Double Blend. From Shadow Style, choose from No Shadow, Drop Shadow, Block Shadow, and Silhouette.

If you select Drop Shadow or Block Shadow, choose Upper Right, Upper Left, Lower Right, or Lower Left from the Shadow Position box. If you select Silhouette, choose Solid, Blend Across, Blend Down, Radiant, or Double Blend from the Shadow Fill box. From Color, choose what you want to color: Text, Text Blend, Outline, Shadow, or Shadow Blend. Finally, make your color selection from the color palette.

**5.** For now, press Cancel to leave this box and go back to the Headline box.

**6.** Select Effect 13 from the custom effects.

**7.** Click on Customize and the Custom Effect box returns. Note the text effect and fill of Effect 13.

**8.** Cancel out of Custom Effect and return to Headline. We will look more closely at Headlines in Chapter 11, "Working with Text and Headlines."

**9.** For now, click OK.

You return to the main window with *WIND SONG*, the name of the ship, now inserted into the headline placeholder on the invitation. You can see what it looks like against the backdrop in Figure 1.8.

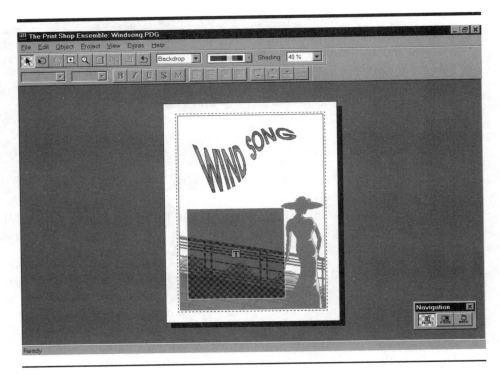

**Figure 1.8:** The headline in place with chosen font and custom effect.

# Editing Text

Next we want to fill the text placeholder to finish off the text on the front of the card.

**1.** Double-click on the text placeholder. This is the gray rectangular box with a T at its center.

The Edit Text dialog box, shown here, pops up. This screen offers a variety of options for font type, style, size, and color. You can also choose how you'd like to justify the text in its placeholder. If you're at a loss for words, you can click on Quotes and Verses to get some ideas or click on Thesaurus to look for alternate words. You can also merge a name list or custom list, or spell check your creation. We'll explore these options in Chapter 11.

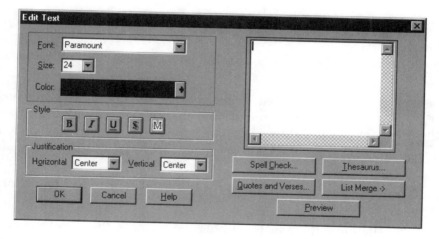

**2.** For our invitation, select Paramount as the Font and 30 as the type Size.

**3.** Select bold by clicking on the B and shadow by clicking on the S as Style options.

**4.** Choose Horizontal Center and Vertical Center to center the type in the text block, both side-to-side and top-to-bottom.

## Entering the Text

Now let's type the text in the text area.

**5.** Click once in the text entry box, then type the following:

A

Bon

Voyage

Party

All finished. Let's take a look at our creation.

**6.** Click on the Preview button. All of the text is are shown in the pre-view window.

## Changing the Text Color

It looks great. Let's do one last thing: change the color of the type.

 The Preview button becomes the Edit button when you are in pre-view mode. If you want to change the text, click on Edit and the text box changes back to normal so you can change or add to the text (the button changes back to Preview at the same time).

**7.** Click on the Edit button; the type goes back to its original plain work font.

**8.** Highlight the type by placing the cursor to the left of the first letter, *A*, holding down the mouse button, and dragging the cursor all the way down through the last letter, *y*. This highlights the complete statement.

**9.** Click on the arrow next to the Color box and a pop-up palette of color chips appears. If you're working in grayscale rather than color, this pop-up palette will offer you shades of gray rather than color.

**10.** Select the color or shade you want your type to be. When you release the mouse button, the selected color shows in the color box.

You can now preview the selection as you did before, but in its new color.

**11.** If all the selections are OK, click on OK and the type will be placed on the front of the invitation. The finished product is shown here.

# Moving Objects

Now that you see the front of the invitation all together, you may want to reposition the text or headline blocks. To move an object:

**1.** First, select it using the Pointer tool. The Pointer tool will be ON by default. If you need to select it, you will need to do so from the Standard Toolbar. If your Toolbars are not on your screen, open them by clicking on the View menu, then Toolbars, and Show Standard Toolbar. You might also want to choose Show Text Toolbar, for later. The Pointer, an arrow pointing up and left, is the first button in the Standard Toolbar, which appears at the top of the main window, below the menu. Click on the Pointer tool, then click once in the headline area; a box will appear around the words WIND SONG.

 It is important to remember that you must select the object or text with the Pointer tool before you can do anything to it. Menus and tool options will be offered based on what you've chosen to edit. If you've selected a graphic, graphic options will be available. If you've selected text, text options will be offered.

**2.** Place the cursor inside the box, then hold down the left mouse button while you drag the box—and the headline along with it—to what you feel is a better position (toward the top of the page, for instance).

**3.** Now do the same to the box that appears when you click on the words *A Bon Voyage Party*. Notice that the text box can be moved to any position on the backdrop, or to any place inside the window, for that matter.

You can also make the box larger or smaller by grabbing the *handles* (the square boxes at each corner) and pulling or pushing on them. Handles appear when you select an object with the Pointer tool. We will tell you more about this feature in Chapter 2, "Discovering Tools."

# Adding a Graphic

The final element for the front of the invitation is an indication that refreshments will be served. We could just put in another text box and type the words, but it might be more fun and creative to put in a graphic.

1. Click on Object on the menu bar at the top of the window.

2. Select Add from the drop down menu; you are offered a choice of graphic shapes that can be added to the invitation.

What we'd like to do is find a graphic of a cold drink or some other refreshment we can place in the bottom-left corner of the invitation. Since most Print Shop graphics are square, let's start with that category.

3. Choose Square Graphic from the list by clicking once. A placeholder for a square graphic appears in the center of the project as shown here.

4. Double-click on the icon in the center of the placeholder and you will be presented with a list of graphics and graphics libraries, shown in Figure 1.9.

By default, the PS Squares library is listed. There are 334 graphics in this library; pretty overwhelming. Let's narrow our search.

5. Click on Search Options, and the Graphics Browser expands to include search criteria just like the Backdrops Browser did.

 Once you turn on search options, they will remain open in all subsequent Browser dialog boxes until you hide them.

6. Click on Category Keywords and take a look at the options offered.

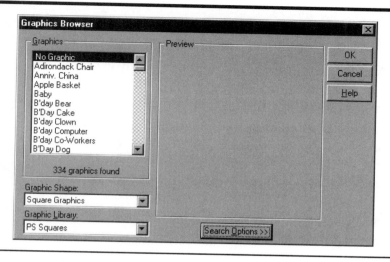

**Figure 1.9:** When you click on the square graphic placeholder, the Graphics Browser presents you with a variety of options.

Unfortunately, the categories offered do not include drinks or refreshments. Food is offered, but this is probably too broad a search criterion.

**7.** Cancel out of this screen and go back to the Keywords box.

**8.** Type Drinks into this box and click on Search.

You're offered a choice of five different graphics. By using the Keywords option, we have narrowed our graphics search from 334 to 5. Pretty neat.

**9.** Click on the graphics offered and take a look. There are some great ones here. Celebrate 3, shown here, looks pretty good. So does Tropical Drinks. Let's go with that one.

You can pull down the names of more graphics libraries if you cannot find what you're looking for in this one. The Print Shop Ensemble III has over 5,600 graphics available for your projects. We'll talk more about graphics and graphics libraries in Part Two, "Managing Graphics."

**10.** With Tropical Drinks selected, click OK and you return to the main project window with Tropical Drinks inserted into the graphic placeholder.

**11.** Select the graphic and, holding down your left mouse button, drag it to the lower-left corner of the invitation, as shown here.

That completes the design for the front of our invitation. On it, we've told our friends three important things:

◆ The location of the party (that is, the name of the ship)

◆ The kind of party we're having

◆ That refreshments will be served

We are now ready to start working on the inside spread page. We can get to the inside page by clicking on the INSIDE navigation tool, shown here, which has defaulted  to the lower-right corner of the screen. These navigation tools—FRONT, INSIDE, and BACK—are used to move you from page to page in a multipage project. You'll only see this toolbar when you're working on multipage projects in Print Shop.

# ◆ Designing the Inside of the Card

Once you've selected INSIDE from the Navigation tools, Print Shop prompts you to select a backdrop for the inside of the card.

## Selecting a Backdrop

You'll see the Backdrops Browser again (the same dialog box you saw when you were designing the front of the card). Selecting a backdrop from those listed should be fairly easy since we've already established the look of the card with the design elements on the front. We just need to find an inside backdrop that matches or complements what we have already done.

The backdrop graphics listed are different from those offered for the front of the card. In this case, the inside of the card is twice the size of the front, and the graphics are designed to fit this new area.

Again, you're offered multiple libraries from which to choose your graphic. And you can still use the search options to find a graphic if you like. Let's take a look at those options.

**1.** Click through the graphics so you can see them in preview. We spotted one called Gradient, shown here. It has an art deco look to it that complements the background we put on the front.

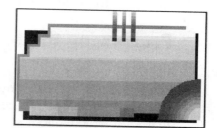

**2.** Select Gradient and click OK.

# Selecting a Layout

At this point the Select a Layout dialog box appears again. The layout options are different from those available for designing the front of the card, because the page size and expected content are different.

## Deciding What Information to Include

Before we select a layout, let's decide what information we want to include so we can pick one that provides the right kind of placeholders. We've already provided the ship's name, but there are still some unanswered questions:

| | |
|---|---|
| What date is the party? | Tuesday, November 4 |
| When does the party start and when will it be over? | 3 to 5 p.m. |
| Where is the ship located? | Pier 39 |
| Where on the ship will the party be held? | In our stateroom, number 112 |

We'll also want our friends to let us know if they plan to attend, so we'll need an RSVP line. And of course we want to let them know that they're invited, so we'll use a headline for that.

Basically, we need to have a layout with four placeholders for all the above information. We'll need a headline placeholder for the "you're invited" text, two text placeholders for the specifics (one for date and time, one for location), and one more headline placeholder for the RSVP.

## Previewing the Layouts

With this information in mind, let's look at the layouts available. (If you can't find one you like, you can always make your own.) All of the choices offered, except one, give us the placeholders we need, so it's just a matter of which layout we like best.

**1.** Choose Gradient 4, shown here.

**2.** Before confirming the layout, click on the box that says Lighten Backdrop. This will make the backdrop lighter and give more emphasis to the text.

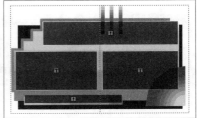

When you do this, you are given additional layout options. You can click through a few of these for practice, but stick with Gradient 4 as the selection.

**3.** When you're finished browsing, select Gradient 4 again and click OK. You return to the main project window with your layout in place.

## Adding Text

Now let's fill the text and headline blocks. You can fill these just as you did on the front of the card. We've chosen to fill these blocks as shown here, using a Double Arch Up headline.

1. Since you've now had some experience with text and headline blocks, try your hand at filling in the placeholders.

Feel free to experiment with different headline types, fonts, or colors.

2. When you're finished with the inside of the card, click the navigation tool that says BACK and go to the back of the card.

# ◆ Designing the Back of the Card

Since this is the first time you've been to the back of the card, you are prompted to select a layout. (No backdrops are offered, since the back of a card is traditionally pretty sparse. Reserve this space to give yourself credit.)

1. Click through the layouts and you'll see that some offer text and graphics.

What we'd like is to have one graphic, plus a text box where we can give directions to the party location. Greeting Card 9 looks like it might work. We'll have to resize the text block to make it bigger, but that's easy enough.

2. Select Greeting Card 9 and click OK.

## Selecting a Graphic

Filling the blocks is easy to do. Let's do the graphic first.

1. Click on the bear icon and you go to the Graphics Browser dialog box. Note that you are working with a row graphic.

Since the *Wind Song* is a sailing ship whose sails are manipulated and trimmed by a computer, let's look for a sailboat for the back of our card.

2. Change the Graphic Library area to All Libraries and type Sailing in the Keywords box.

3. Click on Search.

We're offered four graphics: Father Sail-
boats, Ocean Liner, Sailing Flags, shown
here, and Seaside Dining. None of these
will work. Let's change the row graphic to a square graphic.

4. Click on the arrow next to Row Graphics and select Square Graphics, then All Libraries again.

Now you're presented with a choice of eleven graphics. Click through them.

The first one named Sailboat would be okay. The second Sailboat, the cartoon sailboat shown here, is not a choice we'd make. The one named Sailing looks just like what we had in mind. Let's select this one.

5. With Sailing selected, click OK; it is placed in a square placeholder on the back of the invitation.

## Putting a Frame around the Text Box

We're going to fill the text block with directions, and a frame around the box might be nice. First, we'll need to make it bigger.

1. Click on it to select it, then pull on the handles to resize it.

2. Double-click on the *T* at its center, type the directions (you can just make up something for now), and click OK. You now have an unframed text box with the directions in it.

3. Select the text box once more and pull down the Object menu from the top of the screen.

4. Select Frame and choose a frame for the box. Let's choose Thick Line.

5. Select it and release the mouse. A thick line appears around your text box.

There, the box is framed and we are finished with this project. Check out Figure 1.10 to see what the invitation looks like.

Let's save the project:

1. Click on the File menu at the top of the screen, then select Save.

2. Name the file **Windsong** and click OK.

# ◆ Endnotes

Mission accomplished! You've completed your first Print Shop project, and a complicated one at that: a three-page greeting card. You have:

◆ Selected a project and chosen an orientation, a backdrop, and a layout for it

◆ Browsed for graphics

◆ Created and filled placeholders

◆ Worked in text and headline blocks

◆ Moved and resized objects

◆ Selected color type

◆ Worked a bit with the main menu and with the standard toolbar

You've gotten your feet wet. In Chapter 2, "Discovering Tools," we'll get a bit more serious with a prolonged look at the standard toolbar. You've only just begun. The best is yet to come.

**Front**

**Inside**

**Back**

**Figure 1.10:** Congratulations! You've completed your first Print Shop project.

# Discovering Tools

## Your mission: to discover everything there is to know about tools

◆

Print Shop is designed to be simple to use. With its graphic-oriented base, Print Shop's tools and menus help you to be creative with your project. As you work your way through the book, you'll explore how to make maximum use of these tool and menu commands to customize your projects. We'll talk about the Standard Toolbar in this chapter and menus in the next.

# ◆ Starting the Project

In this chapter we'll explore each of the commands offered on the Standard Toolbar, while using a ready-made sign as our project.

**1.** If you have not opened Print Shop yet, open it now.

**2.** The first screen you see asks you to select a project. Click on Signs & Posters.

**3.** You are given two paths to choose from: Customize a Ready Made or Start From Scratch. Click on Customize a Ready Made.

**4.** Next, you're asked to select a sign theme: Home, Business, Celebration, Community, School, or Photo Projects (see Figure 2.1). Select Community.

You're presented with a list of ready-made signs. As you click on each file, you can see it in the preview area. For this project, we're looking for a

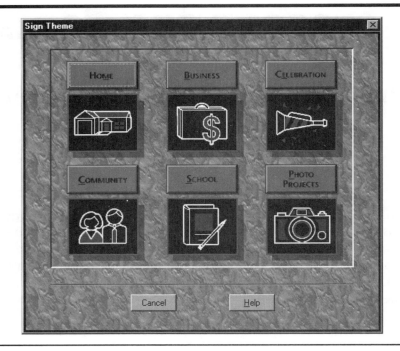

**Figure 2.1:** Select a theme for your ready-made sign.

sign that has graphics, text, headlines, a border, and graduated page coloring—or something along those lines. In other words, we're looking for a sign with lots of stuff on it, like the Car Wash sign (see Figure 2.2).

**5.** Click once on Car Wash and take a look at it in preview. Looks perfect. Click on Select.

Car Wash opens in the project window (see Figure 2.3), ready for you to try your hand with the tools.

 Every ready-made project is complete and can be printed out as is; however the fun of this program is to customize a ready made by adding or deleting objects, changing the backdrop, altering the layout, or changing the page color or anything else. Use your creativity.

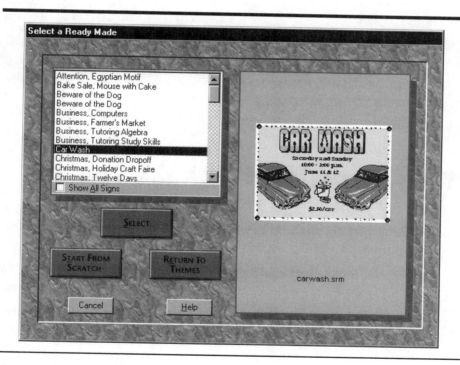

**Figure 2.2:** Select one of the ready-made signs.

**Figure 2.3:** The Car Wash sign opens in the project window, ready for you to print as is or customize as you like.

# ◆ Getting Acquainted with the Toolbar

The Standard Toolbar, by default, is located at the top of the Main Project Window just below the menu. You can, however, move it anywhere on the project page. Let's try this.

**1.** Click on the gray area between any of the buttons and then, holding down your mouse button, drag it anywhere on the screen.

Note that when you do this it acquires a blue bar at the top with the name Standard, for Standard Toolbar, on it.

**2.** Double-click on the gray area between buttons to put it back at the top of the screen.

To place the Standard Toolbar and the Text Toolbar side by side, drag them into this position or double-click on one or the other to place them there.

Print Shop offers you the option of two different size toolbar buttons: Large (32 X 30 pixels) or Small (24 X 22 pixels). You can also select color buttons or grayscale buttons. To change the size or color of the toolbar buttons, select the View Menu and then Toolbars. A dialog box pops up to give you these options as well as a few others.

All these options make it possible to choose a position and size for your toolbar that is both convenient and one that does not conflict with the working area of your project.

Now we're ready to take a look at the commands available on the Standard Toolbar, as shown in Figure 2.4.

 When you place your cursor at the Pointer tool, the tool tips flag will identify it as the Selection tool. This is the only place you will see the Pointer tool identified as the Selection tool. For our purposes, the Pointer tool and the Selection tool are one and the same. In this book, we refer to it as the Pointer tool.

On the toolbar are nine tools, plus an Item Selector, a Color Selector, and a Shading Selector, all of which allow you to select, rotate, move, add, zoom, delete, flip, frame, and color objects in your project.

Some of the toolbar options are also available in the menu bar at the top of the window, but the layout of the toolbar makes often-used commands

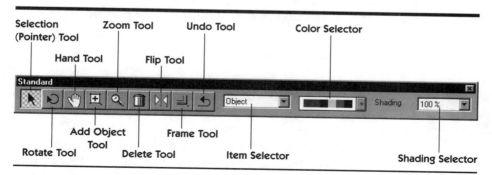

**Figure 2.4:** The Print Shop Standard toolbar.

easier to access and use. Clicking on a button is faster than pulling down a menu command. Of the tools offered, Add Object, Zoom, Flip, and Frame have pop-up menus to help you define exactly what you want to do.

# ◆ Moving and Resizing Objects

The first tool—and the one you will use most often—is the Pointer tool. It allows you to select an object and then change that object in a variety of ways, including moving, resizing, coloring, shading, and inserting graphics or text.

Let's use the car wash sign to take a look at the many ways you can use the Pointer tool. You already have the project on-screen, so let's get to it.

## Moving a Single Object

You can move an object easily using the Pointer tool. Let's try our hand at a few ways to move objects within a window.

**1.** Select the Pointer tool.

**2.** Click on the bucket. A box with squares at each corner appears around the bucket, as shown here. These square corners are called *handles* because you can grab one of these and rotate or resize the object.

**3.** Click again on the bucket and, holding your left mouse button down, drag it to the upper-right corner of the sign. While you're moving the object, you'll see a box the size of the object making the move. The object and its handles will not move yet.

**4.** Once the box is in position, release the mouse button. The object jumps to its new location.

All objects have four corners, regardless of what is inside the object area. The bucket, for example, appears to be just a bucket, but when you select it, you can see it is in a square box. The same would be true no matter what size and shape the graphics or text inside a box. The box always has four corners and four handles.

# Moving Multiple Objects Together

Okay, we've moved a single object successfully. Next let's take a look at how we can move more than one object, keeping them in the same position relative to each other.

1.  First, put the bucket back into its original position: just hold the left mouse button down and drag it back between the two cars.

Now let's move the bucket and the $2.50 text together.

2.  Select the bucket with the Pointer tool.

3.  Hold down the Shift key and click on the $2.50. Both objects are selected. You can tell because both have handles, as shown here.

4.  Hold down the left mouse button anywhere on either of the selected objects and drag both of them to the upper-right corner. Two box outlines appear and move together as you drag your cursor to the new location.

5.  Release the mouse and both of the objects jump to their new location.

So now you know how to move multiple objects at once. Next drag both the bucket and the $2.50 back to their original position using the same technique and we will resize an object.

# Resizing Graphics

You can resize an object, making it larger or smaller, maintaining the aspect ratio or changing it entirely. In other words, you can make a square bigger or you can reshape the square to make it a rectangle.

## Changing a Graphic's Size

Let's do a little graphic resizing using the Pointer tool on the Car Wash sign.

1. Click on the Pointer tool and select the bucket.

2. Now place your cursor on one of the handles and, holding the left mouse button down, pull out to make the object larger.

When resizing an object, you select a handle to pull or push the object to its new size. The opposite handle becomes an anchor for the object and does not move from its original position as you resize. If, for example, you pull on the handle in the upper-right corner, all corners of the object except the lower-left one move.

The object itself does not change as you pull on a handle. Rather, that same outlined box you saw when you moved an object does the resizing. When you release the mouse button, the object jumps to its new size, as shown here. Note that the aspect ratio of the bucket remains the same; it's just larger.

Aspect Ratio is the relationship between the width and the height of an object. For instance, the aspect ratio of the bucket in our sign appears to be 1:1, which means it is a square, just as wide as it is tall. We could resize it, making it larger but keeping it a square. Or we could reshape it, changing the aspect ratio by stretching it or squeezing it into another shape, say a rectangle.

3. We can make an object smaller in the same way. Do that now, pushing the bucket back to its original size.

## Changing a Graphic's Shape

To resize an object, changing its aspect ratio:

1. Select the bucket.

2. Hold down the Ctrl key and the left mouse button at the same time, and push down on the upper-right handle. The bucket changes its aspect ratio: the box becomes a rectangle and the bucket gets short and fat, as shown here.

**3.** Pull the bucket back to its original size, and we'll move on to head-lines and text blocks.

# Resizing Headline or Text Blocks

So that's how you resize a graphic, but what about headline or text blocks? Do you resize them the same way? The answer is yes and no.

To resize headline or text blocks, you do exactly the same thing you've done with the bucket, only the methods for resizing and reshaping are reversed. Let's try it.

## Maintaining the Aspect Ratio

To resize a text or headline block without changing its aspect ratio:

**1.** Click on the Car Wash headline block to select it.

**2.** Hold down the left mouse button and the Ctrl key and pull the lower-left corner of the Car Wash headline down and to the left.

The square outline of the block appears as you pull it to a larger size, while it maintains its aspect ratio.

## Changing the Aspect Ratio

To resize a text or headline block, changing its aspect ratio:

**1.** Select the Car Wash headline block again.

**2.** Hold down the left mouse button and push the lower-left corner up.

The outline of the block appears as you change the size of the text block to a more elongated and smaller size. Text located inside a headline block will resize itself to fit in the block you make. Headline text is designed to fill the box.

On the other hand, text in a text block will *not* resize when you change the size of its box. Rather, the type will remain the same size and will only rearrange itself to fit in the box if it can. If the type can no longer fit because the box is too small, it will disappear outside the box.

Let's see what happens when we make a text box smaller.

**1.** Click on the text box that begins with "Saturday and Sunday..."

**2.** Push on one of the handles, making the box smaller.

Some of the text disappears. It no longer fits in the box and is hidden outside, as shown here. The text is not gone; it's just hidden. You can reclaim it by making the type smaller or the box larger.

Before we go on, drag all the objects in your Car Wash sign back into their original positions and shapes. Next we'll learn to rotate objects.

 By linking items together, you can resize two or more objects simultaneously in exactly the same way that you would resize one. You link the objects together by selecting them all using the Pointer tool and your Shift key. If one of the linked objects is a graphic, you follow the procedure for resizing graphics. If all of the linked objects are text or headline blocks, use the process for resizing text or headline blocks.

# ◆ Rotating Objects

 The Rotate tool allows you to pivot objects on the handle you select. You can select and rotate one object or several objects at the same time.

## Rotating a Single Object

Let's try it on the Car Wash sign.

**1.** Select the Rotate tool by clicking on it. Your cursor becomes a semicircle with an arrow head on one end (it will look just like the Rotate tool button).

2. Now select the car on the left side by clicking on it with the rotate tool. Handles appear at the four corners of the object.

3. To rotate the object, put the rotate arrow directly on one of the handles and drag the box in a clockwise or counter-clockwise direction. The object rotates, as shown here.

4. Rotate the car back to its original position, or select Edit, Undo Rotate Object.

# Rotating Multiple Objects Together

Like the Pointer tool, the Rotate tool allows you to select more than one object and turn them all at the same time. Try this.

1. Select the car at the left.

2. Hold down the Shift key and select the car at the right, then the bucket. You have now selected three objects.

3. Put the arrow cursor on any one of the handles on any one of the objects.

4. Now rotate. All three objects rotate together, maintaining their positioning from each other, as shown here.

5. Rotate until all objects are back in their original position and click anywhere outside the project to deselect the objects.

# ◆ Moving around in the Document

Occasionally you'll want to view a project at a size larger than the main window allows. You can zoom in to focus on a certain part of the document, but then how do you see the parts that moved off-screen? The Hand tool allows you to move the document around in the window so you can see elements that may be hidden when the project is larger than the window.

 The Hand tool is not available when a project fits inside the viewing window, since no part of the project is hidden from view.

This is a handy option when you want to compose in actual size or larger than actual size to see colors, objects, or text options better. Let's try using the Hand tool now. First we'll need to change how we are viewing the project.

1. Click on the Zoom tool (the magnifying glass), and select Actual Size from the options offered by clicking on it.

The Car Wash sign no longer fits in the window, as shown in Figure 2.5. Note that the Hand tool changes from a shaded button to an outlined button to indicate that it is now available.

2. Click on the Hand tool. When you move your cursor back onto the document, you'll see a hand, indicating that this tool is active.

3. Now click anywhere on the sign and, holding down the left mouse button, move the hand cursor around. The document moves with the hand so you can see the portions of it hidden outside the window.

 You can also move around a project that is larger than the viewing window by using the scroll bars at the right and bottom edges of the window. Click on the button located inside the scroll bar and drag the button to move through the project. You'll notice that when you use the Hand tool, the scroll bars move as you move around.

Use the Zoom tool to change your view back so that the sign fits in the window, because we're off to add a few objects to the project using the

**Figure 2.5:** At actual size, the Car Wash sign no longer fits in the project window.

Add Object tool. See "Changing the View" later in the chapter for more about the Zoom tool.

# ◆ Adding Objects

With the Add Object tool we can add objects to our project. A pop-up menu offers these choices: Graphic, Square Graphic, Row Graphic, Column Graphic, Text, Headline, Word Balloon, Horizontal Ruled Line, Vertical Ruled Line, Border, Mini-Border, Mini-Backdrop, Seal, Signature Block, Title Block, and Import...

When you select an option, a placeholder for the object will appear in the middle of your project page. Some options do not use a placeholder but rather place the object directly in the project, and selecting "Graphic" or "Import" will take you directly to a dialog box to select the item you want to add.

Before we go on to actually adding the objects, let's find out what a placeholder is, what it does, what it looks like, and which objects can be added using a placeholder.

# Understanding Placeholders

Placeholders create a space for an object. Just as there are objects of different sizes and shapes, there are placeholders of different sizes and shapes. At the center of many placeholders is an icon that indicates what kind of placeholder it is. Placeholders and their default shapes and icons are as follows:

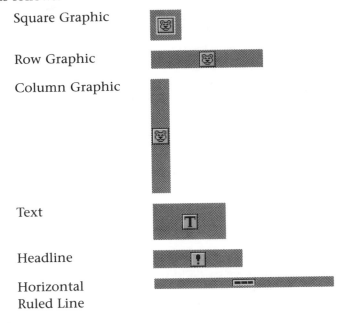

Square Graphic

Row Graphic

Column Graphic

Text

Headline

Horizontal
Ruled Line

Vertical
Ruled Line

Border

Mini-border

Mini-backdrop

Seal

Signature Block

Title Block

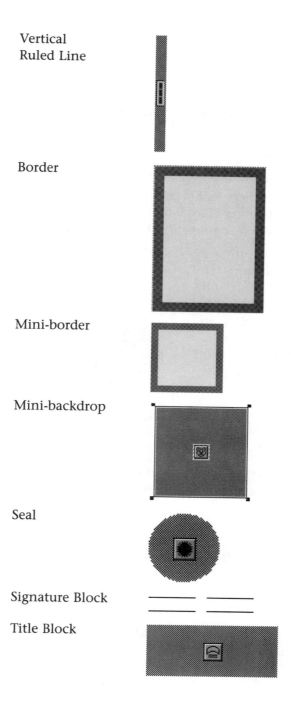

As we mentioned in Chapter 1, you fill a placeholder with an object by double-clicking on the placeholder, then either selecting a graphic or typing in text.

## Adding Objects with Placeholders

Let's practice working with placeholders by adding a few objects to the Car Wash project.

**1.** Click on the Add Object tool; a pop-up menu offers the choices listed in "Understanding Placeholders," plus Graphic (meaning all graphic shapes), Word Balloon, and Import (a graphic).

**2.** Select Square Graphic; a square placeholder appears, as shown here. The default position for a new object is the center of the project, so that's where the placeholder appears. You can always move it or resize it using the Pointer tool.

Let's select a graphic for the placeholder.

**3.** Double-click on the placeholder and the Graphics Browser appears. Scroll through the graphics and highlight Elephant Forgets, as shown in Figure 2.6.

**4.** Click OK.

You immediately return to the project window. The placeholder is gone and in its place is the Elephant Forgets graphic inside a box with handles. Now you can move and resize the new graphic as you did with the objects that were originally part of the sign.

We're going to learn a different way to add objects, so let's get the one we just added out of the way.

**5.** The Elephant Forgets graphic is already selected so just hit the Delete key on your keyboard. The graphic disappears.

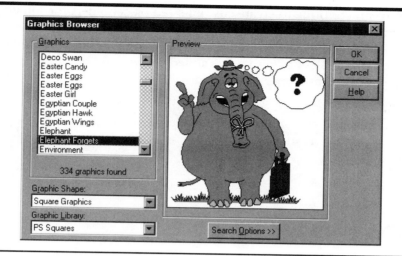

**Figure 2.6:** The Elephant Forgets graphic is shown in the preview window.

# Customizing Placeholders

Using the Ctrl key, you can add custom-sized placeholders for most of the objects offered by the Add Object tool. That is, you can draw a placeholder to your own specifications before you insert the object in it. Custom-sized placeholders can be drawn for square graphics, row graphics, column graphics, text, headlines, horizontal ruled lines, vertical ruled lines, mini-borders, and mini-backdrops. You cannot customize a border or an imported graphic in this way.

Let's try it.

1. Hold down the Ctrl key and click on the Add Object tool, then select the object type. Again, let's add a square graphic.

2. Release the Ctrl key and the mouse button and move your cursor into the project area. A small box appears as your cursor.

3. Click in the upper-right corner of the sign, then drag down and to the left. A box appears and follows your movement as you drag. When the box fills the space to the right of the large Car Wash headline, release the mouse button.

You can continue to create custom-sized placeholders for square graphics until you select another tool or a different object. Practice drawing placeholders until you've got the hang of it. When you're done, delete any extra placeholder boxes you've added. Leave only the one we drew first in the upper-right corner of the sign.

4. Double-click on the bear icon in the remaining placeholder and insert the Elephant Forgets graphic, as shown here.

## Changing the View

As we've already discovered, we can change our view of the project using the Zoom tool. When you click on the Zoom tool, a pop-up menu offers you the options of Zoom In, Zoom Out, Fit to Window, 25%, 50%, Actual Size, 150%, and 200%. You will find it convenient to be able to change the view in order to work on more detailed aspects of the project.

Let's take a closer look at the elephant.

1. Click on the Zoom tool and select 200%. The project becomes bigger than the window so we can no longer see all of it.

2. Click on the Hand tool and move the project window around until you can see the elephant.

3. Select the elephant and adjust it as necessary (resize it, move it around, whatever you need to do) to better fit it on the page next to the Car Wash headline, as shown in Figure 2.7.

4. Click on the Zoom tool again and change the view back to Fit to Window.

## Deleting Objects

The icon for the Delete tool is, appropriately, a trash can. Anything highlighted is deleted when you click on this button.

**Figure 2.7:** Zoom in to 200% so you can better see the elephant's position on the page.

Give deleting a try.

**1.** Select the elephant, then click on the Delete tool. The elephant disappears.

**2.** Now click on the Undo tool and the elephant returns to its former position.

 If you wish to regain what you just deleted, click on the Undo tool, the U-shaped arrow on the toolbar. Only the last thing you deleted can be restored. See "Undoing or Redoing Your Last Action" later in the chapter for more on the Undo tool.

## Flipping Objects

The Flip tool does just what you'd expect: it lets you flip an object horizontally, vertically, or both. This gives you a lot of flexibility with graphics.

Let's give it a try.

1. Using the Pointer tool, select the car on the left side.

2. Click on the Flip tool. A drop down menu appears, offering you the choice of Horizontal, Vertical, or Both. Note that when you begin, the car is facing toward the right.

3. Click Horizontal, and the car faces left. Then click Vertical, and the car turns upside-down, as shown here.

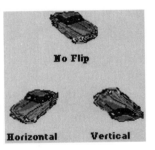

4. To return the car to its original position, select Both from the Flip menu. It flips both vertically and horizontally and once again faces right.

Not all objects can be flipped. Text, Headlines, Word Balloons, Borders, and imported WMF and EPS graphics cannot be flipped. (Imported graphics are discussed in Chapter 9.)

## Framing Objects

As the name indicates, the Frame tool allows you to put frames around objects. You can frame any object except a border, mini-border, seal, or ruled line. When you click on this icon, a menu offers None, Thin Line, Thick Line, Double Line, or Drop Shadow. If the object already has a frame, a check mark appears next to one of these selections.

Let's add a frame to the bucket.

1. Select the bucket.

2. Click on the Frame tool. You'll note that on the menu, None is checked, indicating that the object does not have a frame.

**3.** Click on Thin Line. The menu goes away and the frame appears around the graphic.

You'll note that when you put a frame around the bucket, the background around it changes to white. This is a default color for the inside of an object box. We can change this so we can see through to the page color or change it to another color entirely. More on this in "Coloring and Shading an Area" later in this chapter.

Experiment with the different frames offered by the Frame tool. All the framing options are shown in Figure 2.8.

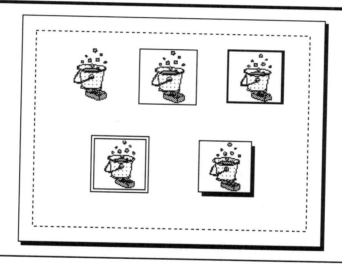

**Figure 2.8:** Your framing choices are None, Thin Line, Thick Line, Double Line, and Drop Shadow.

**4.** When you're done, select None from Frame options to return the bucket to its original state.

Note that any frames you add will be black. This is the default color for frames. You can change this color, choosing from a selection of different colors offered on the palette in the Color Selector. We'll talk about that in "Coloring and Shading an Area" later in this chapter.

# ◆ Undoing or Redoing Your Last Action

The Undo tool reverses the last action you performed. It can act as both an Undo tool to reverse the last action and a Redo tool to reverse the last Undo command.

## Undoing Your Last Action

Use the Undo tool to reverse your last action, whether it was deleting, moving, changing a color, changing a backdrop, or anything else.

Let's try the Undo tool on a graphic change.

1. Double-click on the bucket, and the Graphics Browser opens.

2. Select a new graphic (any one will do) and click OK. The new graphic you selected replaces the bucket.

3. Click on the Undo tool, and the graphic changes back to the bucket.

## Redoing Your Last Action

If you change your mind again, never fear. The Undo tool becomes a Redo tool immediately after an Undo command. Let's give it a try.

1. Click on the Undo tool. The graphic you selected to replace the bucket reappears, since this was your last undo in the exercise above.

2. Click on the Undo tool again and the bucket returns.

If you've performed any actions after clicking the Undo tool, the tool will not act as a Redo tool; instead, clicking it will undo the most recent change.

# ◆ Coloring and Shading an Area

With the next three items on the toolbar—the Item Selector, the Color Selector,

and the Shading Selector, shown below—you can change the color of an object or the shading of a multicolored object.

First you must select what you want to shade or color. Then, using the Item Selector, choose the area of that object you want to apply the shading or color to. The choices offered by the Item Selector will vary depending on the object selected:

| Object | Options |
|---|---|
| Graphic | Object |
| | Behind Object |
| | Frame |
| | Page |
| | Page Blend |
| Headline | Behind Object |
| | Frame |
| | Page |
| | Page Blend |
| Imported Graphic | Frame |
| | Page |
| | Page Blend |
| Signature Block | Signature Text |
| | Autograph |
| | Behind Object |
| | Page |
| | Page Blend |

| Object | Options |
|---|---|
| Seal, Border, Mini-Border | Object |
| | Behind Object |
| | Page |
| | Page Blend |
| Text | Text |
| | Behind Text |
| | Frame |
| | Page |
| | Page Blend |
| Word Balloon | Text |
| | Balloon |
| | Page |
| | Page Blend |
| No Object | Page |
| | Page Blend |
| | Backdrop (if one is part of the project) |

Make your choice, then change the color with the Color Selector or the shading with the Shading Selector.

 You cannot change colors for a multicolored object, but you can change the saturation of these colors in increments of 10%. The lower the percentage, the lighter the color.

Now let's change our sign using the Item Selector, the Color Selector, and the Shading Selector.

**1.** Select one of the cars with the Pointer tool.

**2.** Select Object from the Item Selector.

The Color Selector changes to multiple colors, as shown here (in grayscale, it appears as various shades of gray), because the car is more than one color. Note also that the Shading Selector reads 100%. We cannot change the color of the car because it is multicolored, but we can change the color saturation.

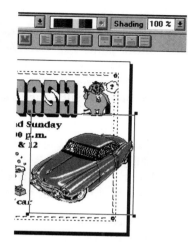

3. Click on the arrow at the right edge of the Shading Selector. A list pops up, offering options from 100% to 10%. Click on 50% and see the car change to a lighter shade.

4. To change the color of the area behind the object, select Behind Object from the Item Selector. The color in the Color Selector reads Clear. This is the present color of the area behind the object. The Shading Selector has become light in color, meaning that it is not available for use, while the Color Selector is dark in color, indicating that it is available.

5. Click on the arrow on the right side of the Color Selector and a color palette pops up, offering a wide choice of colors. Run your cursor over the color palette; the color in the Color Selector changes as you move around the color palette. Select one of the colors, say green. The color of the area behind the car changes to your choice.

6. To add a colored frame to the car, select the Frame tool from the toolbar and put a thick line frame around the car. Select Frame from the Item Selector and you'll see that the color of the frame is black. Change it by clicking on the Color Selector and selecting a new color, say blue.

You have just put your multicolored car into a green box with a thick blue line around it. Cool.

In some cases, the graphic may cover the entire object area. When this happens, you cannot color behind the object because there is no area behind the object that you can see.

The Page option on the Item Selector always refers to the full page of the project. You can color the page, provided the backdrop does not cover the entire page. Our Car Wash sign does not have a backdrop and the page is colored. Click on any part of the page and take a look at the Color Selector. You'll see that the page is a shade of yellow. We can change the color of the page with the Color Selector just as we changed the area behind the car.

The Page Blend option blends two different colors in a pattern across the page. The Item Selector is used only to select the two colors; the actual blend is done using the Project menu. We'll take a more in-depth look at page blending in Chapter 3.

Selected text can be colored using the Item Selector and the Color Selector, but headlines cannot. Headlines can only be colored in the Headline dialog box.

## ◆ Endnotes

Mission accomplished. You now know everything there is to know about the Print Shop toolbar. You can:

- ◆ Select, rotate, move, add, flip, frame, or color an object
- ◆ Zoom in or out of a project
- ◆ Add color to a page, object, or background
- ◆ Delete and undo

Now on to the main menu to see how it works with the toolbar. Do not close your Car Wash sign. We'll be using it in Chapter 3, "Mastering Menus."

# Mastering Menus

## Your mission: to learn the main menu backward and forward

◆

Print Shop's main menu, shown below, offers all the commands that the toolbar does, plus more. It trades the one-click convenience of the toolbar for a more complete list of command options. From

| File | Edit | Object | Project | View | Extras | Help |

the main menu, you can open, print, save, view, or change a project in numerous ways.

In order to look at the main menu, you need to open a file. The Car Wash sign from Chapter 2 should still be open. If it's not, open it again following the instructions in Chapter 2. The main menu bar appears above the toolbar across the top of the project window.

To access a menu command, click on an item, such as File, in the main menu. A submenu listing various commands drops down, as shown here; click on any of these commands to select it. A command followed by an ellipsis (...), like New, brings up a dialog box when you select it, while a command followed by a triangular-shaped arrow (➤), like Preview, brings up a secondary drop down menu. If a command is light gray in color, like Revert to Saved, it is currently unavailable.

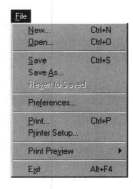

Some commands can also be accessed using keyboard shortcuts. Where applicable, these shortcuts are noted next to the corresponding menu commands. For example, in the File menu you can see that the keyboard shortcut for the Open command is Ctrl+O. The next time you want to open a project, you can just press Ctrl+O instead of selecting File ➤ Open.

You can also access some menu/tool options by right clicking on graphics or text in your project. If you right click on a graphic, for example, a drop down list gives you the option of Edit, Cut, Copy, Paste, Delete, Shadow, Frame, Flip, and Duplicate. If you click on a text box, the options are Edit, Cut, Copy, Paste, Delete, Frame, and Duplicate.

All of these options let you develop your own style of working with the program. Let's take a look at how we can use the menu commands.

## ◆ Using the File Menu

File menu commands perform housekeeping chores such as starting a new document; opening an already-existing document; selecting project preferences; saving, previewing, and printing a project; and exiting the program. These commands are generally the same as those in other programs (such as word processing programs), with some slight differences specific to Print Shop.

Let's take a look at the File menu's ten commands: New, Open, Save, Save As, Revert To Saved, Preferences, Print, Printer Setup, Print Preview, and Exit.

## Starting a New Project

Print Shop can only open one project at a time. Thus, if you are working on a project when you click on New, Print Shop closes the open project to make room for the new one. If you haven't saved the open document, a dialog box like the one

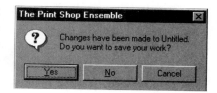

shown here pops up. If you haven't made any changes to the active project since you last saved it, this dialog box does not appear and the project closes automatically.

**1.** With the Car Wash sign open, select File ➤ New.

**2.** Click No at the Do you want to save your work? prompt.

The Select a Project dialog box appears. We just lost any changes we made to the Car Wash sign, but it still exists as a ready-made sign. So let's just open it again.

**3.** Click on Signs & Posters and reopen the ready-made Car Wash sign.

## Opening an Existing File

The Open command in the File menu opens an existing Print Shop file, either one you have created and saved or one of the ready-made projects. As with the New command, if you have an open project a dialog box asks if you want to save your changes or just exit without saving.

**1.** With the Car Wash sign open, select File ➤ Open. If you have made changes to the Car Wash sign, a dialog box will ask if you want to save your changes. If you have made no changes, no prompt will appear.

The Open dialog box appears with the default settings that show you all the Print Shop files you have created (Show Project Files and All as the Files of Type selected). If you have a Print Shop project already saved, you can highlight it to see it in the Preview area. The Wind Song invitation from Chapter 1 is listed as one of the files available.

**2.** Click once on Windsong.pdg. As you can see in Figure 3.1, the front page of the invitation is displayed in the preview area.

In addition to your own projects, you can preview and open all the ready-made projects provided by Print Shop.

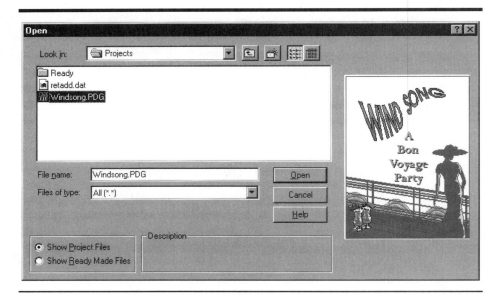

**Figure 3.1:** When you click on the Wind Song file, you can preview the first page before you open it.

**3.** Click on Show Ready Made Files at the bottom of the dialog box. Since your Files of Type still says All, all ready-made files are listed in alphabetical order.

You can specialize your search by changing the Files of Type setting to any one of the projects available in Print Shop.

**4.** Choose Sign from the list. Scroll through the ready-mades and highlight Carwash.srm to see the car wash sign in preview, shown here in Figure 3.2.

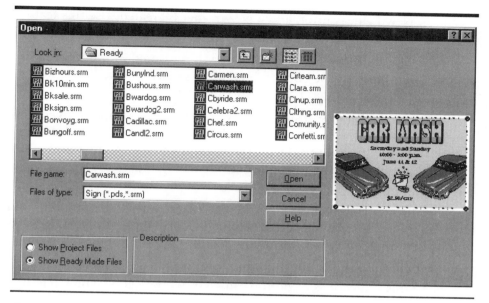

**Figure 3.2:** Ready-made projects appear in alphabetical order with the selected project shown in preview.

At the top of the Open dialog box are four buttons, shown here in Figure 3.3, which help you navigate through your files. Let's take a look at these.

**Figure 3.3:** Navigate through your files with these four buttons: Up One Level, Create New Folder, List, and Details.

**5.** Up One Level, the first button, takes you to the folder immediately above the one you currently have open. Right now you are in the Ready folder. Click on the Up One Level button. You move up to the Projects folder. Double-click on Ready again to return to the list of ready-made sign projects.

**6.** The second button, Create New Folder, creates a new folder and places it in the folder you currently have open. Click on the Create

New Folder button and a New Folder is created. Use this feature to create folders for your own projects.

**7.** The third button, List, lists everything stored in the folder that is currently in the Look in box. In this case, you are in the Ready folder looking at the ready-made signs.

**8.** The last button, Details, gives you information about saved files, specifically their name, size, type, and the last date and time modified. Click on the Details button and you see all the information about the ready-made sign files, including the date they were last modified by Brøderbund.

Finally, the Open dialog box includes a Description box that tells you if the project you have selected has any coordinating elements. Let's take a look at this.

**9.** Highlight Confetti.srm and in the Description box you'll see that this project has a coordinating Banner, Envelope, and Greeting Card, shown here in Figure 3.4.

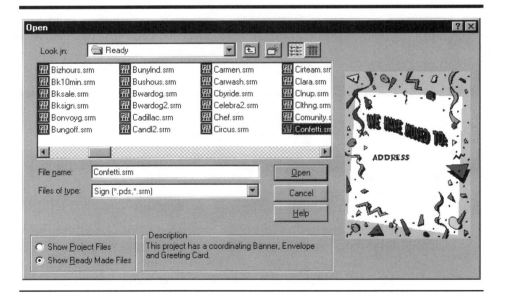

**Figure 3.4:** The selected project has a coordinating Banner, Envelope, and Greeting Card.

The question mark in the upper-right corner of the box can be dragged to specific areas on the dialog box to get quick, short answers to questions you may have. For more detailed help, you can click on the Help button.

Let's go on to Saving a File.

**10.** Select Cancel from the Open dialog box and you revert to the Car Wash sign.

The Print Shop Ensemble III gives you the ability to open files using a drag and drop feature. To use this feature, select Microsoft Windows Explorer, then select The Print Shop Ensemble III project you want to open and drag it onto The Print Shop Ensemble III icon to open it.

## Saving a File

This command saves an active file for the first time or updates a file already saved.

**1.** Click on File ➤ Save.

If the project has been saved before and already has a file title, no prompt appears. The active file is simply updated. If the project has not been saved previously (and therefore does not have a file name), the Save As dialog box appears.

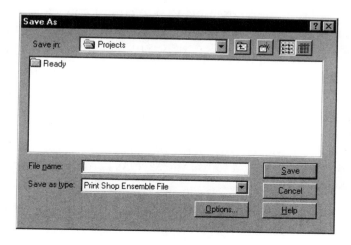

**2.** To save the file, type **CAR** in the Filename box. The file type will be selected for you based on the project type. CAR is a sign so it will be saved with the extension .pds.

**3.** Click on the Options button to access the Save Options dialog box, shown here.

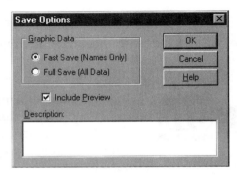

The Graphic Data section of this dialog box allows you to choose between Fast Save (Names Only), which is the default, or Full Save (All Data). Fast Save speeds up each save and takes up less disk space. The Include Preview check box lets you choose whether to show a preview of the project when you click on it in the Open dialog box. Again, you might wish to uncheck Include Preview in order to speed up saves. Finally, you can include a description of the project in the Description box below if you choose, noting coordinating projects you may have created or some other information that will be helpful later.

**4.** Click on OK and you return to the Save As dialog box.

The default file format in the Save as type box in the lower-center is a Print Shop Ensemble File. You can also save the file as a Windows Bitmap file, a Windows Metafile, a TIFF Bitmap file, or a JPEG file.

Note the folder where the file is being saved. The default is c:\Program Files\The Print Shop Ensemble III\Projects. If you want the project saved to a different drive or folder, use your mouse to point and click your way through the drive and folder choices installed in your computer.

**5.** Once you've made your selections, click on Save to save the file.

Once the file is saved, the Save As dialog box will disappear and the newly saved file will remain active. Whenever you click Save after this, the file will be saved automatically using the options you selected above; you won't see the Save As dialog box again. If you want to change the save options, you need to use the Save As command, as explained in the next section.

# Saving As

To change the save options of an already-saved file or to save it under a new name or to a new drive or folder, click on Save As. This brings up the Save As dialog box, and you can select your preferences as before. For projects not previously saved, you can use either Save or Save As to give the file a name and location.

You can also rename or reroute an already-saved file with the Save As command. This is a good way to experiment without endangering the original file. You can save the project under another name or in another location, make all the changes you want, and still be able to access the original project under its old name or in its old location. Let's save the CAR file under a new name.

1. Click on Save As. As with a first-time save, the Save As dialog box appears.

2. Type **CAR2** in the Filename box.

3. Select any preferences you have from the Save Options dialog box and click on OK to return to the Save As box.

4. Click on Save to save the file under its new name.

Now you can experiment on CAR2 as you please without ruining CAR. This procedure isn't really necessary with the ready-made CAR, but if you've spent hours perfecting your own project you can recognize the value of saving under another name.

# Reverting to a Previously Saved Version

Another way to protect your original project is using the Revert to Saved command. When you choose this option, any changes you made in a document since the last time you saved it are ignored and the document reverts to what it was the last time you saved it. When you click on Revert to Saved, a dialog box gives you the opportunity to change your mind.

# Choosing Preferences

Clicking on the Preferences option in the File menu brings up a Preferences dialog box with three tabs, shown here, which lets you change certain defaults in the Print Shop program.

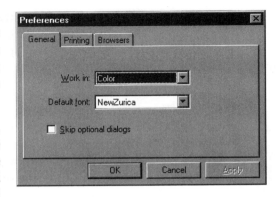

Before we select the preferences, let's open a new file. Select File ➤ New ➤ Banners ➤ Customize a Ready Made ➤ Birthday and select the ready-made file called Birthday/Child, Mouse Party. Note that you have opened a three-page banner. Dotted lines separate the pages, as shown here.

Okay, we have our working project. Let's take a look at the preferences.

**1.** Select File ➤ Preferences.

In the Preferences dialog box, you'll see a dialog box with three tabs— General, Printing, and Browsers.

**2.** Select Work in Grayscale from the tab labeled General. (If you are printing in black and white, you might want to work in grayscale instead of color so that you have a better idea of how your project is actually going to look.)

**3.** Click on Apply. The banner changes from color to grayscale without closing the Preferences dialog box. This allows you to preview your change before exiting the box.

**4.** Select Color again and Apply it to the project.

The next option is the default font. The designated default font is used for headlines and text blocks that do not have a font set by the layout or by you. Change this if you like.

Select Skip optional dialogs for a more direct route to the main project window. If you select this option, you will bypass the Select a Path, Backdrops Browser, and Select a Layout dialog boxes (except if you're working with banners, labels, or calendars). With this option, you'll need only to select a project and then choose an orientation. You might want to do this if you're importing backdrops or other objects or if you want to create your own layout.

**5.** Click on the tab labeled Printing. On it, shown here, you'll find some printing defaults you can set.

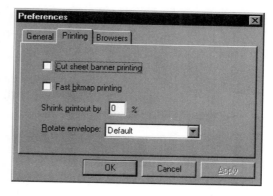

One of the defaults is called Rotate envelope. This option is used only if you are having problems printing envelopes. At the Default setting, the program will adjust the rotation of the envelope output according to the printer you are using. At the Always setting, the program will always rotate the output 180 degrees. At the Never setting, the output will never be rotated.

If you are printing a banner, you can tell Print Shop to print on a cut sheet printer (such as a laser printer) rather than a continuous feed printer. If you're having difficulty printing on a continuous feed printer, select this option to tell Print Shop to treat your printer as a cut sheet printer.

Another option, Fast bitmap printing, may solve printing problems if you are having difficulty flipping or rotating bitmap graphics.

Finally, you can shrink the size at which Print Shop prints if you are having difficulty printing the entire image. If the image is being cut off on the edges, shrink the image slightly to solve the problem. Note that the option is phrased "Shrink printout *by*," not "Shrink printout *to*," so, for example, be sure to type 5% if you want the image to print at 95% of its original size.

**6.** Click on the tab labeled Browsers to reset some browser defaults, shown here.

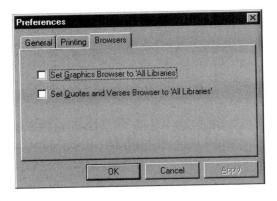

First, you can Set Graphics Browser to All Libraries. With this default set, all libraries will be displayed when you look for a graphic of any kind. For example, if you add a square graphic placeholder and click on it to find a graphic, you will automatically be shown All Libraries containing Square Graphics. For now, do not select this option.

Second, you can set Set Quotes and Verses Libraries to All Libraries, which is also a helpful option at times. Leave this box unselected, make sure your preference is set to Color on the General box, and click on OK to return to the project.

# Printing a Project

When you click on Print, the Print dialog box, shown here, appears. Here you can set up your printer, choose how many copies will print, and determine the print quality, among other things. Also, in some projects you can make your project larger or smaller by scaling it up or down. You can also type a number from 10 to 400 in the Scale Percentage text box to have the document print at anywhere from 10 to 400 percent of its actual size. A project printed at 400 percent will print on 16 pages; a project at 300 percent, on 9 pages; and a project at 200 percent, on 4 pages. This option is not available for banners, so it does not appear on the Print dialog box shown here. Let's take a look at some of the options offered when you select the Print menu.

The Print Shop Ensemble III gives you the ability to print files using a drag and drop feature. To use this feature, select Microsoft Windows Explorer, then select The Print Shop Ensemble III project you want to print and drag it onto the printer icon. The Printer dialog box will appear where you can choose your options and then print.

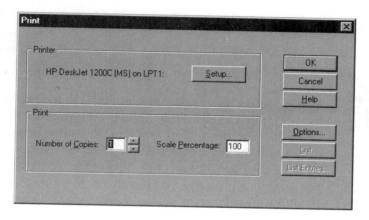

**1.** Select File ➤ Print. The Print dialog box appears. Here you can specify the number of copies and access other dialog boxes by clicking on Setup, Options, List, or List Entries. Let's quickly run through some of these options.

**2.** Click on Setup and select your printer from the Printer Setup dialog box.

**3.** Click on Setup in the Printer Setup dialog box and you will be offered additional options based on your own printer.

These options are presented on a dialog box with a series of tabs. Ours has four tabs, one each for Paper, Graphics, Fonts, and Device Options. The number of tabs you have and your print options will depend on your printer. Browse through your tabs and then we'll go back and look at several interesting print options offered by Print Shop.

**4.** When you've finished browsing, cancel out of the tabbed boxes until you are again at the Print dialog box.

**5.** Click on Options, shown here.

**6.** Select Coloring Book (print outline only) and click OK. The
image prints with text and
graphics in outline. This is an interesting variation for a project.

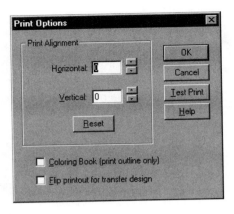

 On sign projects (and only sign projects) in the Print Options dia-
log box, you'll be offered the option "flip printout for transfer
design." Using this option, you can flip your sign project so you
can print it out on special transfer paper, which can then be used
to place the sign onto a t-shirt. Text blocks and Word Balloons do
not print when flipping, so keep this in mind when designing your
T-shirt projects.

Another option lets you adjust the print alignment to better align the
project on the page, moving the project in small increments up to one
inch with the inch divided into 15 parts. You can set the alignment
between –15 to +15, nudging the project up or down or right or left. (The
effects vary from printer to printer.) The Reset button resets alignment
to zero.

To test the alignment of your project on the page, select Test Print. The
dialog box closes and "Welcome to Print Shop" prints with a box outline
around the outer edges of the print page.  In the case of the three-page
banner, Test Print will print on three pages with a box outline around the
outer edge of each page. If your printer does not print the test as indicated above, check your printer settings before going on.

The Print dialog box offers additional options for certain projects. See
Chapter 5, "Understanding Print Shop Projects," and Chapter 14,
"Printing Made Easy," for information about printing specific projects.

# Setting Up Your Printer

When you click on Printer Setup, a dialog box allows you to set up your printer. We just looked at these setup boxes in "Printing a Project" above. Some of the options offered are specific to your printer. Since we may not have the same printer as you have, we'll pass on discussing these here. If you need help, consult your printer's manual or ask somebody who knows about printer settings.

# Previewing a Project

To preview a project in full screen before you print it out, select from the choices offered on the Print Preview

pop-up list, shown here. You can preview a project in color, in Grayscale, or in coloring book format. Let's take a look at the Mouse Party banner in coloring book format.

1. Select File ➤ Preview.

2. From the Print Preview pop-up list, click on Coloring Book. Mouse Party is previewed in coloring book format, as shown below. When you're finished looking, click on Done.

3. Click File ➤ Print Preview again and select Grayscale to preview the banner in grayscale. Click on Done.

4. Click File ➤ Print Preview and select Color to preview in color.

5. Click on Done to return to the main project window for the next File menu command, Exit.

## Exiting the Program

Exit, the last command on the File menu, exits the Print Shop program. (Don't do this now! We're not done exploring the menus.) If you have not saved your project (or if you have not saved your most recent changes to a project), a prompt will ask if you want to save it. If you click on Yes, you'll be asked to name the file (unless you have previously saved and named it). If you have saved your project and all its edits, or if you're working with a ready-made project and you haven't changed anything, Print Shop will close without a prompt.

## ◆ Using the Edit Menu

The Edit menu offers the following options: Undo, Cut, Copy, Paste, Delete, Duplicate, and Select All. These commands are pretty self-explanatory, but let's run through them quickly.

You must select an object before you can use most of the Edit commands. If no object is selected, the only edit option available is Select All.

## Undoing an Action

Undo reverses your last action. If you delete something or make a change in the project and then change your mind, just select Edit ➤ Undo. You can undo an insertion, a deletion, a move, a color change, or anything else you've done. Keep in mind, though, that Undo only works for your most recent action. You cannot use it to put things back the way they were three actions ago.

The Undo command changes to match the last action. For example, if you delete an object, the Undo command reads Undo Delete Object. If you change the backdrop, the Undo command reads Undo Backdrop Change. If you change a color, the command reads Undo Color Change, and so on.

1. Click on the Pointer tool, then select the large graphic in the Mouse Party banner that includes the table and several mice.

2. From the Edit menu, click on Delete; the graphic is deleted.

3. Now from the Edit menu, select Undo Delete Object and the graphic returns.

Once you have used Undo, the command changes to Redo. For example, if you delete an object and then click on Undo Delete Object, the command will change to read Redo. If you click on it, the object will be deleted again.

4. Pull down the Edit menu again; the Undo command now says Redo. Click on Redo and the table and mice disappear again.

5. Undo the deletion again to put the banner back the way it was.

## Cutting Objects

The Cut command removes whatever is highlighted and stores it in the Clipboard (a Windows temporary storage area), where it remains until it is replaced. Once you have placed material in the Clipboard, you can paste it elsewhere in the document (or in another document) with the Paste command. The Cut command competes for storage in the Clipboard with the Copy command; every time you use the Cut or Copy command, the Clipboard erases what it has stored previously and replaces it with the new material.

When using the Cut command, make sure you paste the material in its new location as quickly as possible to prevent losing it in case you forget and cut or copy some new material. The Cut command is a good way to move material from one project to another or move material to a program other than Print Shop, assuming the file formats are compatible.

Using the Mouse Party banner, we'll practice cutting.

1. Click on the duck standing on the table.

2. Click on Edit ➤ Cut and the duck disappears. The duck graphic is now stored in the Clipboard.

3. Since we're not quite ready to paste it, select Edit ➤ Undo Cut to put the graphic back where it was.

# Copying Objects

The Copy command makes a copy of whatever is highlighted and stores it in the Clipboard to be pasted elsewhere. Unlike a cut item, an item that is copied remains in the project. Every time you use the Copy command, the last item copied to the Clipboard is replaced by the new item. As noted already, Cut and Copy compete for the storage space in the Clipboard, so if you copy right after you cut, the item copied will replace the item cut.

Using the Mouse Party banner again, let's make a line of mice bringing in cake for the party.

1. Click on the mouse in the upper-left corner.

2. Click on Edit ➤ Copy and the object is copied. The original does not change at all.

The mouse graphic (called Mouse & Slice from the Special Occasions square graphics library) is now stored in the Clipboard. We'll paste it in the next section.

# Pasting Objects

The Paste command pastes whatever is stored in the Clipboard into a project wherever you place the cursor. If nothing is stored in the Clipboard, the Paste command is light gray in color, indicating that it is unavailable.

We just copied the Mouse & Slice graphic, so let's paste it now.

1. Click on Paste. The second mouse graphic is placed on top of the first one. The mouse graphic on top is selected, waiting for you to move it to its new location.

2. Drag the mouse graphic so it's just in front of the first mouse.

3. Click on Paste again and move this third mouse just in front of the second one. Using paste once more, move the fourth mouse just in front of the third one, as shown here. Your mice will probably cover up some of the headline and they will probably step on a teddy bear and a duck but don't worry about this. We'll take care of this little

problem in a minute. Now you have a bunch of mice coming to the party, each one bringing cake. Yummm.

# Deleting Objects

The Delete command serves the same function as the trash can icon on the toolbar and the Delete key on the keyboard. It erases whatever is highlighted or selected by the Pointer tool.

Let's delete the teddy bear and the duck under the feet of the parade of mice.

**1.** Click on the teddy bear and then, while holding down your shift key, click on the duck. Both are selected. If you're having trouble selecting these two graphics because the feet of the mice are in the way, move one or more of the mice aside until you can delete the duck and the teddy. Then you can move the mice back into position.

**2.** Click on Edit ➤ Delete. The teddy bear and the duck disappear.

Don't worry about these little guys. We'll bring them both back to the party (or at least exact duplicates of them) when we duplicate objects in the next section.

# Duplicating Objects

The Duplicate command makes one copy of the item(s) selected, placing it on top of and to the side of the item duplicated. Multiple copies can be made by continuing to click on Duplicate once you've selected an object. Use the Pointer tool to move the copied object into its desired location in the project.

Let's use Duplicate to bring our deleted teddy and duck back and double the size of the party at the same time. Take a look at your banner. You have three duck and three teddy graphics. Each one is a separate graphic.

1. Click on one of the ducks and then holding down the Shift key, click on the other two ducks and the three teddys. All six graphics will be selected (all have handles).

2. Select Edit ➤ Duplicate. A second set of three ducks and three teddys is created and placed on top of the first. Select Edit ➤ Duplicate once more and make a third set.

3. Click outside your duplicated graphics to deselect them all. Then select each one and drag it to a position on your banner. Take a look at our party in the graphic in the next section.

## Selecting All

The Select All command selects everything in the project, including text, headlines, and graphics. Once selected, you can copy, cut, or duplicate everything with one command.

You can use the Select All command to identify all the objects in a project. This is particularly useful when you're working with a ready-made project and are not quite sure, for example, where one text block ends and another begins, or whether an image is one large graphic or a combination of several graphics.

Let's select everything in the Mouse Party banner.

1. Click on Select All and all objects acquire boxes and handles, as shown below.

**2.** Click on any object and drag everything off the banner area.

You'll notice that two objects are left on the banner, as shown below.

One of them is the headline box. This box is permanently locked. (You can tell it's locked because its handles are smaller.) You cannot move or delete a headline box in a banner. You can add headline boxes but you cannot delete one that was part of the original layout.

The other unmovable object is the border. Borders cannot be moved or resized unless they're mini-borders. Mini-borders can be both moved and resized.

**3.** Pull down the Edit menu and select Undo Move Object; your banner returns to its previous state.

## ◆ Using the Object Menu

The Object menu lets you add or manipulate objects in your project. The Object menu commands are Add, Edit, Shadow, Border Size, Frame, Order, Scale, Rotate, Flip, Lock, Unlock, and Align. Many of the commands offered in this menu are also available in the toolbar, including the commands under Add, Frame, Rotate (with some variations), and Flip. The others are available only from this menu.

### Adding Objects

The Add command offers the following choices: Graphic, Square Graphic, Row Graphic, Column Graphic, Text, Headline, Word Balloon, Horizontal Ruled Line, Vertical Ruled Line, Border, Mini-border, Mini-backdrop, Seal,

Signature Block, Title Block, and Import (a graphic). Do these commands look familiar? They should: they are exactly the same—and function the same way—as the options for the Add Object tool on the toolbar. Please refer to "Adding Objects" in Chapter 2 for details.

# Editing Objects

You can edit an object by selecting it and clicking on Object ➤ Edit. If the object selected is a graphic, you will see a dialog box that allows you to select a new graphic, replacing the current one. If the object selected is a text or headline block, you'll see a dialog box that allows you to change the font, color, and text style and add customized touches.

You can also trigger the Edit command by double-clicking on any object. Let's take a look at different types of editing using the Object ➤ Edit menu.

## Replacing a Graphic

First, let's edit a graphic.

**1.** In the banner, select one of the ducks. We're going to select the duck at the top of our teddy bear pyramid.

**2.** If you like, select the View menu and change the view to 150% so you can get a closer look at your duck.

**3.** Select your duck and then select Edit from the Object menu or double-click on the duck. The Graphics Browser dialog box pops up.

**4.** Select the Elephant Forgets graphic in the graphic library called PS Squares to replace the duck.

**5.** Click OK and you return to the project window. The elephant has replaced the duck as the top of the teddy pyramid.

**6.** Resize the elephant to make it larger and heavier, as shown here, so everyone can be impressed by the strength of the teddys.

# Editing a Banner Headline

Now let's edit our headline. First, pull down the View menu and select Fit to Window so you can see the complete banner, if you're not already there.

1. Now select the banner headline. (This is the only text block in this banner, for now anyway.)

2. Click on Object ➤ Edit and the Banner dialog box appears. This text box appears only in banners.

All the specifications are noted: font, size, color, style, and justification. You can change any of these specifications and you can add or delete text. Clicking on the Preview button will accurately preview the text's font, size, color, and style in the text box.

Let's change the text:

3. Delete Emily, as shown here.

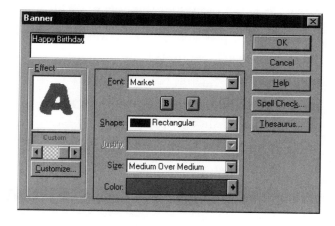

4. Click OK and you return to your project with the new text in place.

# Editing Headlines

Now let's add a headline.

1. Select Object ➤ Add ➤ Headline.

**2.** With the new headline box selected, click on Object ➤ Edit or double-click on the box and the Headline dialog box appears, as shown below. This is the same dialog box that appeared in Chapter 1 when we added 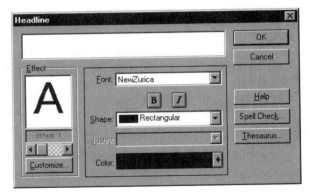 the headline to the front of the party invitation. Here we can select all the characteristics of our headline text, including effect, font, shape, justification, and color.

**3.** Click on the arrow to the right of the Shape box and a list drops down offering 21 different headline shapes. Change the headline shape from Rectangular to Arc Down.

**4.** Move the slider bar under the Effect box all the way to the right so it's on Custom. Change your font to Market and change the color of the type to fit the banner. (For more information, see Chapter 11, "Working with Text and Headlines.")

**5.** Type **Emily** in the Edit box.

**6.** Next click on the Customize button and the Custom Effect dialog box appears, as shown here. Here you have even more options for changing the text with effects, fill, shadow, position, color, color saturation, and more.

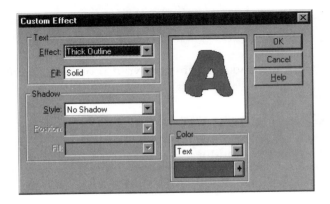

7. Change your Text Effect to Thick Outline. Your outline color will be black by default. This will be fine, so click OK.

8. Click OK again and you return to the banner with a new headline.

9. Move and resize the headline so it fits with your banner design. We placed the headline in the hands of our teddy bear pyramid, as shown here.

# Adding Shadows to Objects

The next option on the Object menu is the Shadow command. You can add shadows to square, row, and column graphics, giving the graphics a somewhat three-dimensional look. This type of shadow differs from the shadow you can put behind a frame in that it falls behind the graphic itself.

Let's take a look at shadows. First, let's invite another guest to the Mouse Party.

1. From the Object menu, select Add, then click on Square Graphic. A placeholder for a square graphic is added to the banner.

2. Double-click on the bear icon in the center of the square graphic. The Graphics Browser pops up. Choose PS Squares as your library.

3. Click on Baby and then OK. The Baby graphic is placed in the square graphic box.

4. Select the Elephant and hit the Delete key on your keyboard. The elephant will disappear. Next drag the baby so it's at the top of the teddy pyramid, as shown here.

**5.** Now pull down the Object menu and select Shadow, then On. The baby now has a shadow.

Not all graphics benefit from the Shadow option. Some have so many elements in them that adding a shadow just confuses the subject. Others have built-in shadows, making an additional shadow unnecessary. The size of the graphic on the project page will be a factor in whether the shadow works or not. Obviously, on larger graphics a shadow will be more visible than on smaller ones.

It's best to take a look at graphics with and without shadows to see if the effect works. The baby is shown here with and without a shadow. Does the shadow add anything to the graphic? (You may wish to change the view to a larger size in order to see better.) If you decide it does not, you can reverse the procedure by selecting either Object ➤ Shadow ➤ Off or Edit ➤ Undo Shadow Object.

Shadow    No Shadow

# Framing an Object

The Frame command in the Object menu has the same options and works the same way as the Frame tool on the toolbar. For specifics, please refer to "Framing Objects" in Chapter 2.

# Putting Objects in Order

Print Shop's default is for the last object placed on the page to be the uppermost object, covering the objects below it. If, however, you want text to print on top of a graphic or one graphic to print over a portion of another graphic, you can use the Order command to designate the objects' order of placement.

The Order commands available and their designated functions are as follows:

| | |
|---|---|
| Bring Forward | Moves object forward one layer |
| Bring to Front | Moves object to the topmost layer |
| Send Backward | Moves object backward one layer |
| Send to Back | Moves object to bottommost layer |

 You cannot place an object behind the backdrop; it will always be the bottom layer of the project. And you cannot place an object in front of a border; it will always be the top layer. (If you really want to place an object in front of a border or a backdrop, there's a way around this: make a mini-border or mini-backdrop and stretch it to fit the page. You *can* place objects in front of a mini-border or mini-backdrop.)

Let's use the Order command to clean up our banner. Right now our banner headline is covered up by cake. We can easily remedy this.

**1.** Click on one of the cake-carrying mice marching in on the left side of the banner. Now hold down your Shift key and select the other three mice. All four should be selected.

**2.** Next, select Order from the Object menu and click on Send to Back. The mice move behind the banner headline, as seen here.

## Scaling an Object

So far we've resized objects by selecting them and pulling or pushing on their handles. Another way is to use the Scale command, which scales objects by a specific percentage. This is a good way to fit an object precisely into a given space.

**1.** Select the baby graphic.

**2.** Select Object ➤ Scale. The Scale dialog box, shown here, appears.

The percentage defaults to 100%, representing the object's current size. You can either type the percentage you

want or use the arrow keys to move the percentage up or down. When you scale a graphic or headline box, the graphic or headline changes its size to fit into the new box.

**3.** Type 50 in the scale dialog box and click OK; the dialog box disappears and the baby graphic shrinks down to 50% of its original size.

**4.** Select Object ➤ Scale. Note that the Scaling box reads 100%, as it did before. Any time you scale a graphic, its present size is always 100%, regardless of any scaling you have done before. Type 200, and click OK. Now the baby is twice the size it was.

**5.** Select Object ➤ Scale one more time, type 25, and click OK. The baby returns to its original size.

# Rotating an Object

The Rotate command on the Object menu is more precise than the Rotate tool on the toolbar. You'll remember from Chapter 2 that the Rotate tool allows you to grab an object and physically turn it. The Rotate menu command takes you one step further. It allows you to designate an exact angle of turn for objects and to turn them automatically. The Rotate menu offers you the option of rotating: Left 90°, Right 90°, or Other.

Let's make the baby stand on one foot by using the Rotate menu command.

**1.** Select the baby.

**2.** Click on Object ➤ Rotate ➤ Other. The Rotate dialog box appears.

**3.** Click on the arrows to change 0 to 330, as shown here. The angle of rotation you've selected is indicated on the angle clock.

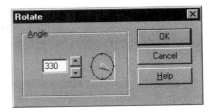

**4.** Click OK and the baby will stand on one foot. Reposition the baby so its foot is held up by one of the teddys.

# Flipping Objects

The Flip command in the Object menu offers the same options as the Flip tool in the toolbar: Horizontal, Vertical, and Both. Refer to "Flipping Objects" in Chapter 2 for details.

# Locking and Unlocking Objects

Once you have an object in the right position, you can lock it in place to keep it from moving around while you are working on other objects. A locked object will not move until you unlock it.

Now that we've got the baby where we want it, let's lock it.

**1.** Select the baby and from the Object menu, click on Lock. The handles on the bubble become smaller, indicating that it is locked.

**2.** To unlock the baby, select it and click on Object ➤ Unlock. The handles change back to their normal size to indicate that the object is not locked.

# Aligning Objects

Aligning makes it easy to place two or more objects in exact relationship to each other. You can arrange the objects in eleven different ways:

Aligns objects by upper-left corners

Aligns objects by upper edges

Aligns objects by upper-right corners

Aligns objects by left edges

Aligns objects by centers, vertically and horizontally

Aligns objects by right edges

Aligns objects by lower-left corners

Aligns objects by lower edges

Aligns objects by lower-right corners

Aligns objects by centers, horizontally

Aligns objects by centers, vertically

Let's try aligning several of our ducks, putting them all in a row.

**1.** Select all the ducks by clicking on one, holding down the Shift key, and then clicking on the others. Note how the ducks are positioned right now.

**2.** Select Object ➤ Align and the alignment options pop up, as outlined above.

**3.** Click on each of the options offered; as you click each one, its description appears in the lower portion of the screen.

**4.** Select the one that "aligns objects along vertical midlines" and click OK. The ducks are now all in a row, top to bottom.

Aligning objects in this way is a faster and more accurate way to align your objects than trying to align them by sight alone. If you don't like the results of an alignment you've performed, remember you can always undo your action by clicking the Undo tool or choosing Edit ➤ Undo as long as you do it immediately.

# ◆ Using the Project Menu

The Project menu offers options for changing the basics of your project. The first two commands in the Project menu for all projects are always Change Backdrop (except a Label project) and Change Layout. The other commands vary depending on the project type.

# Changing the Backdrop

You can change the backdrop of your project at any time by clicking on Change Backdrop. If you have a backdrop already, a dialog box pops up letting you know that if you change the backdrop, you'll lose your current backdrop. If you have no backdrop (as is the case with our Mouse Party banner), you go directly to the Backdrops Browser.

As usual, the backdrops available appear in the preview box as you click on them. If you decide not to add or change the backdrop, you can click on Cancel to return to the project unchanged.

 When you change a backdrop, all the layout elements remain the same and maintain the same position they had with the previous backdrop.

Let's try a few of the backdrops on the Mouse Party banner.

1. Click on Project ➤ Change Backdrop.

2. Select Cupids and click OK. The Cupids backdrop appears underneath the banner, but it makes everything too confusing.

3. Select Edit ➤ Undo to change the banner back the way it was.

4. Click on Project ➤ Change Backdrop again.

5. Select Hot Dog, shown here. This is certainly different, but not very appropriate.

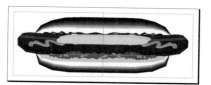

6. Click Cancel.

 If you've experimented with several backdrops and you want to go back to having no backdrop at all, you won't be able to use the Undo command, since that only removes your most recent action. But you can still return to a blank background by scrolling to the top of the list of graphics and selecting Blank Page.

## Changing the Layout

When you click on Change Layout, a dialog box pops up letting you know that changing the layout will erase the current project. When you select a new layout, all objects in your project are deleted and replaced by the new layout.

Let's do a practice run without actually changing the layout of the banner.

**1.** Select Project ➤ Change Layout.

**2.** In the dialog box that appears, click on Yes.

**3.** The ready-made layout options appear in the Select a Layout dialog box. Click on a few of these layouts to see what they look like, but don't click on OK. You don't want to lose all your work.

**4.** When you're through looking at the layout options, click on Cancel. You will return to the project and no changes will have been made to the original layout.

## Changing the Banner Length

When you're working on a banner, Banner Length is one of the command options on the Project menu. Clicking on Banner Length displays the dialog box shown here, which allows you to specify in inches where you want the length added: in front of the type (leading space) or behind it (trailing space).

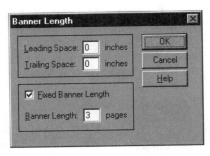

The Fixed Banner Length option, which automatically adjusts the number of pages in the banner to fit the text, is selected by default. If you prefer, you can change the length manually by typing a number in the Banner Length box below. Right now, the Mouse Party banner is set to print on three pages. Let's change it to five pages.

**1.** Click on Project ➤ Banner Length and type **5** in the Banner Length box. Do not change the leading or trailing spaces.

**2.** Click OK and the banner appears on five pages, as shown below (dotted lines appear between the pages). You can see that the banner headline stretched to fit the new size but the graphics did not change in size.

 Changing the banner length stretches the backdrop and any headlines that were part of the original layout, but does not stretch any graphics on the banner or any headline added to the project. All these stay in essentially the same position as they were before the stretch. You'll need to grab handles and manually stretch graphics to fill the new space.

Let's look at another banner to see if it automatically adjusts.

**1.** Click on the File menu and select Open.

**2.** From the Open dialog box, click on Show Ready Made Files, and in the box files of type, select Banners from the drop down list. Then select the file called Room.brm, and click open.

**3.** A prompt will ask you if you want to save your Mouse Party banner. Click on Yes and type Mouse Party in as the name of the banner. It will be saved in the Projects folder where we can open it later. Once the project is saved, the Room banner, shown below, will open.

You have a brand new banner in your project window. Let's adjust its length.

4. Select Project ➤ Banner Length.

5. Change the length to **5** pages and click OK. Everything on the banner stretches to fit five pages, as shown below. The reason the items on this banner stretch to fill five pages is that they are all either backdrop or headline, and backdrops and headlines stretch to fit the space available.

6. Now select Project ➤ Banner Length again, and this time change the leading space to **3** inches.

7. Click OK. The word *Francine* has been moved to the right three inches.

Browse through the ready-made banners and take a look at the variety of styles. Try changing the banner lengths and adjusting the leading and trailing spaces to see the effects.

# Blending the Colors on a Page

Banners do not offer the Page Blend option, so you will not find it on the Project menu at the moment. The command appears in almost every other project, however. With Page Blend, you can add texture to a page color by applying one of six different designs that blend the color in varying shades.

## Using Page Blend Alone

Let's take a look at Page Blend.

1. Pull down the File menu, select New, and click No when asked if you want to save the existing project.

2. Select Signs & Posters as your project, then choose Start From Scratch from the Select a Path dialog box, then Tall from the Sign Orientation dialog box, Blank Page from the Graphics Browser, and

finally No Layout from the Select a Layout dialog box. You end up in the main project window with a blank piece of paper.

3. The Item Selector shows that Page is selected and the Color Selector indicates that the page color is white. Change the color by pulling down the Color Selector and choosing from the colors offered. Your page will become the color you selected.

4. Pull down the Item Selector and select Page Blend.

5. The default color for a page blend is black. Again pull down the Color Selector and change the color.

The page in your main project window does not change color, because Page Blend is the secondary color and only shows up when you actually blend the colors using Page Blend from the Project Menu. Let's do that now.

6. Pull down the Project menu and select Page Blend. Solid is selected by default; this means that only the primary page color is in effect. Blend this color with the secondary page blend color by selecting Blend Across. The page changes, blending the two selected colors across the page as shown here.

7. Pull down the Project menu again and select Page Blend ➤ Blend Down. The page colors blend again, but in a different direction, as shown here. Continue through the list until you've seen all the blends.

## Using Page Blend with a Backdrop

Let's try using Page Blend with a backdrop. First, select one of the Page Blend options, choosing whatever colors you like. When your page is blended and colored just right, begin.

1. From the Project menu, select Change Backdrop.

**2.** From the Backdrops Browser, select Calendar. Your page now shows the Calendar graphic over the blended page.

**3.** Try some of the other backdrops and see how they work. You might want to change your page blend colors as well.

Some backdrops fill the entire page and, when they do, you cannot see the page color at all. If the backdrop graphic is black in color, its color can be changed using the Item Selector and the Color Selector. Backdrop graphics that are multicolored can be lightened using the Shading Selector.

We'll cover this more in Part Three, "Managing Graphics."

## Choosing Other Project Commands

Other commands that are specific to particular projects appear on the Project menu. When you're working on a greeting card, for instance, options include Front of Card, Inside of Card, and Back of Card. Click on these to move between the different pages of the card. When you're working on a calendar, options include Change Month, Edit Day, Change Year, and Calendar Options. These options change based on whether your calendar has a daily, weekly, monthly, or yearly format.

We'll cover the options specific to different types of projects in Chapter 5, "Understanding Print Shop Projects." For now, just remember that when you're working on different projects you will find other commands on the Project menu than those we've seen here.

## ◆ Using the View Menu

The View menu lets you change the way you view your project. Many of the commands in this menu are the same as those affiliated with the Zoom tool on the toolbar. The commands repeated here are Zoom In, Zoom Out, Fit to Window, 25%, 50%, Actual Size, 150%, and 200%. The result will be the same whether you select these commands from the Zoom tool or from the View menu. Refer to "Changing the View" in Chapter 2 for details.

The commands available only on the View menu are Hide (Show) Backdrop, Hide (Show) Placeholders, Toolbars, and, for greeting card and postcard projects, Hide (Show) Navigation Toolbar. Toolbar has a dialog box, shown here, attached to it. On it, you can

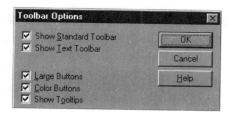

choose to show or hide the Standard Toolbar or Text Toolbar. You can also choose to have Large or Color Buttons on your toolbars. And you can choose to be shown Tool tips (the drop down box that identifies the tool by name).

If your screen is getting crowded, you may wish to hide one or more toolbars, backdrops, or placeholders to make a little more room. When an element is visible, the command on the View menu says Hide. When an element is hidden, the command changes to Show. For example, if you hide a toolbar, the command says Show (that) Toolbar.

# ◆ Using the Extras Menu

Commands offered on the Extras menu include Smart Graphics, Custom Libraries, Select List Type, Edit Address List, Edit Custom List, Edit Return Address, Export and Print Graphics, and Internet Connection.

## Using Smart Graphics

Smart Graphics allow you to create customized graphics, such as the stylized initial (Initial Caps) shown here, to use in your projects. Other Smart Graphics options include Numbers, Timepieces, and Custom Borders. The Numbers option gives you the ability to customize numbers, much as the initial is customized. Timepieces allows you to customize a clock, choosing a graphic and time. And with Custom Borders, you can create a border, mini-border, or certificate border. You will learn more about all these in Chapter 8, "Creating Special Graphics."

## Customizing Libraries

The Custom Libraries command allows you to merge and modify graphics libraries. See Chapter 7, "Working with Graphics Libraries," for a complete discussion of this command.

## Accessing Lists

The Select List Type, Edit Address List, Edit Custom List, and Edit Return Address commands provide you with access to address and custom lists and let you merge these lists into your projects. This feature is particularly useful for signs, labels, mailing lists, and name tags. See Chapter 12, "Creating and Merging Lists" for more information.

## Exporting Graphics

The Export and Print Graphics command allows you to export graphics directly from the project window. (This command is also available in the Select a Project, Extras, Graphics Exporter dialog box when you first open the program.) See Chapter 10, "Exporting Graphics," for information.

## Connecting with the Internet

The Internet Connection command takes you through a simple setup operation for extablishing a direct connection to the Internet, so that you can send Online Greetings to friends and colleagues, and you can access The Print Shop web page. See Chapter 6, "Creating Online Greetings" for more on making your Internet connection.

# ◆ Using the Help Menu

Print Shop Ensemble III comes with an extensive Help library online. When in doubt, click on Help on the main menu bar and you'll be offered three options: Contents, Using Help, and About.

Contents takes you to the main Help screen, from which you can access the information you need directly or by performing a specific search. See Chapter 4, "Getting Help," for complete instructions. Using Help gives you specific instructions using three search areas: Contents, Index, and Find. About gives credit to all those great creative types at Broderbund who worked on Print Shop.

See Chapter 4, "Getting Help," for complete instructions on Help.

# ◆ Endnotes

Mission accomplished. You now know everything you ever wanted to know about menus. You know:

- ◆ How to open, close, save, and print files
- ◆ How to choose your working preferences
- ◆ How to undo an edit or cut, copy, and paste objects
- ◆ How to duplicate everything in the project window or one object only
- ◆ How to add, edit, shadow, frame, move to the front, push to the back, flip, rotate, lock down, and align objects
- ◆ How to change a backdrop or a layout, adjust a banner length, and change the page blend or page color
- ◆ How to view the project in any size you like
- ◆ A bit about special projects filed under the Extras Menu
- ◆ Where to find Help when you need it

You're well on your way to mastering this program.

In Chapter 4, "Getting Help," we'll take a look at how to effectively use the online Help system in The Print Shop Ensemble III.

# Getting Help

## Your mission: to understand Help, where to find it and how to use it

◆

In Chapter 3, you received a brief introduction to Help by way of the main menu. In this chapter, we'll explore all that Help has to offer: the various screens, dialog boxes, links, and other elements that help you find the information you need.

From the main project window select Help and a drop down list offers you Contents, Using Help, and About. Selecting Contents will take you directly to the Print Shop Ensemble III Main Help Screen. Selecting Using Help will take you to a help area that will give you information about using the Windows help system, not help on Print Shop. The last selection About takes you to information on the program itself, including a complete credit list you can scroll through.

# ◆ Using the Main Help Screen

The main Help screen, shown in Figure 4.1, is reached by clicking on Help ➤ Contents. The left side of the screen lists five chapters designed to walk you through specifics of the program: The Basics, The Projects, Tools and Menus, Graphics Exporter, and Troubleshooting. This list also includes a Glossary to help you understand terminology. You can click on any one of these buttons to reach more specific information.

The right side of the Help screen contains some informative welcome text. Some of the words are green and underlined; this special text indicates a link to information on a related topic.

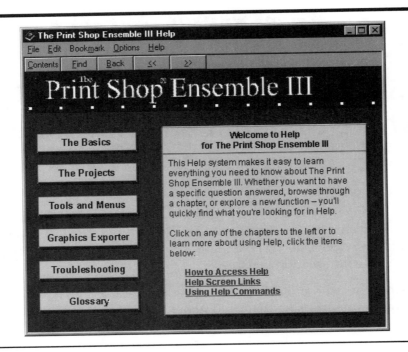

**Figure 4.1:** Print Shop's main help screen.

Help screens have three different linked elements—pop-up boxes, jumps, and notes. Whenever you move your cursor over one of these links, the cursor will change to a hand, indicating a link command. Green text is linked to a pop-up box that offers additional information about the current subject. Underlined green text is linked to a jump, which takes you directly to another Help screen. A note icon offers additional information on the current topic or a related topic when you click on it.

# Using Links

Let's give it a try.

1. Select File ➤ Open ➤ Mouse Party, stored in your Projects folder, to open the banner we created in Chapter 3.

2. In the main project window, click on Help, then on Contents. The Print Shop Ensemble III Help screen appears.

3. Read through the welcome text. There are three jumps (green underlined text) in the welcome text: How to Access Help, Help Screen Links, and Using Help Commands. Click on How to Access Help, and the text box is filled with a brief explanation, telling you to click on a Help button if one appears or to click on the Help menu to access Help at any time.

4. At the top of the Print Shop Ensemble III Help dialog box, click on the button labeled Back, and you will return to the previous screen.

5. Click on Help Screen Links, and information on pop-ups, jumps, and notes appears. Read through it.

6. Click on Back again, then on Using Help Commands. Here you'll find an explanation of the buttons at the top of the Help dialog box, as follows:

| Button | Action |
| --- | --- |
| Contents | Returns you to the initial Help screen |
| Find | Calls up the Find dialog box, which allows you to search by word, phrase, or subject |
| Back | Returns you to the previous screen |

| Button | Action |
|---|---|
|  | Moves you back one screen |
| | Moves you forward one screen |

**NOTE** The left arrow button moves you between screens but does not necessarily return you to the last screen, since there are topics embedded in screens. If you want to go to a previous screen, use Back.

**7.** Click on Back again to return to the initial Print Shop Ensemble III Help screen.

## Using the Help Chapters

Let's take a look at the Help chapters.

**1.** Click on The Basics. A list of basics replaces the welcome information in the preview window to the right of the Print Shop Ensemble III Help dialog box, as shown here. You can select from this list to see information on a topic.

> To learn more about the basic skills needed to work with The Print Shop Ensemble III, click any of the items below. Browse through all the topics for a comprehensive lesson.
>
> Initial Selections
> Working with Backdrops
> Layouts
> The Main Window
> Graphics
> Working with Text
> Design Options
> Saving Your Project
> Printing Your Project
> Quitting the Program
> Drag and Drop Features
> Tooltips
> Status Bar

**2.** Click on Initial Selections and you jump to that screen. Note that this screen has a series of jumps, represented by green underlined type. There is one in the first paragraph and a list of them at the end of the screen.

**3.** Click on the Contents button at the top of the screen to return to the initial Print Shop Ensemble III Help screen.

You can continue your search for help in this way by clicking through the other chapter options, or you can search for help on a specific subject, as described in "Searching Help" later in the chapter.

# ◆ Setting Up Help

The first time you select Help ➤ Contents, you will be prompted to choose how you want to set up your help section using the Find Setup Wizard dialog box, shown here in Figure 4.2.

 The Find Setup Wizard dialog box is available anytime, if you want to change your help setup, by clicking on the Rebuild button that appears in the Find dialog box, discussed in the next section.

Here you can choose from three options:

◆ Minimize database size (recommended)

◆ Maximize search capabilities

◆ Customize search capabilities

This Help setup makes it possible for you to control your database size and even customize Help by adding other help libraries. This ability will prove to be a great time saver.

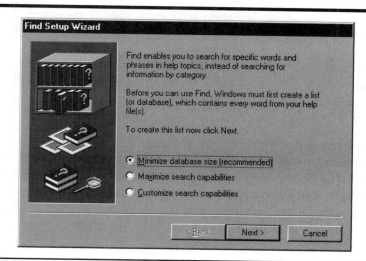

**Figure 4.2:** The Find Setup Wizard will help you set up your help area so it best suits your needs.

# ◆ Searching Help

You can narrow your search criteria by using the Find dialog box, shown below, which is accessed by clicking on the Find button at the top of the Print Shop Ensemble III Help screen.

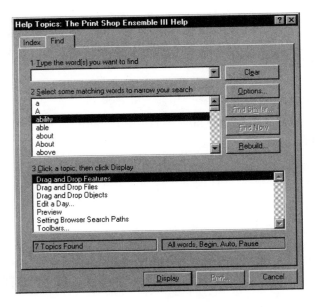

Your cursor will appear in the number 1 text box: Type the word(s) you want to find. A list of your most recent searches will appear when you click on the arrow next to this box, giving you easy access to previous screens. If this is your first search, nothing will be listed.

Below this is a number 2 box: Select some matching words to narrow your search. This second box includes a list of every search word and symbol presently in your help setup. You can scroll down this list and highlight a word or symbol that corresponds to the subject on which you need help. Or you can type a word, phrase, or symbol in text box number 1. If you type in a word or symbol, Help searches for that word or symbol in the list appearing in box number 2.

If no word or symbol is found that matches what you typed in, all boxes go blank with the notation "0 topics found" at the bottom of the screen. If no topics are found, you can attempt the search again by clicking on the Find Similar button. Help will look for similar words that may fit your need. Searching for similar words is an option you choose when you set up with Find Setup Wizard. If you have not selected this option, the Find Similar button will always be dim, indicating this option is not available to you.

If topics are found, they are listed in box 3: Click a topic, then click "display." Choose the topic that best fits your need and click on Display to read the help screen.

The Find Options dialog box, shown here, is accessed by clicking on the Options button in the Find dialog box. Here you'll find options for

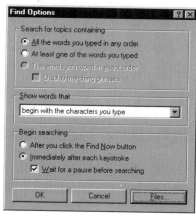

fine-tuning your search preferences including searching for all words in any order, searching for at least one of the words typed, searching for words in exact order, and displaying matching phrases. This dialog box also has options that allow you to set how you want to begin a search and how Help searches for a word you typed. The Files option takes you to a dialog box where you can search help in other programs, other than Print Shop. This is not an option you'll need, at least not for working with Print Shop.

The Index dialog box, shown here, is hidden behind the Find box. Click on Index to move it to the front position, putting Find in the back. The Index includes a complete list of all topics in your Help system. You can scroll down the list, looking for help, or you can type a word or phrase in box number one. Just keep in mind that the search looks for a word or phrase included in the topic name, not inside the topic itself.

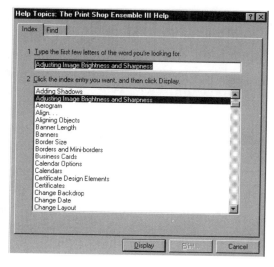

Let's search for help on backdrops.

1. In the Print Shop Ensemble III Help dialog box, click on the Find button. Type backdrops or scroll through the list and highlight backdrops. You may find more than one backdrop. If you type in backdrop, all the versions of backdrop in the list will be highlighted so you can see a complete list of all topics. If you scroll down the list and want to select all the versions of backdrop, select the first one and then hold down the Shift key and select the last one. All will be highlighted and all topics will be listed.

2. From the topics, select Banners and double-click or click on the Display button.

3. The Banners help screen opens. You'll note that this Help file includes a graphic and various jump commands that take you to other relevant Help files if you click on them.

4. Click on Contents to return to the initial Help menu.

# ◆ Using the Help Menu Bar

The Help menu bar offers additional options for searching, including menus for File, Edit, Bookmark, Options, and Help. Let's take a look at each one.

## Using the File Menu

The File menu offers options including Open, Print Topic, and Exit. Open allows you to open help files in other programs outside Print Shop. Print Topic prints whatever appears on your Help screen. Exit closes Help.

## Using the Edit Menu

The Edit menu offers two ways to copy or mark Help text: Copy and Annotate. Let's work our way through these.

1. Click on the Find button. The Find dialog box appears. Highlight *backdrops* in box number 2. Make sure you select the entire word in all lowercase letters.

**2.** You are presented with several topics in box 3.

**3.** Double-click on Banners to reach the Banners Help screen.

**4.** Select Edit ➤ Copy to save the entire screen (without the graphic) in the Clipboard. This information will remain in the Clipboard until it is replaced by new information from another copy command. You can paste this Help topic into any word processing program, or you can paste it into an annotation. We'll choose the annotation route.

**5.** Click on Edit ➤ Annotate. The Annotate dialog box pops up. You can use this dialog box to add your own comments to Help or to create your own links from one Help screen to another.

**6.** Click on Paste; all the text you just copied into the Clipboard is pasted into the Annotate dialog box, as shown here.

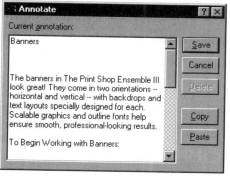

**7.** Click on Save. You return to the Banners Help screen, which shows a paper clip at the beginning of the screen. This lets you know that you have created a note here.

**8.** Click on the paper clip to access the note. The Annotate dialog box appears again with the note in place.

**9.** Click on Delete; the annotation and the paper clip disappear.

This is a great way to create reminders for yourself about new ways you have devised to make the program work more efficiently for you.

## Using the Bookmark Menu

Another useful Help technique is to mark a particularly helpful screen with a bookmark so that you can find it again easily.

**10.** Select the Bookmark menu ➤ Define.

**11.** The Bookmark Define dialog box, shown here, opens with the current Help screen in the Bookmark Name box. You can click on OK to leave this as the name of the bookmark or you can type another name. For this example, leave it at Banners and click on OK.

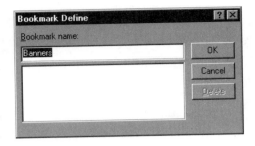

The Bookmark Define dialog box disappears and you're back in the Banners Help screen. Even though there is no visual indication, you have placed a bookmark on this page.

**12.** Click on Back to return to the initial Help screen.

**13.** Click on the Bookmark menu. Now the drop down list includes not only Define but Banners as well. We've also added a bookmark at Contents, as shown here, so you can see what happens when you add a second bookmark.

**14.** Select Banners and you jump immediately to the Banners Help screen.

To delete a bookmark, select Bookmark menu ➤ Define, highlight the bookmark you want deleted and hit the Delete button.

## Using the Options Menu

The Options Menu lets you set up how you see your help screen. Options include:

- ◆ Keep Help On Top
  - ◆ Default
  - ◆ On Top
  - ◆ Not On Top
- ◆ Display History Window

◆ Font

    ◆ Small

    ◆ Normal

    ◆ Large

◆ Use System Colors

Use these options to make your search life even easier.

## Using the Help Menu

The Help menu gives you information on the version of Print Shop Help you are using, as well as copyright information on Windows 95.

# Finding Help in Dialog Boxes

You can get instant help from many dialog boxes by clicking on their Help buttons. The Help system is context-sensitive, so a click on a Help button in a dialog box will take you instantly to a Help screen on that particular subject.

On some dialog boxes you will find a question mark (?) in the upper-right corner. This question mark serves the same function as a Help button on the dialog box. Clicking on this question mark takes you to the help screen attached to that dialog box.

# Endnotes

Now you'll never be at a loss if you need help. You know how to:

◆ Access the main help screen and the special Using Help library

◆ Use Help's main topics, links, buttons, and menu bar to access the information you need

◆ Search for help on specific words, phrases, or subjects

◆ Get context-sensitive help from any dialog box

Now that you've learned how to use Print Shop's toolbar, menus, and Help system, we'll take a closer look at the individual projects Print Shop offers in Chapter 5, "Understanding Print Shop Projects."

# Understanding Print Shop Projects

## Your mission: to maximize your knowledge of the Print Shop projects

◆

There are twelve great projects you can create with Print Shop. This is your introduction to eleven of them. We'll take a look at the twelfth one in the next chapter, "Creating Online Greetings."

◆ Greeting Cards      ◆ Calendars

◆ Letterhead      ◆ Signs & Posters

- ◆ Envelopes
- ◆ Labels
- ◆ Banners
- ◆ Postcards
- ◆ Certificates
- ◆ Business Cards
- ◆ Photo Projects

All are different and yet all share common design steps that lead to a creative conclusion. In this chapter, we'll explore the design elements that are unique to individual projects. But first, let's review the common design elements.

# ◆ Common Design Elements

PS Ensemble III simplifies the creative process. Many of the steps and most of the design elements available in Print Shop are common for all projects. The first step, of course, is to select which type of project you want to work on. Next, you must select a path.

## Selecting a Path

You'll recall from Chapter 1 that the first step after choosing the project is to decide if you will create the project using ready-made design selections or if you will start from scratch. An exception is a Stationery project that requires you to select a path after you select Stationery and then select the specific project such as Letterhead, Envelopes, Postcards, or Business Cards.

### Customizing a Ready-Made Project

A ready-made project may include backdrops, text, headlines, graphics—in other words, any of the available design elements—combined to create a project. While they are complete projects that can be printed as they are, this does not mean that you must keep the exact design as it's presented. Another way to look at ready-made projects is as a group of design elements created to get you started, then to be changed and modified to suit your creative vision.

You can make modifications to almost all of the individual elements that make up a particular ready-made design, as we did with the Open House banner in Chapter 3 and the Car Wash sign in Chapter 2. We say *almost all* because some elements are locked and cannot be changed. (See "Locking and Unlocking Objects" in Chapter 3 for an explanation of locked objects.)

Some ready-made projects have other projects coordinated to match. For example, a greeting card may have a coordinating envelope or banner.

Let's take a look at a greeting card with a coordinating envelope.

**1.** In the Select a Project dialog box, select Greeting Cards ➤ Customize A Ready Made ➤ Quarter-Page ➤ Invitation.

**2.** Click on the first Baby Shower, Umbrella Invite to preview it. Below the preview, shown here, there is a note indicating that it has a coordinating banner, business card, envelope, and sign.

**3.** Click on Cancel four times to return to the Select a Project dialog box.

**4.** Select Signs & Posters ➤ Customize a Ready Made ➤ Celebration.

**5.** From the list, select Baby Shower, Umbrella and the coordinating sign appears in the preview window, as shown here.

Take a look at the other coordinating elements, shown here, by selecting the project—Banner, Envelope, Business (Place) Card—and choosing Baby Shower, Umbrella from the Ready Mades for each of these projects.

babshwr.brm
This project has a coordinating Bus. Card, Envelope, Greeting Card and Sign.

babshwr.erm
This project has a coordinating Banner/Bus. Card/Quarter Page Greet. Card/Sign.

babshwr.bcr
This project has a coordinating Banner, Envelope, Greeting Card and Sign.

Coordinating projects are available for many Print Shop projects and have similar or same names from one project to another to make them easy to locate.

## Starting from Scratch

When you start from scratch, it is up to you to choose every aspect of the design. The next few sections of this chapter deal specifically with the choices offered when you elect to start from scratch.

## Choosing an Orientation

When you select Start From Scratch from the Select a Path dialog box, the next screen you see in most projects will be one asking you to select an orientation for your project. Orientation refers to how the design elements will initially be laid out. For example, if you are creating a banner, your selections are Wide or Tall, as shown here.

Eventually, you will have to choose an orientation for any project you create from scratch, except letterhead, envelopes, and

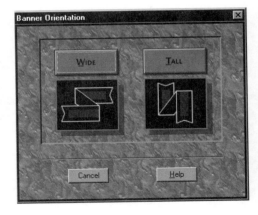

labels. With these projects, the project orientation is chosen in a different way. For example, if you've chosen stationery and letterhead as your project, you will be asked to choose between single page and notepad. Choose envelopes and you will be asked to choose between quarter page card size or business size, while labels will give you a list of label sizes from which to choose.

# Browsing for a Backdrop

After you've selected the appropriate orientation, you will be prompted to select a backdrop. The exception to this rule is label projects, which do not have backdrops due to their size.

The Backdrops Browser defaults to PS Backdrops, showing you those backdrops that fit the orientation of your current project. You can expand your backdrop choices by changing the selections to All Libraries or to a library that sounds like it might better suit your requirements, such as Business Backdrops.

You may also want to use the Search utility to see if there's a specific theme backdrop that fits your design. Figure 5.1, for instance, shows the Backdrops Browser for a wide backdrop after a search on the keyword sports. (See Chapter 1 for complete search instructions.)

When you select the Search Tall and Wide Backdrops option, the graphic will automatically adjust to your current page size. In other words, if you're working on a wide page format and the chosen backdrop was designed for a tall page format, the graphic will resize itself to fit in the wide format.

This might create backdrops that look stretched or squished, but in most cases, the graphics work just fine. You, of course, will be the judge of whether it works for your project.

# Selecting a Layout

After you've selected your backdrop, you will be asked to select a layout. A layout is a variety of shapes and sizes of placeholders for headlines, text, graphics, and other objects that may be included in your design. The layouts offered in the Select a Layout dialog box, shown in

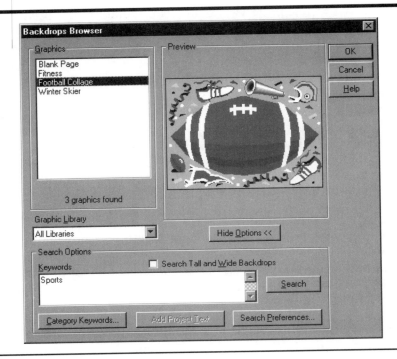

**Figure 5.1:** A search on the keyword sports in PSD backdrops finds only three backdrops.

Figure 5.2, are designed to creatively maximize the page surface of the project. PS Ensemble III gives you the option of selecting a layout and then adding additional placeholders or modifying or deleting placeholders from the selected layout once you reach the main project window.

A larger selection of predesigned layouts is available if you check the Lighten Backdrop box. This makes the backdrop less dominant, so it's possible to put more graphics or text over it without looking too busy.

Select the Lighten Backdrop box on the Select a Layout dialog box to lighten the backdrop by 40%. You might find this useful if the backdrop is particularly busy or you want to add additional graphics. When you select Lighten Backdrop, you will be given additional layouts to choose from.

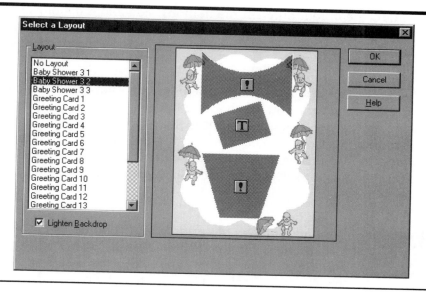

**Figure 5.2:** The Select a Layout dialog box offers a wide variety of layouts to choose from, or you can click on No Layout and create your own.

Now that you've taken care of the preliminary design issues, it's time to proceed to the precise details of your project's design. In the sections ahead, we'll describe those elements that are unique to each project in PS Ensemble III.

# ◆ Project-Specific Design Elements

The design elements available to you in Print Shop will vary depending on the type of project you undertake. Let's take a look at each type of project.

## Designing Greeting Cards

You can create unique greeting cards for invitations, announcements, or special occasions, choosing from an array of graphics and text options and styles. Greeting cards come in two different sizes: half page or quarter page. Half page greeting cards fold a letter or legal size page in half while quarter page folds it in fourths. Both half page and quarter page greeting cards come in four different orientations: side-fold, side-fold spread, top-fold, and top-fold spread. Spread-type cards let you fill the entire area inside the card. Non-spread cards let you use only half of the inside of the card as a design area.

When you go through the initial steps of choosing a backdrop and layout for a greeting card, you are choosing these elements for the front of the card only. When you move to the inside of the card for the first time, you are prompted to select a backdrop and layout for this part of the card. And when you navigate to the back of the card for the first time, you are again prompted to select a layout (backdrops are not available for the back of a greeting card).

 Greeting cards and postcards (discussed under "Designing Stationery" later in the chapter) are the only multipage projects in Print Shop. To move from page to page in these projects, you use the Navigation toolbar. (See Chapter 1 for more information about the Navigation toolbar.)

Let's take a look at some greeting-card-specific design elements.

**1.** Open the ready-made birthday card called Frog Birthday. (From the Select A Project screen, select Greeting Cards ➤ Customize A Ready Made ➤ Quarter Page ➤ Birthday ➤ Birthday/Child, Frog.)

 The Print Shop Ensemble III gives you the ability to drop and drag files to open them. From Microsoft Windows Explorer, select the Print Shop Ensemble III project icon you want to open and drag it to the Print Shop Ensemble III application icon. The project will open. This same drop and drag feature can be used to print a project or delete a project.

**2.** Click on the Project menu. Note the options to go to the front of the card (you are already there, so this one is checked), the inside of card, or the back of card. These Project menu commands duplicate the Navigation toolbar.

**3.** Select Inside of Card. Inside, you can see that this is a side-fold spread card with no backdrop, only a colored page with four square graphics.

4. Click on Project ➤ Change Backdrop. The Backdrops Browser dialog box opens. Note that you have 49 backdrop graphics available.

5. Click on the arrow next to Graphic Library and change the selection to All Libraries. Now you have 87 backdrops available.

6. Click on the Search Options button and select the Search Tall and Wide Backdrops box.

7. Click on Search. Now you have 523 backdrops available. (Remember, you're filling a wide space in the side-fold spread card, so tall backdrops will be stretched to fit.)

8. Select Bon Voyage from the list of backdrops. This is the same backdrop you used in Chapter 1 for the front of the party invitation. Notice how it is elongated to fit the spread area, as shown here.

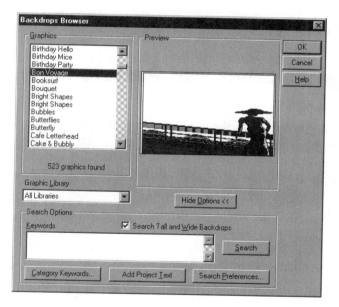

9. Click on OK to return to the main project window.

10. Click on the Navigation toolbar to go to the back of the card.

11. Click on Project and note that the Change Backdrop option is available for the back of the card. So, while you are not prompted to select a backdrop when you first create a greeting card, you can

add one after you are in the main project window if you choose to do so. Many people use the back of a greeting card to give themselves credit for designing such a great card.

Here's an idea: create a miniature coloring book for someone special using the greeting card project. Fill the four pages of the greeting card with graphics, add a headline personalizing the "book," then print the project in coloring book format. (See "Printing a Project" in Chapter 3 for instructions. For some more great ideas, see "Using The Idea Guide" in Chapter 13.)

Quarter page and half page greeting cards print differently. Quarter page greeting cards print on one side of one page and you fold the page twice to make the card. Half page greeting cards print on both sides of the paper and fold only once. To print a half page greeting card you must first print one side of the greeting card and then run the paper back through again to print the other side of the card. The Print dialog box will let you select to print either the Front/Back or Inside of the card.

## Designing Signs and Posters

When you choose Signs & Posters from the Select a Project dialog box, you can make a whole array of different projects. Yes, you can make a sign or poster for a garage sale, car wash, school dance, or notice of hours, but you can also make bookmarks, gift wrap, bumper stickers, and more.

Let's look at three great projects. We'll start with a bumper sticker.

1. Select File ➤ New ➤ Signs & Posters ➤ Start From Scratch. Next, hold down the Ctrl key and select Wide for the orientation. You are taken to a wide, blank page in the main project window.

2. Select Object ➤ Add ➤ Mini-border. A mini-border placeholder appears on the page.

3. Double-click on the mini-border, choose All Libraries, select Memo Planes, and click on OK.

4. Move and resize the mini-border to fit into the lower half of the page (see "Moving and Resizing Objects" in Chapter 2 for instructions). Leave the top half of the page blank.

5. Select Object ➤ Add ➤ Square Graphic. A square graphic place-holder appears on the page.

6. Move the graphic placeholder inside the mini-border on the left.

7. Add a second square graphic placeholder in the same way, only this time place it on the right, inside the mini-border.

8. Double-click on the placeholder on the left, choose Wildlife Squares Library, select Eagle, and click on OK. An eagle appears inside the mini-border on the left.

You can select a graphic by searching in All Libraries. If you would then like to know in what library that graphic can be found, add the graphic to the project, then double-click on the graphic to go back to the Graphics Browser. The Browser will tell you the library location.

9. Double-click on the right placeholder, choose the Special Occasions Library, select Turkey, and click on OK. A turkey appears inside the mini-border on the right.

10. Adjust the two graphics to make them fit neatly inside the mini-border, the eagle all the way to the left and the turkey all the way to the right.

11. Select Object ➤ Add ➤ Text. A text placeholder appears in the project.

12. Double-click on the placeholder and type **How can I soar with Eagles when I work with Turkeys?** in the Edit Text dialog box. Select a text color and style. We highlighted the word *Turkeys* and selected the U button to underline this one word. When you're finished, click on OK to place the text in the project.

13. Move and resize the headline to fill the area inside the mini-border between the two graphics.

14. You should now have a completed bumper sticker filling half of your project page. Click on Edit ➤ Select All to select all the items in the project.

15. Click on Edit ➤ Duplicate. The bumper sticker is duplicated.

16. Move the duplicate copy to fill the upper half of the project page, so you have a page with two bumper stickers as shown here.

17. Print the project on full-page peel-off paper and cut it in half to create two bumper stickers.

You can also make a sheet of gift wrapping paper by using a backdrop with repeating elements such as lips or red balloons, as shown here. The limitation on this idea is the size of paper your printer will accept, which will generally be regular letter or legal size.

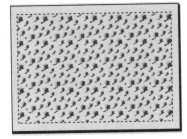

Bookmarks are a good project; you can create just one or a whole pageful, as shown here. Select the tall orientation, stretch (resize) any graphic (column and row graphics work particularly well), then use the duplicate option to create a pageful. You can print your bookmarks directly on card-stock paper or print them on regular paper and photocopy them onto card-stock.

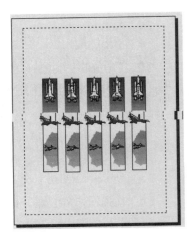

# Designing Banners

Banners are great for announcing a grand opening or a special sale, a school dance or a new recycling program. Banners can be coordinated to match a party invitation or an announcement or a sale flyer by using the same graphic elements in both projects.

Unlike most other projects, banners require you to select a layout (you cannot skip over the Select a Layout dialog box). Once you've chosen a layout for a banner, you'll find that some of its design elements cannot be changed because the placeholders are locked. Locked objects cannot be moved or resized, but some can be deleted. As previously mentioned, the locked elements have smaller handles than unlocked ones, allowing you to identify them easily.

Banners can be wide (horizontal) or tall (vertical). You can change the length of either of these to print on 2 to 35 pages (only 6 pages will be readable in preview). To change the length, click on Project ➤ Banner Length (the only extra command in the Project menu for banners) and type a new number of pages in the Banner Length dialog box.

Here you can also change the position of the message on a banner by adjusting the leading space before the message begins and the trailing space after the message. If you add more space to either of these dimensions, it will move the graphic farther away from the edges. (These techniques are discussed in "Changing the Banner Length" in Chapter 3.)

You add text to a banner by double-clicking on a banner text box to reach the Banner dialog box, shown here. This dialog box looks similar to the Headline dialog box, but keep in mind that banner text boxes do not behave the same as headline boxes. Unless you resize it manually, a headline box remains the same size no matter how much text you put in it; the text inside spreads or shrinks to fill the box. A banner text box, on the other hand, grows larger as

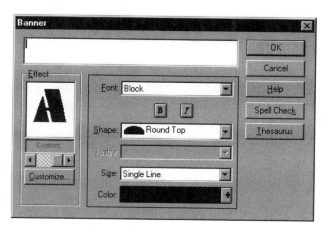

you add text, increasing the length of the banner. You can type a total of 63 characters into the box at the top of the Banner dialog box.

The Banner dialog box shown above is for a horizontal banner. Horizontal banners can have one or two lines of text, and you can choose from various font, style, shape, justification, size, color, and custom effect options. (Vertical banners do not offer shape, justification, or size options due to the orientation of the text on the page.) The Size option lets you designate the size of one line of banner text as it relates to the other (if any), as follows:

Single Line

Small Over Large

Large Over Small

If the layout of your banner contains a locked text placeholder but you do not wish to add text to it, double-click on the placeholder and, in the Edit Text dialog box that appears, type a couple of spaces and click OK. The text placeholder will disappear with no text added to the project.

## Designing Certificates

Certificates are a great way to recognize a special achievement for the highest sales, the most improved player, the highest grades, or the greatest Mom or Dad. The certificate project category has many creative options. For instance, you can make a plain piece of white paper look like an expensive piece of watermarked parchment. Let's give this a try.

**1.** Select File ➤ New ➤ Certificates ➤ Start From Scratch ➤ Wide and then click on the Watermarked Text button. The Watermarked Text dialog box, shown here, prompts you to enter the text you'd like to use.

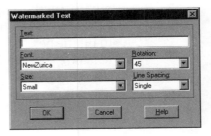

2. Type your text. (Initials are a good choice.) Customize the text, selecting its size, rotation, spacing, and font.

3. Click on OK and the watermarked text is previewed in the Backdrops Browser. The default color is a light gray, shown here. You can experiment with the color in the main project window using the Color Selector.

If you would like to use watermarked paper in a project other than a certificate, you can. Just start a certificate project, create your watermarked paper, and go to the main project window with no other objects added. Save the project as a Windows Bitmap, Windows Metafile, TIFF Bitmap file, or a JPEG file, and you can import this file into any other project and size it to fit the area you want watermarked, either part or all of the page.

Because most certificates are signed, you can add signature blocks for a number of signers in different layouts. Two more items that certificates generally have are a place for the recipient's name and an official seal. All of these elements can be added by clicking on Object ➤ Add, then making your selection from the drop down menu, as described in "Adding Objects" in Chapter 3. See Chapter 11 for instructions on adding signature blocks and Chapter 8 for designing seals.

When there are a number of awards to prepare, the names in the title block can be changed from one recipient to another automatically by using the Name List option (more on this in Chapter 12, "Creating and Merging Lists").

# Designing Stationery

Under the Stationery category, you can create single-page or notepad letterheads, envelopes in two sizes, postcards, or business cards.

Selecting ready-made stationery gives you an added bonus: coordinating projects. As noted above, ready-made letterheads may have coordinating envelopes, business cards, or postcards. Some even have coordinated labels. See "Starting with a Ready-Made Project" near the beginning of this chapter for instructions.

You can create coordinated stationery of your own design by selecting the same graphics and text options when you design the letterhead as when you design the envelope. (An even easier way is to copy and paste graphics and text boxes from one project to another.) The secret to coordinating projects is to save them the right way. Here's an example.

1. Once you have the coordinating projects completed, select File ➤ Save As. The Save As dialog box appears.

2. Click on the Options button and type a description in the Save Options dialog box. For example, if you are saving the letterhead for a coordinating letterhead and envelope set, type **coordinating envelope** in the Description area. For the envelope, type **coordinating letterhead**. That way when you open either of these files, your description will appear below the project as it is previewed and you'll know that there is a matching project you can access as well.

3. When you save the coordinated letterhead and envelope, give them the same name. They will automatically be given different extensions (.pdl for the letterhead and .pce for the envelope).

Some letterhead and notepad layouts contain a large text block that allows you to type a letter or note to be printed as part of the project. (You can always add this text block if it is not a part of the layout.) Keep in mind that notepads are half the size of a regular piece of paper and automatically print two to a page.

Another stationery project is postcards. As with greeting cards, Print Shop's other multipage project, you use the Navigation tool to move from page to page, but postcards have only two pages, while greeting cards have three. Postcards are great as customer contact cards, informal invitations, moving notifications, or special announcements.

When you print a postcard, you will need to feed the paper into your printer twice, once to print the front of the card and once to print the back. You can purchase postcard paper stock for your printer to print on. (All Print Shop postcards are $4^1/_4''$ by $5^1/_2''$.) Let's take a look at the special print options you'll see for postcards.

1. Select File ➤ New ➤ Stationery ➤ Customize A Ready Made ➤ Post Cards. Open whichever ready-made postcard you like and click on File ➤ Print. The Print dialog box pops up, as shown here.

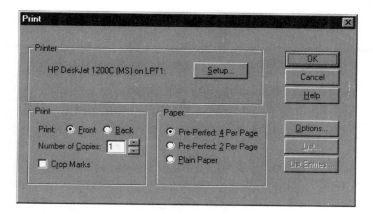

2. Look at the Paper options at the bottom of the dialog box—Pre-Perfed: 4 per page, Pre-Perfed: 2 per page, and Plain Paper. Here you can designate whether you want to print two or four postcards on a page of pre-perfed (pre-perforated) postcard paper or to print on plain paper.

3. Check the Crop Marks option if you're printing on plain paper. This will give you guidelines of where to cut the paper to separate the postcards. You won't need crop marks with perforated card paper.

4. Select either Front or Back to indicate which side you're printing, and click on OK to start printing.

One other interesting postcard option is to select a postcard layout that is approved by the U.S. Postal Service. (Just choose USPS Layouts at the layout stage.) You can also designate a return address to appear on all postcards that you create. See Chapter 12, "Creating and Merging Lists," for details about both of these options.

# Designing Calendars

You can create a calendar that reflects your style, your business, or your goals using the Calendar option. Whether they are ready-made or created from scratch, you can personalize calendars with your own chosen graphics, notes, and red-letter days.

Calendars can be yearly, monthly, weekly, or daily, as shown in Figure 5.3.

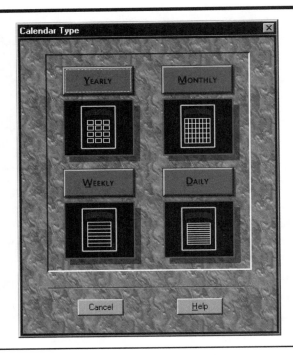

**Figure 5.3:** Choose a yearly, monthly, weekly, or daily calendar.

If you select Yearly, you'll be prompted to choose a calendar year. If you select Monthly, you'll be asked to choose a month and year. If you select Weekly, you'll need to choose a week, month, the year, and the starting date. You can specify any day as the beginning of your week. For instance, you can begin your weekly calendar on Thursday instead of Sunday if you like. And finally, if you choose Daily, you will be prompted to select the day, month, year, and time period for the calendar. You can choose any 10-hour period using either a 12- or a 24-hour clock.

Let's create a daily calendar and see what calendar-specific options are available in the main project window.

**1.** Select File ➤ New ➤ Calendars ➤ Start From Scratch ➤ Daily.

**2.** Complete the Calendar Day dialog box as shown here. Choose December 1999, then click on 7 for the date. Select the 12-hour clock option and choose 8:00 AM to 5:00 PM for the time frame.

**3.** Select the orientation, backdrop, and layout of your choice in the dialog boxes that appear next. As with banners, you must select a layout for a calendar.

**4.** In the main project window, click on the Project menu and you'll see three commands specific to calendars. When working with a daily calendar, these commands are Edit Hour, Change Day, and Calendar Options.

**5.** Click on Edit Hour and the Edit Hour dialog box pops up, as shown in Figure 5.4.

To add text to an hour of the calendar, click on that hour, then on the Edit Text button. A text box will appear in which you can type your note. When you're done, click on OK. To add a graphic, click on an hour, then on the Select Graphic button. The Graphics Browser appears, from which you can select the graphic to include. Click on OK to place the graphic in the hour. You can also double-click on the text or graphics placeholder at the top of the dialog box to reach the text box or the Graphics Browser, respectively.

**6.** Make your graphic and text selections and click OK to return to the main project window.

**7.** Click on Project ➤ Change Day. The Calendar Day dialog box reappears so you can change the day if you like. When you do this, a dialog box appears warning you that graphics and text may change position if you proceed. On this box you can elect to have the

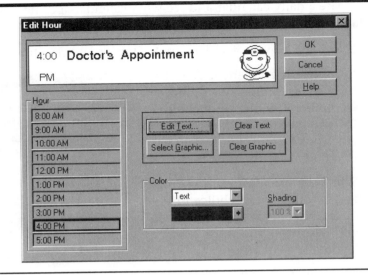

**Figure 5.4:** You can add graphics, text, and design elements to a daily calendar in the Edit Hour dialog box.

items remain in the Same Positions, Same Times, or Erase. Before you proceed, you would want to select the appropriate options. For now, click on cancel to return to the main project window.

8. Select Project ➤ Calendar Options and the Daily Calendar Options dialog box pops up, as shown here. Here you can select the font and text style, change the type of clock, and choose a language: English, French, Spanish, German, or Italian.

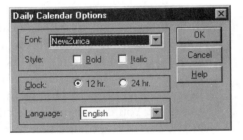

9. Click on OK to return to the main project window, then select the calendar box that contains the calendar lines.

10. Now click on the Item Selector and you'll note that there are three calendar-specific options—Calendar Lines, Behind Calendar, and Calendar Text.

**11.** Click on Calendar Lines and change the color of the lines using the Color Selector (see "Coloring and Shading an Area" in Chapter 2 for instructions). You can change the color behind the calendar or the color of the calendar text in the same way.

When you're working on a weekly, monthly, or yearly calendar, the Project commands are similar to the options for a daily calendar, with slight variations. For instance, the Edit Day command for a weekly or monthly calendar offers options that are similar to those offered by the Edit Hour command for a daily calendar. (Yearly calendars do not have either command.)

When you click on Project ➤ Calendar Options for a weekly calendar, you will be offered the same choices as with daily calendars. The calendar options for monthly and yearly calendars are a bit different.

The Monthly Calendar Options dialog box includes three extra options: Month Thumbnails (shown here), which places thumbnails of the preceding and following months at the bottom of your calendar; Preceding/Following Days, which includes the ending days of the preceding month and the beginning days of the following month on your calendar, as space allows; and Red Sundays, which prints Sundays in red. The Yearly Calendar Options dialog box offers the same Red Sundays option and lets you choose whether you want the month blocks to appear plain, underlined, or boxed in your calendar.

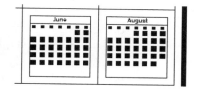

# Designing Labels

With Print Shop Ensemble III you can create custom labels for letters, packages, video and audio tapes, computer disks, file folders, or anything else. Labels can be designed to print on a variety of label shapes and, of course, print multiple copies per page.

First, let's look at a ready-made label.

**1.** Select File ➤ New ➤ Labels ➤ Customize A Ready Made. Choose whichever ready-made label you like.

2. In the main project window, click on File ➤ Print. (A note may pop up telling you that the label text will be scaled down to 99% of its original size in order to fit on the label. If you see this note, just click on OK.)

3. The Print dialog box, shown here, pops up. Note that the number of labels to be printed is already set (in this case, it's set to 14). This is the number of labels that will fit on a page, given the size of the chosen label.

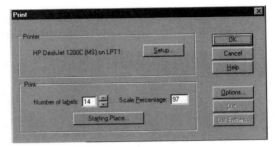

4. Click on the Starting Place button at the bottom of the dialog box. The Starting Place dialog box, shown here, pops up. This is the layout of your label page. You can click on any of the label squares to designate where you want to begin printing your labels. This is particularly useful if you are not using an entire sheet of labels. When you return to the Print dialog box, note that the number of labels you'll be printing changes to match your starting place selection.

 You can also Scale Percentage. Remember a prompt has already told you that the label text will be scaled down to 99% of its original size. You can scale this farther if you like.

Now let's design a label from scratch.

1. Select File ➤ New ➤ Labels ➤ Start From Scratch.

**2.** The Select a Label Type dialog box, shown here, pops up. At the top of the dialog box, you can choose between laser or pinfed labels. (The default is laser labels.) Select the label type appropriate for your printer and click through the list of labels to see the different types displayed in the preview area to the right.

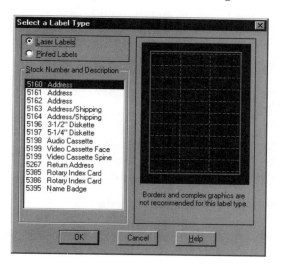

**3.** Select a label type and click on OK to go directly to the Select a Layout dialog box. Since labels are small and usually text-intensive, backdrops are not available for labels.

**4.** Select a layout and click on OK to move to the main project window. From here on your options will be the same as with ready-made labels.

# Designing Photo Projects

Print Shop Ensemble III has a brand new project, Photo Projects. This new project gives you some tips on creating a project using photographs, either your own or one from the over 100 that are provided on the Print Shop CD. In addition to providing photos along with the ability to import your own, Print Shop has included a special Photo Accessories graphics library where you can choose from a variety of objects and frames that will enhance your photograph and add to the message you wish to send.

Photo Projects is not reached when you Start From Scratch and is not available at the Select A Project screen. You'll find Photo Projects as one of the Ready Made Themes in the following projects: Greeting Cards, Signs & Posters, Banners and Certificates.

Photos can be imported into ANY project (ready-made or from scratch) from the Main Project Window by selecting Object ➤ Import and selecting a photo file compatible with Print Shop. More on this in Chapter 9, "Importing Images."

Let's take a look at one of these.

**1.** Select Signs & Posters ➤ Customize A Ready Made ➤ Photo Projects. Select the first Wanted. The project, seen here, opens in the Main Project Window.

**2.** Double-click on the photograph and the Open dialog box pops up, where you can choose another photograph if you like. You can find a whole collection of photographs provided with The Print Shop Ensemble III on the Print Shop CD. Browse through those if you like. When you're finished, cancel to return to the Main Project Window.

**3.** Double-click on the headline box that reads, "Type Name Here." Type in a name, change font, color, or any other text attributes and click OK to place the text in the project.

Now let's add an accessory.

**4.** Select the Object Menu ➤ Add ➤ Square Graphic or select the Object tool ➤ Square Graphic.

**5.** Click on the square graphic placeholder and in the Graphics Browser, and change the Graphic Library to Photo Accessories.

Browse through the 171 graphics offered. You'll find hats, wigs, glasses, masks, and a variety of frames, both normal and humorous, for your photographs or the people in them, as shown here.

While this library is called Photo Accessories, any of the graphics in it can be used over other graphics in any other project as well. Remember that you have the option of selecting the Order of the graphics by selecting Object ➤ Order, putting the accessory behind rather than in front of another graphic.

## ◆ One Last Tip

There will come a time when you want to cover up part of an object in a project, maybe a portion of a locked graphic or a border that interferes with something else on your project. When this happens, the Print Shop

Ensemble III has given you some erasers you can use to cover up unwanted parts of a graphic. Let's take a look at these. You should still have your Wanted poster open.

1. In the main project window, click on the Object Menu ➤ Add ➤ Square Graphic.

2. Double-click on the graphic placeholder.

3. From the Graphics Browser, choose the graphic library called Symbols. In this library, you'll find a filled circle, a filled hexagon, a filled octagon, a filled pentagon, a filled spade, a filled square, a filled star, a filled teardrop, and a filled triangle. The fill color in all these graphics is black. In the main project window we can change the fill color from black to any other color.

4. Select the Filled Square and click on OK.

5. You'll return to the main project window with a black square on your project. Move and resize it so it covers the photograph.

6. Now from the Item Selector, select Object, then change the color of the box to match the color of the background surrounding the box, in this case, a light gray. The box disappears and now you have a blank wanted poster.

These symbols can be used in combination and resized to cover anything on your Print Shop project. Keep these in mind. You'll find them a big help in manipulating graphics and projects to cater to your own creative ideas.

# ◆ Endnotes

You now know the projects, their common design elements, and their project-specific design elements. You also know:

◆ That the basic design options are the same from project to project but that some commands are unique to certain projects

◆ How to lighten a backdrop to increase your layout options

◆ How to create a personal coloring book or special wrapping paper

◆ How many characters you can type into a banner text block

◆ How to create coordinating letterhead, envelopes, and labels, then save them so you can locate them easily

◆ When to add crop marks to a printout of a postcard

◆ How to watermark a page and copy that page into another project if you want

◆ How to pick a day on a calendar, make a note about a meeting, and add a graphic

◆ How to print a series of labels, starting where you designate on the sheet of labels

◆ How to add a little humor to a Photo Project

In Chapter 6, "Creating Online Greetings" we'll take a look at our twelfth Print Shop Ensemble III project, a new and exciting way to create and send Print Shop greetings over the Internet.

CHAPTER SIX

W W W

World Wide Web

# Creating Online Greetings

## Your Mission: To create and send a Print Shop greeting over the Internet's World Wide Web

◆

One of the most exciting projects and features available in The Print Shop Ensemble III program is the ability to create Online Greetings and connect to the Internet from within Print Shop.

The Online Greeting project lets you send a Print Shop greeting on the World Wide Web (WWW) to anyone with an e-mail address. The recipient of an online greeting does not need to have the Print Shop program in their computer to read your greeting. Creating this special greeting to spruce up your e-mail is as easy as making any other project in Print Shop.

The Internet Connection feature allows you to visit The Print Shop Connection Web site or surf the net from within Print Shop.

Let's take a look at how easy it is to make and send an online greeting on the Internet with The Print Shop Ensemble III.

# ◆ Creating an Online Greeting

An online greeting is a one-page greeting project, available at the Select a Project dialog box, that is sent as a JPEG (Joint Photographics Experts Group) file attached to an e-mail message.

To create this special greeting project:

**1.** Select Online Greetings from the Select a Project dialog box.

**2.** Select either Customize a Ready Made or Start From Scratch.

If you choose Start From Scratch, you'll be prompted to select a backdrop from the Backdrops Browser and a layout from the Select a Layout dialog box.

**3.** For this exercise, select Customize a Ready Made.

**4.** Select a ready-made called Get Well, Monkey. The project, shown here in Figure 6.1, opens in the main project window where you can customize it, adding or changing text or graphics.

It's that simple. Once your greeting is created, you're ready to send it via the Internet.

# ◆ Sending an Online Greeting

To send an Online Greeting from within Print Shop, you'll need direct access to the Internet through an Internet Service Provider (ISP), such as AT&T WorldNet, NetCom, or uuNet.

If you already access the Internet through a private network such as AOL, Compuserve, or Prodigy, you have what is called "indirect Internet

**Figure 6.1:** An online greeting project is a one-page greeting that is sent as a JPEG file attached to an e-mail message.

access" and will not be able to access the Web and send your greeting from within Print Shop. You will need to add an ISP in order to use the Print Shop features Online Greetings and Internet Connection.

To send an online greeting via an Internet Service Provider, you'll need a modem installed and operational and you'll need to tell Print Shop two things:

◆ how you access the Internet
◆ your recipient's e-mail address

The Print Shop Ensemble III uses the Internet network to reach an e-mail address where you can drop off a special greeting to someone equally special. To connect your computer to the Internet, you'll need a modem. A modem is the device that uses your telephone line to connect your computer to another computer using the Internet as the connection between them.

After your modem is installed and configured, it's a simple matter to tell Print Shop how to reach your Internet Service Provider.

You can send your online greeting directly from Print Shop using an ISP. The first time you do this you'll need to set up your connection, telling Print Shop specifically how you access the Internet's World Wide Web. You can set up your Internet connection either at the Select a Project screen or at the Main Project Window.

# Setting Up Your Internet Connection

To tell Print Shop how to set up your system to send your online greeting, do one of the following:

◆ at the Select a Project screen, select Extras ➤ Internet Connection

◆ at the main project window, click on the Extras menu ➤ Internet Connection

In either case, you'll be offered the choice of configuring your WWW access with one step or two steps, as shown here. Most Internet browsers (i.e., software that lets you view the Internet and the WWW) come with dial-up networking capabilities. If this is the kind of web browser you have, click the One Step button. You will need to know the name and location of your Internet Browser.

If you use a dialer application, you will use the two-step process. You will need to know the name and location of the dialer application you use.

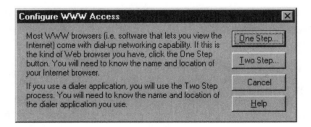

The ISP you have chosen will determine which of these buttons you now select. The one-step process will take you to a dialog box where you can

search for your web browser, such as the Microsoft Internet Explorer or Netscape Navigator. The two-step process takes you to a dialog box where you can search for your dialer application, such as AT&T WorldNet.

**1.** Click on One Step to go to the Find and Select Your Web Browser dialog box. Here you can look through your folders to locate your web browser. We have one installed, Netscape Navigator, located at C:\Windows\Net.exe, as you can see in Figure 6.2.

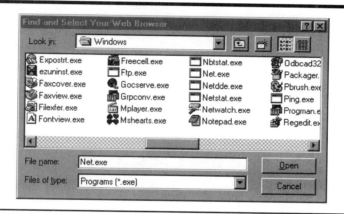

**Figure 6.2:** Look through your drives and folders to locate your web browser.

If you access the web with a dialer such as AT&T WorldNet, click on the Two Step button to reach the Choose a Dial-Up Networking Connection, shown here.

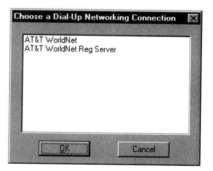

**2.** Highlight your Internet Service Provider. Our list includes the AT&T WorldNet. Once you've chosen your provider, click OK and you go to Find and Select Your Web Browser, the same dialog box you saw with the one-step process.

3. You're asked to find and select your browser. Our browser is Netscape Navigator located at C:\Windows\Net.exe, as you already know. Select Net.exe and click Open.

The Web Browser dialog box, shown here, pops up. Whenever you click on Internet Connection, this dialog box will appear, offering you the opportunity either to go directly to the Internet or to reconfigure your Web access. You will probably not need to reconfigure your Web access unless you change your Internet provider.

At this point you can close the Web Browser dialog box and continue with sending your online greeting, or you can choose Access the Web. For now, click Cancel to close the Web Browser dialog box. We'll come back in a minute and check out the Access the Web option.

## Sending the Greeting inside Print Shop

To send an online greeting, you will need to prepare a brief message to accompany the greeting and to enter the e-mail address of your recipient. You also have a few housekeeping chores to do.

1. Select the File menu ➤ Send. The Prepare Your Message dialog box, shown here in Figure 6.3, appears.

You'll need to type some information here but first:

2. Click on the button labeled Configure. The Internet Mail Information dialog box, shown here, appears. Enter your e-mail address and your name. This information will serve as your return address to the recipient of your online greeting.

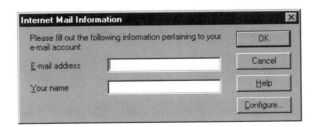

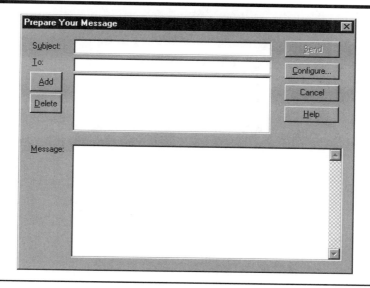

**Figure 6.3:** When you select File ➤ Send, you are prompted to choose a title, designate the recipients, and type in a message to accompany your online greeting.

Notice that there is a Configure button on this dialog box also. Click on this button to configure your Internet connection, if you have not already done so. We have already set up our Internet connection but let's take a look at the options offered.

**3.** Click on Configure. The Configure Your Internet Connection dialog box, shown here, pops up, giving you three options:

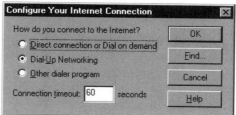

♦ Direct connection or Dial on demand

♦ Dial-Up Networking

♦ Other dialer program

This is another opportunity to set up your Internet connection if you have not already done so. Since we have already configured, Dial-Up Networking is already selected. The ISP we have selected, AT&T WorldNet, is considered dial-up networking.

**4.** Click OK and return to the Internet Mail Information dialog box.

**5.** Click OK again and return to the Prepare Your Message dialog box.

Type in the requested information:

◆ Subject:   Give the message a title.

◆ To:   Type in the e-mail address of the recipients. You can have one recipient or many. After each address click Add to add an address to the list of recipients. If you decide you'd like to delete a recipient, just highlight that e-mail address and click Delete.

◆ Message:   Add a brief e-mail message to accompany your file if you'd like. You do not have to include a message if you do not want to.

**6.** When you have prepared your message, click on Send.

You may see a dialog box asking you if you want to connect to your ISP, or you may be connected automatically. Either way, once you are connected, your online greeting will be sent automatically as a JPEG file attached to your message. We'll take a look at how the message is retrieved and viewed in a moment but first, let's look at how we'd send the same online greeting through an Online Service Provider (OSP).

## Sending as an Attachment

If you access the Internet and the WWW through an Online Service Provider (CompuServe, America Online, etc.), you will not be able to send your online greeting directly from the main project window in Print Shop. You'll need to first save your online greeting as a JPEG file and then send it as an attachment to an e-mail message you prepare at your OSP.

Let's take a look at how to do this. After you've created your online message:

**1.** Click on File ➤ Save As and save your online greeting as a JPEG file.

**2.** Exit Print Shop.

**3.** Open your Online Service Provider, such as the Microsoft Network, CompuServe, America Online, or Prodigy.

**4.** Create an e-mail message or send a file.

**5.** Attach the JPEG file to that message.

**6.** Send the e-mail message just like you'd send any other one you'd create in your OSP.

It's that simple.

Now let's see how your online greeting can be retrieved and viewed.

# ◆ Viewing an Online Greeting

Whether you send it through an ISP or an OSP, your Print Shop online greeting arrives as a JPEG file attached to an e-mail message. To receive an online greeting, the recipient must have:

◆ a computer equipped with Microsoft Windows

◆ a modem

◆ an Internet connection

Retrieving and opening an online greeting is just as simple as opening any e-mail message.

**1.** Retrieve the message.

**2.** Open the message.

The e-mail message and the Print Shop JPEG file should open simultaneously when the message is opened. If the JPEG file does not open:

**3.** Double-click on the JPEG file icon. It should open.

If you have problems opening a Print Shop greeting, consult your e-mail software manual or WWW browser manual to make sure your software supports JPEG files. If you have a problem opening a greeting sent via an OSP, consult your Online Service Provider to make sure they support attached JPEG files.

And that's all there is to sending a online greeting created in The Print Shop Ensemble III.

# ◆ Accessing the Print Shop Connection

The Internet Connection feature of The Print Shop Ensemble III takes you to an exciting Print Shop Web page. At The Print Shop Connection Web page, you'll find the latest from Print Shop, including free graphics, project ideas, technical support, and more. And, if you like, you can access other sites on the World Wide Web from within Print Shop through Internet Connection.

**1.** To reach the Internet Connection feature:

◆ From the Select a Project screen, click on Extras ➤ Internet Connection

◆ From the main project window, click on the Extras menu ➤ Internet Connection

The Web Browser dialog box pops up, offering you the option of configuring or accessing the web.

**2.** Click on Access the Web.

You will be connected to The Print Shop Connection Web page. You will need an Internet Service Provider to access this page through Print Shop.

If you'd like to go to this Web page outside of Print Shop, use a Web browser to look for http://www.broderbund.com/printshop on the WWW.

Check this Web page out for more exciting features and news from Print Shop and Broderbund.

# ◆ Endnotes

Now you're online with Print Shop. You can:

◆ Set up so Print Shop knows how to access the World Wide Web

◆ Send an Online Greeting

◆ Retrieve and open an online message and the accompanying JPEG file

◆ And you know how to access an exciting new Print Shop Web page

Now you're on the web with The Print Shop Ensemble III.

Let's move on and check out Print Shop graphics in a series of chapters that cover all the different art offered by the program. We'll start with Chapter 7, "Working With Graphics Libraries."

# Part Two:

## Managing Graphics

# Working with Graphics Libraries

## Your mission: to learn to navigate Print Shop's graphics libraries and to create and modify your own custom libraries

◆

Print Shop Ensemble III has possibly the most comprehensive graphics library of any desktop publishing program available today. With over 5,500 graphics, there's bound to be more than one graphic that not only fills your creative needs for a project but offers you new ideas that expand your creative vision. This great diversity is made even better by the added ability to search the libraries and to create your own custom libraries.

More than 80 graphics libraries offer you images in a variety of sizes and on a wide range of subjects. There are so many graphics in this program it's unlikely you'll ever see all of them unless you go exploring. If you do, make sure you note the location of graphics you find interesting so you can make a custom library of your favorites later.

The size of the available libraries makes it absolutely critical that you know how to get around in this graphics world quickly and efficiently. Let's look at the structure of the libraries so we can negotiate through the graphics maze.

# ◆ Types of Graphics

There are three main types of graphics stored in libraries: backdrops, layouts, and graphics. Of these three, you will have direct access to only two in a library format: backdrops and graphics. Layouts are available only from the Select a Layout dialog box and they are not really graphics but rather a collection of placeholder layouts.

◆ Backdrop libraries are opened with the Backdrops Browser, which appears automatically when you create a project from scratch, or when you select Change Backdrop from the Project menu of an open project.

◆ Layout libraries are opened using the Select a Layout dialog box, which appears automatically when you create a project from scratch, or when you select Change Layout from the Project menu of an open project.

◆ Graphics libraries are opened from the Graphics Browser, which appears when you double-click on a placeholder or an existing graphic.

Graphics libraries are divided into graphic shapes: squares, rows, columns, ruled lines, mini-backdrops, borders, and certificate borders. Different graphic shapes appear in different libraries. When you click on a square graphic placeholder, for example, the Graphics Browser that pops up will offer you these graphic shapes: square, column, row, and mini-backdrops. When you click on a border placeholder, the Graphics Browser that pops up will offer borders and certificate borders.

 To reach a Graphics Browser that offers all graphic shapes, select Object ➤ Add. The first item listed is Graphics. Click on this instead of one of the shapes offered and you go immediately to a Graphics Browser where you can search all shapes and all libraries. Selecting All Shapes and All Libraries as a search criterion is a quick way to search every graphic available at the same time.

Backdrop libraries are divided into backdrop shapes: tall and wide, with both options available on every Backdrops Browser.

All libraries have descriptive names designed to help you find the graphics you're looking for. For example, the Animals library contains—what else?—animal graphics. You can search graphic libraries or backdrop libraries by selecting a specific library by name or by selecting All Libraries and searching all libraries at once.

## ◆ The Libraries

The graphic libraries you'll find in Print Shop cover just about every subject, every type, and every orientation you can think of and more. And, as you'll discover in this chapter, you can create even more libraries by adding your own graphics, or you can modify existing libraries to delete, rename, or add graphics.

The over 5,500 graphics available in Print Shop Ensemble III are stored as square graphics, column graphics, row graphics, mini-backdrops, ruled lines, borders, certificate borders, and backdrops.

| Name of library | No. of graphics | Name of library | No. of graphics |
| --- | --- | --- | --- |
| **SQUARE** | | Calendar Icons | 26 |
| Animals | 51 | Carmen | 65 |
| Assorted | 196 | CC Amazing Animals | 102 |
| Business | 32 | CC Amusements | 32 |

| Name of library | No. of graphics | Name of library | No. of graphics |
|---|---|---|---|
| **SQUARE** (cont.) | | Food & Dining Beverage | 23 |
| CC Cool Cats | 38 | Food & Dining Edibles | 71 |
| CC Dapper Dogs | 63 | Food & Dining Service | 33 |
| CC Dynamic Dinos | 100 | Going Places | 17 |
| CC Fabulous Food | 100 | Icons | 73 |
| CC Hardware | 36 | Initial Caps | 35 |
| CC Home & Office | 72 | Jewish | 51 |
| CC Letters & Numbers | 55 | Letters & Numbers | 184 |
| CC Letters & Numbers Plain | 55 | Modern Living | 28 |
| CC People Play | 115 | Nature | 18 |
| CC People Work | 122 | People | 78 |
| CC Science & Nature | 82 | Photo Accessories | 121 |
| CC Travel & Transportation | 43 | Postmarks | 14 |
| Celebrations | 50 | PS | 334 |
| Christian | 45 | Recreation | 22 |
| Comic Characters Holiday | 28 | Sampler | 30 |
| Countries | 229 | Special Occasions | 27 |
| Crazy | 144 | Sports | 49 |
| Cultural | 35 | Stamps | 15 |
| Decorative Numbers | 21 | Symbols | 27 |
| Education | 92 | Wildlife | 71 |
| Flags | 224 | **COLUMN** | |
| Food & Beverage | 40 | Business | 13 |
| Food & Dining Atmosphere | 53 | Carmen | 9 |
| | | Celebrations | 22 |
| | | Christian | 33 |

| Name of library | No. of graphics | Name of library | No. of graphics |
|---|---|---|---|
| **COLUMN** (cont.) | | **MINI-BACKDROPS** | |
| Food & Dining | 40 | Business | 43 |
| Jewish | 21 | Carmen | 9 |
| PS | 199 | PS | 432 |
| Sampler | 16 | Sampler | 39 |
| Sports | 22 | **RULED LINES** | |
| Wildlife | 10 | Business | 20 |
| **ROW** | | PS | 81 |
| Business | 16 | Sampler | 19 |
| Carmen | 25 | **BORDERS** | |
| Celebrations | 32 | Business | 25 |
| Christian | 35 | PS | 111 |
| Food & Dining | 45 | Sampler | 25 |
| Jewish | 29 | **CERTIFICATE BORDERS** | |
| PS | 259 | PSD Certificate | 26 |
| Sampler | 63 | **BACKDROPS** | |
| Sports | 30 | Business | 20 |
| Wildlife | 22 | Carmen | 6 |
| | | PS | 101 |
| | | Sampler | 20 |

# ◆ Navigating the Graphics Browser

The task of sorting through more than 5,500 graphics to find just the right one would be insurmountable were it not for the Graphics Browser, shown in Figure 7.1. It makes short work of searching for a graphic by offering you a search strategy. Finding the right graphic for a project is as

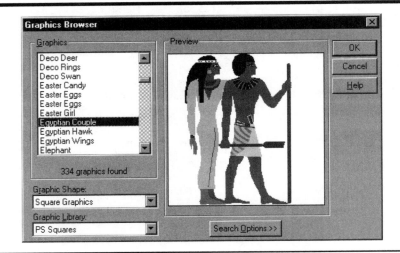

**Figure 7.1:** The Graphics Browser makes short work of searching for a graphic from the thousands available.

simple as making some basic decisions about your project, then searching the libraries for graphics that fit the search criteria.

In the Graphics Browser, you can search by graphic library or graphic shape, or you can do a more specific search by clicking on Search Options and selecting a search choice.

## Starting a Project

First, what is the subject of your project? A birthday? A trip? A school dance? Once you've defined the subject, you can search for the right graphic by key words, either words that relate to the subject or theme or words that are a part of the text of the project.

Let's say your subject is a kids' burger party with dinosaurs as the theme. It might sound crazy to think you can find a graphic that fits this idea, but let's try.

Start a new project.

1. If you still have an open project, select File ➤ New ➤ Stationery ➤ Start From Scratch ➤ Postcard. If you're at the Select a Project dialog box, select Stationery ➤ Start From Scratch ➤ Postcard.

2. At the orientation screen, hold down the Ctrl key and select Wide to go directly to the main project window.

In all the projects except Labels and Calendars, you can quickly reach the main project window from the Orientation screen by holding down the Ctrl key while clicking on the orientation of your project. This action bypasses the backdrop and layout options.

## Broadening the Search Options

Now search for the perfect graphic, a burger-eating dinosaur.

1. Click on the Add Object tool and select Square Graphic. A square graphic placeholder appears in the center of your blank page.

2. Double-click on the placeholder; the Graphics Browser pops up with Square Graphics selected under Graphic Shape. The default library is PS Squares, with 334 available graphics.

You can change the type of graphic in the Graphics Browser window. While you started with a square graphic in this search, you could switch to a column graphic, row graphic, or mini-backdrop by simply selecting one of these from the Graphic Shape drop down list. The placeholder in the project will change its shape to accommodate the new graphic choice.

3. Click on the drop down list arrow next to PS Squares and you'll see all the libraries available for square graphics. You could search this list by library name for a burger-eating dinosaur, or you could broaden your search category by changing the Graphics Library choice to All Libraries. Because All Libraries will yield a lot more options, click on All Libraries. The graphics list now shows more than 3,700 square graphics available.

**4.** Narrow this list down by clicking on the Search Options button.

The Graphics Browser expands, as shown in Figure 7.2, to include some search options that enable you to specify narrower search criteria: Keywords, Category Keywords, Add Project Text (this option is light gray, meaning it's not available now, because we do not have any text in our project yet), and Search Preferences.

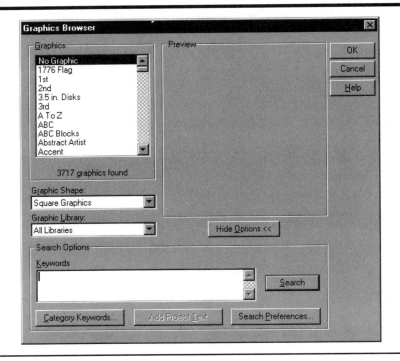

**Figure 7.2:** More options are displayed when you click on the Search Options button.

# Searching by Category

Let's begin with Category Keywords.

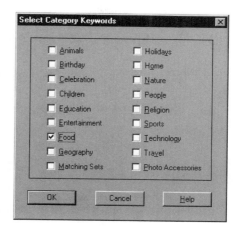

**5.** Click on the Category Keywords button, and up pops a list of 18 different keywords to aid in your search, as shown here. Because we're talking burgers, click on Food, then on OK to return to the Graphics Browser.

**6.** The word *Food* appears in the Keywords box. Now click on Search; the Graphics Browser searches All Libraries for square graphics with a food theme.

The search finds 205 graphics that in some way include food; much fewer than 3,700, but still too many.

# Searching by Multiple Keywords

Try narrowing the search further by adding *dinosaur* as a keyword.

**7.** In the Keywords box, type **dinosaur** next to *Food*. Include a space between the words but don't worry about upper- and lowercase—it doesn't matter to the search.

At this point you could click on Search to begin again. However, just separating two keywords by a space activates the Match Any Keywords default, which would find graphics that relate either to food or to dinosaurs, but not necessarily to both. If you began another search now, the Browser would find 312 graphics; we would have added *more* graphics by searching for food *or* dinosaurs.

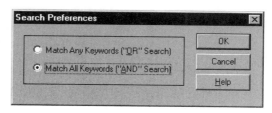

**8.** Because you're looking for a graphic with dinosaurs *and* food, click on Search Preferences. In the Search Preferences dialog box that appears, select Match All Keywords ("AND" Search), as shown here, to search for a graphic that has both food and a dinosaur. Click on OK.

9. Now search again. The graphic selection has dwindled to six graphics (that's more like it).

10. Click through the choices in the graphics list; as you do so, check the preview window to see what they look like. They are all dinosaurs that are either eating, preparing to eat, or have eaten already. Amazingly enough, one of them—Brachiosaurus—is a dinosaur eating a burger, as shown in Figure 7.3. This is a great demonstration of how diverse the Graphics Library really is.

**Figure 7.3:** Searching on the keywords **Food** and **Dinosaur** finds six graphics, including this burger-eating dinosaur.

You could have found this dinosaur much faster by searching with the keywords *burger* and *dinosaur* from the very beginning. Let's try it.

1.  Delete *Food* in the Keywords box and type Burger. Leave the word *Dinosaur*.

2.  Click on Search Preferences and make sure Match All Keywords ("AND" Search) is still selected; you'll search for a graphic that matches both *Burger* and *Dinosaur*.

3.  Now click on Search, and bingo! There's our burger-eating dinosaur, the Brachiosaurus. It is now the only graphic found in the search.

 When a search is in progress, the Search button changes to a Stop button. If you want to stop the search, click on it.

Searching for an image is, as you've seen, easiest when you narrow your search by using specific keywords from the start. You can always broaden the search to less specific categories if you do not find a graphic right away.

## Searching with Project Text

You can also search for a graphic by using any text you already have in the project, including text in word balloons, headlines, or text blocks. Let's try it.

1.  Click on Cancel to return to the main project window. You still have a blank page except for the square graphic placeholder. Click on the Add Object tool and select Text to add a text placeholder to the project.

2.  Double-click on the text placeholder and, in the Edit Text dialog box that appears, type **HAVE A DINO BURGER**. Click on OK, and the text will be placed on your page.

3.  Now double-click on the graphic placeholder to return to the Graphics Browser.

4. Select Search Options if they are not visible and click on Add Project Text. Text from the text box in your project now appears in the Keywords box: *HAVE DINO BURGER*. (Words like *a, an, and, the, from, to, by,* and *so* do not appear in the keywords box.) *HAVE* is not a word that will yield any results in the search, so delete it from the keywords box. *DINO* may or may not help in the search. The program may know that *DINO* refers to a dinosaur, and it may not. Because we're not sure, leave it as a keyword.

5. Click on Search Preferences and select Match Any Keywords ("OR" Search); the Browser will search for graphics that match either the word *BURGER* or the word *DINO*. Click on OK.

6. Under Graphics Library, select All Libraries, then click on Search. The search produces 13 graphics, one of them the burger-eating dinosaur and quite a few of them burgers.

When you add project text, any keywords you already have in the keywords box will be replaced by the new project text.

Searching for graphics is that easy. Define your criteria and search either individual libraries or all of them at once. We find that searching All Libraries at once is by far the best route.

Being able to browse the libraries for a suitable graphic is a great feature of Ensemble III. In the next section, you'll learn how to create a custom library that includes only the graphics you use most often; this consolidation will further shorten your search time.

# ◆ Merging Graphics Libraries

You can create a custom library by merging two or more libraries. Merging libraries gives you the opportunity to create libraries that cater to your particular Print Shop usage. When you merge libraries, you do not affect the original libraries; they remain intact. What you're really doing is merging copies of the libraries you've selected to create an entirely new library.

You cannot modify the original Print Shop libraries. The program will not allow you to delete graphics from the original libraries, so don't worry about deleting graphics by mistake. However, once you've merged original libraries into a new custom library, you can delete, rename, or add to the copied graphics.

# Preparing to Merge Libraries

Let's try our hand at merging libraries.

1. At the Select a Project dialog box, select Extras.

2. The Extra Features dialog box, shown in Figure 7.4, appears; choose Custom Libraries.

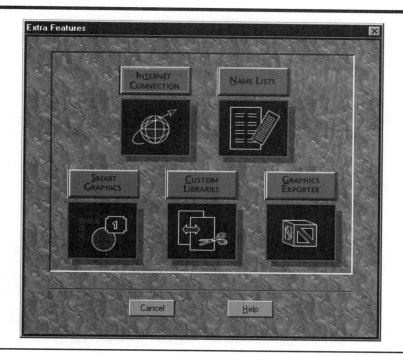

**Figure 7.4:** Clicking on Extras in the Select a Project dialog box brings up the Extra Features dialog box.

**3.** In the Custom Library dialog box, shown here, select Merge Library.

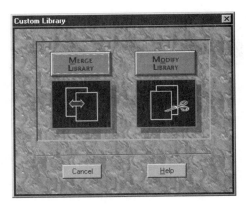

You'll see the Merge Libraries dialog box, shown in Figure 7.5. Because Square Graphics is selected in the Files of Type box, all square graphics libraries are listed. You can click on the Files of Type drop down list arrow to access all Print Shop libraries, as follows:

Square Graphics (*.PSG—i.e., files ending in .psg)

Certificate Borders (*.CBR)

Borders (*.PBR)

Column Graphics (*.PCG)

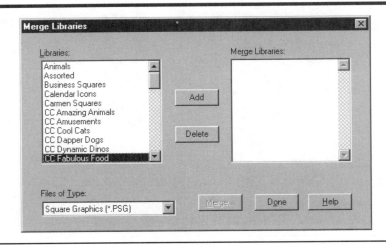

**Figure 7.5:** The Merge Libraries dialog box presents you with options for merging libraries.

Row Graphics (*.PRG)

Ruled Lines (*.PRL)

Seal Edges (*.PSE)

Seal Centers (*.PSI)

Keep in mind that these are libraries, not specific graphics. You cannot pick and choose graphics to merge into a library here. You must first merge libraries and then modify your new custom library by deleting or renaming graphics. See "Modifying Graphics Libraries" later in the chapter for more information.

## Starting the Merge

Now for the actual library merge:

1. Select Square Graphics (*.PSG) under Files of Type. The square graphics libraries appear in the Libraries area.

2. Select the libraries you want to merge; first highlight the Animals library and click on Add. The Animals library appears in the box labeled Merge Libraries.

 If you change your mind and do not want to merge the Animals library, highlight it in the Merge Libraries box and click on Delete. It is removed from your merge list.

3. Now select another library (your turn to choose). Highlight it and click on Add.

4. To merge the libraries, click on the Merge button. The Name Graphic Library dialog box, shown here, pops up. Give your new library a name.

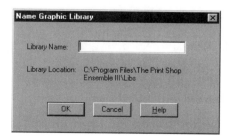

**5.** Let's call it TEST ONE. Type this in and then click on OK. The program will give the file an extension of .psg (meaning it's a square graphics library), and the merge is complete.

Scroll through the available files again; the new custom library called *TEST ONE* will now be listed, as shown here. It's that simple.

You can further customize your new library by using the Modify Library option, as we'll discuss next.

**6.** Select Done to return to the Select a Project screen.

# ◆ Modifying Graphics Libraries

User-created custom libraries can be modified by deleting any unwanted graphics or by renaming graphics. As stated above, original Print Shop graphics libraries can only be modified if you first merge them into a custom library. They cannot be modified in their original form.

## Preparing to Modify a Library

In order to modify a library, you need to use the Modify Library dialog box:

**1.** At the Select a Project dialog box, select Extras.

**2.** The Extra Features dialog box appears; choose Custom Libraries.

**3.** Select Modify Library.

The Modify Library dialog box appears, as shown in Figure 7.6. While this dialog box lists all libraries, you will be able to modify only your custom libraries.

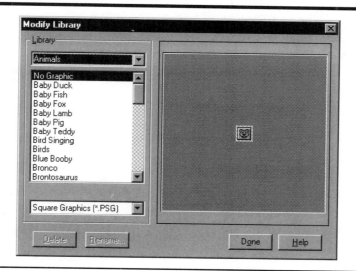

**Figure 7.6:** The Modify Library dialog box offers you options for modifying a custom library, including deleting or renaming graphics.

This dialog box also includes the option of selecting the graphic shape. If you have a lot of custom libraries, this option might be helpful. For now, we have only one custom library, TEST ONE, which we just made. This is the only library we can modify.

## Modifying a Library

When you first enter the Modify Library dialog box, the default library selected is Animals.

**1.** Click on the arrow next to Animals and select TEST ONE from the list of libraries. All graphics stored in the library TEST ONE are listed.

**2.** Highlight any graphic in the list. It will appear in the preview window.

**3.** Click on Delete; the graphic will be deleted from the file.

 When you delete a graphic, there is no prompt asking you if you're sure you want to delete it. Once you have hit the Delete key, the graphic is gone and you cannot undo the deletion. But because the custom library was created by merging two Print Shop libraries, the graphic still exists intact in one of the two Print Shop libraries you merged. Therefore, you could retrieve the graphic from its original file. If the deleted graphic is one you created, however, it's gone for good, unless you stored it in another library as well.

**4.** Highlight another graphic.

**5.** Click on Rename; the Rename Graphic dialog box, shown here, opens up with the old name highlighted in the text box. Give this graphic a new name of up to 16 characters. (You can include spaces between words if you like.) Click on OK to give the graphic its new name.

Before we go on, let's do one more thing.

**1.** From the Library drop down list, select Wildlife Squares. This is an original Print Shop Library. As noted above, you will not be able to modify this library. Let's see what happens if you try.

**2.** Highlight one of the graphics and click on Delete. A prompt pops up, shown here, warning you that you can delete only user-created libraries.

**3.** Click on Rename; the Rename Graphic dialog box pops up. You can type in a new name, but when you click on OK the same prompt appears, letting you know you cannot rename the graphic because it's an original Print Shop graphic.

That's all there is to it. With the Merge and Modify options, you can create a library that exactly fit your needs.

 Print Shop Ensemble III gives you the ability to drag and drop a file to the recycle bin. If you want to delete a Custom Library, for example, go to Microsoft Windows Explorer, highlight the library you want to delete and then just drag it to the recycle bin.

## ◆ **Endnotes**

You are now graphics library literate. You know how to:

◆ Recognize the file types in Print Shop libraries

◆ Browse for graphics and find a burger-eating dinosaur

◆ Set search options and use text in a project to find a graphic that creatively illustrates and enhances the text

◆ Create a custom library by merging two or more other libraries

◆ Modify a custom library

◆ Get a graphic back if by some chance you delete one you really want

You are a graphics library whiz—and now you're ready for Chapter 8, "Creating Special Graphics."

# Creating Special Graphics

## Your mission: to make some great special graphics

◆

The subject of this chapter is one of the most exciting and creative parts of PS Ensemble III: creating your very own designs—your chance to add that bit of pizzazz you've wanted for your projects. These are the design elements that will place your presentations in the realm of the most original ever seen by humankind.

OK, that statement may be a bit grandiose. What we're saying is that you can make some really great graphics with the special elements we'll cover in this chapter. All of this amazing creativity is reached through the most unassuming parts of this program, Smart Graphics and Seals.

# ◆ Customizing Smart Graphics

With Smart Graphics you can create special square graphics to use in your projects. There are three Smart Graphic styles available in PS Ensemble III: initial caps, numbers, and timepieces. (Actually, there are four: the fourth is borders, but since borders are a totally different kind of graphic than the other three, we'll deal with them separately.)

Let's get started.

1. From the Select a Project screen, select Extras. The Extra Features dialog box pops up, offering Internet Connection, Name List, Smart Graphics, Custom Libraries, and Graphics Exporter.

2. Select Smart Graphics. The Smart Graphics dialog box pops up (see Figure 8.1), offering four choices: Initial Caps, Numbers, Timepieces, and Borders.

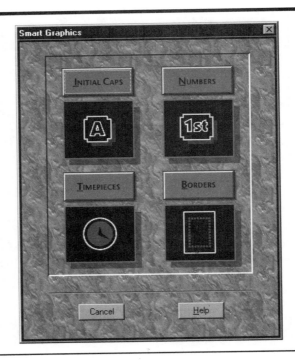

**Figure 8.1:** The Smart Graphics dialog box offers four different graphics to create.

You can also reach smart graphics from the main project window by selecting Extras from the main menu, clicking on Smart Graphics, and choosing from the drop down list offering Initial Caps, Numbers, Timepieces, and Custom Borders. If you select Initial Caps, for instance, the Create an Initial Cap dialog box will pop up.

# Designing an Initial Cap

The process of designing an initial cap takes place in the Create an Initial Cap dialog box, shown in Figure 8.2. This dialog box gives you a choice of upper- or lowercase letters in four text effects, 21 shapes, a range of Print Shop fonts (you may have more fonts available from other programs installed in your computer), two shadow effects, a choice of colors for text or text effects, and a variety of graphic backdrops. All of these elements enable you to create a unique initial cap that you can use to start a paragraph, embellish a letterhead, add style to a business card, customize a greeting card, or create your own personal monogram.

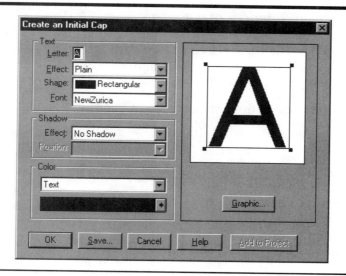

**Figure 8.2:** The Create an Initial Cap dialog box gives you a wide choice of fonts, styles, and colors, as well as a variety of graphic backdrops.

The design elements offered in the Create an Initial Cap dialog box are not limited to upper- and lowercase letters. You can type anything into the Letter box, including numbers or symbols. You can also design number graphics by choosing Smart Graphics ➤ Numbers, but special symbol graphics can only be designed in the Initial Cap area.

Let's go through the steps of designing an initial cap.

**1.** From the Smart Graphics dialog box, select Initial Cap to reach the Create an Initial Cap dialog box.

The default font is New Zurica, and the default letter is a capital *A*. Leave both of these as they are for this first creation. The Effect box in the Text area defaults to Plain, meaning that you have just a plain letter *A* without embellishment or modifications. Let's start to bring the letter *A* to life by seeing what our choices are and how they change the letter.

**2.** Click on the arrow next to the Effect box. There are three options available to modify the letter's initial appearance. You can add a thin outline, a thick outline, or a highlight.

**3.** Click on each option to see how it changes the look of the letter *A*; the results are shown here. Note that the Highlight selection leaves a space between the letter and the outline.

**4.** When you're done looking, select Plain.

**5.** The next step is to change the shape of the letter. Click on the arrow next to the Shape box, and a drop down list gives you 21 different shapes from which to choose. Go ahead and click on each choice so you can see how it changes the shape of the letter. All 21 options are shown here.

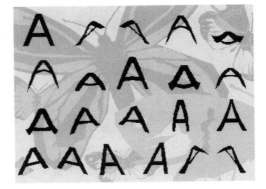

As you click through the options, you'll see that some distort the letter beyond recognition. Note how a change in shape can give the letter an added subtle meaning. Perspective Right, for instance, might say "movin' in," while Perspective Left could say "movin' on." Admittedly this example might be a little obscure, but this is the kind of reasoning used by many graphic designers in their design decisions. Let's face it: visual stimulation does motivate us to do a lot of things, even though it can be as subtle as the shape of a letter.

**6.** With the Effect option in the Shadow area, you can add a drop shadow or a silhouette to the letter, as shown here. If you choose Drop Shadow, the Position box will let you place the shadow to the upper-right, upper-left, lower-right, or lower-left of the letter. Experiment with these choices to see how they look.

**7.** Next, you can change the color of the text, outline, or shadow. The Color box defaults to Text, but you can click on the arrow next to the box to access the other choices. Click on the colored box below to choose a new color for the element you want to change.

**8.** Finally, you can add a graphic backdrop. Click on the Graphic button, and the Graphics Browser pops up. The default library is Initial Caps, offering 35 graphics; however, you can select a graphic from any square graphic library, so you actually have over 3,700 graphics available.

To see how you can add meaning to a letter, try adding some specially designed initial caps to projects. We'll help get you started.

**1.** Cancel out of the Create an Initial Cap dialog box and select File ➤ New to access the Select a Project dialog box.

**2.** Select Certificates ➤ Customize A Ready Made ➤ Achievement. Then scroll through the list of ready-made projects and select Dancercise; it opens in the main project window.

**3.** Note the text box in the center. The text size here might be small enough to be unreadable, appearing only as a gray block. Double-click on this text box and the Edit Text dialog box pops up. The first word of the text is *Dancing*. Delete the letter *D* and click OK to return to the main project window.

**4.** Now save the certificate with the Save As command from the File menu. Name the new file *dance art*.

Your design challenge is to create an initial cap that will look like a dancing *D* to begin the word *dancing*.

**5.** Click on the Extras menu to start. Then select Smart Graphics ➤ Initial Caps and begin your design work.

**6.** First change your letter from *A* to *D* by just typing in a **D**.

**7.** Select Arc Up as your shape. Add a gray drop shadow in the lower-right position and dark blue text with a light blue, thick outline in the New Zurica font.

**8.** When you have a design that you like, you'll want to see what it looks like on the certificate. Click on the Add to Project button.

**9.** You'll be prompted to save the initial cap as a graphic (you must do this before you can add it to the Dancercise Certificate). Click on OK; the Save Graphic In Library dialog box pops up, as shown here. Type **Dance1** for the file name, since you might want to create a dance2, -3, -4, etc. until you get just the right design.

**10.** Note the Graphics Library name box in the Save Graphic In Library dialog box. Here you can select the custom library where the graphic will be stored. In the graphic shown here you see only one custom library, TEST ONE, which we just created in Chapter 7. You could store it in that library by just clicking OK.

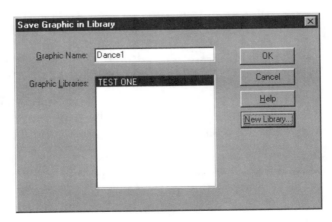

**11.** If you want to create a new library for your graphic, click on New Library and the Create a New Graphic Library dialog box, shown here,

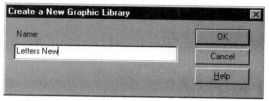

pops up so you can give this new custom library a name. Since this is a letter, let's create a library called *Letters New*.

**12.** Once you've given it a file name and clicked OK, the graphic will be saved in your new library and then placed in the center of your project. Resize and move it around to the right position, as shown here.

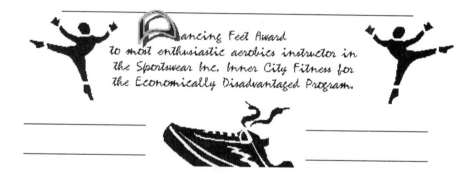

If you save an initial cap without adding it to the project (by clicking on the Save button instead of the Add to Project button), you can retrieve it by adding a square graphic and double-clicking on its placeholder to reach the Graphics Browser. Change the library to your library name (in this case Letters New), find the graphic (Dance1), and insert it into the project.

Here's another idea. Let's create an original initial cap similar to those created by the scribes in ancient times, an initial cap designed to catch the reader's eye for a special piece of stationery.

**1.** Select Extras ➤ Smart Graphics ➤ Initial Caps to open the Create an Initial Cap dialog box.

2. Click on the Graphic button under the preview window. The 35 square graphics in the Initial Caps library are listed. Choose Pedestal to get started with the idea of creating a rather formal monogram for a notepad.

3. Click on OK and the Pedestal graphic becomes the backdrop for the letter *A*. Change the *A* to your initial. We changed ours to *C*.

4. Resize the letter until it sits on the pedestal. As you can see here, the New Zurica font does not work well with the Pedestal graphic.

We need a font with a serif or even additional elements to create the formal look we had in mind. After reviewing some of the styles included with PS Ensemble III, we've selected Percival as just the right font.

5. Change the font to Percival.

6. Next, the letter needs to be more prominent. Choose the Silhouette option from Shadow Effect and separate the background from the letter with contrasting colors. The completed Initial Cap is shown here.

These are just a few examples of how simple it is to create your own initial cap, giving added pizzazz to a project. You can design numbers in Initial Caps as well, but the Numbers design area gives you the additional option of adding a suffix.

## Designing a Number

Sometimes you want a number to stand out in your project. Let's say you want the world to know that you're number one in your business. You need to create a look that is instantly recognizable to both your old clients as well as the new ones you would like to acquire.

1. Start by selecting File ➤ New, then select Stationery ➤ Customize A Ready Made ➤ Letterhead ➤ Business Travel.

2. To design your special number graphic from the main project window, click on Extras ➤ Smart Graphics ➤ Numbers.

The Create a Number dialog box pops up, as shown in Figure 8.3. The options offered here are the same as those offered in the Create an Initial Cap dialog box, except that you have the option of adding a suffix to your number, and when you click on the Graphic button, the default library is different.

**3.** The default number 1 has a suffix added to it so that it reads *1st*, not *1*. But "we're number first" doesn't make sense. To eliminate the suffix, uncheck the Suffix box next to the Number box. When this box is checked, it adds the suffixes *st*, *nd*, *rd*, and *th* to numbers as appropriate. Without the suffix, the number 1 is ready for you to begin your design work.

Here are some of the things that we did that you might want to try. We like the looks of the *1* in Tribune font with a shape of Perspective Right and a drop shadow in the upper-right position, as shown here. Perspective Right opens the number slightly to invite the viewer in. The drop shadow reinforces this feeling, and its upper-right position makes the number stand out.

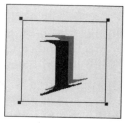

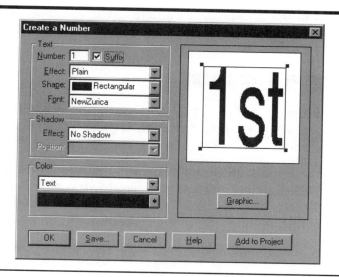

**Figure 8.3:** The Create a Number dialog box offers you four text effects, 21 text shapes, a variety of fonts, two shadow effects, a choice of colors for text or text effects, and a variety of graphic backdrops.

**4.** Make the appropriate adjustments so your number looks like ours, or choose your own look.

**5.** When you're done experimenting, click on the Graphic button; you're offered 35 graphics in the Initial Caps library. We could increase the number of graphic choices to over 3,700 by changing the Graphic Library box in the Graphics Browser to All Libraries. Instead, select a library called Decorative Numbers and a graphic named Burst. Click OK.

**6.** Resize the number and move it to fit over the graphic. The finished Number graphic is shown here.

**7.** Click on the Add to Project button, and you will be reminded that you must save it before you can add it to your letterhead. Save it as *one1* since you might decide to try another design or graphic selection. Save it to a library called Numbers. Click OK and the number is added to the project.

**8.** As usual, your new number graphic appears in the center of the project. Move and resize it as necessary, then add text blocks for your business information and the "We're number" text preceding the 1.

## Selecting a Timepiece

The Extras menu also gives you the opportunity to choose a timepiece to add to a project to make sure that the recipients of a meeting memo or party invitation know what time to show up.

**1.** To reach the Timepiece design area, select File ➤ New, and from the Select a Project dialog box, select Extras ➤ Smart Graphics ➤ Timepieces. (You can also reach the design area from the main project window by selecting the Extras ➤ Smart Graphics ➤ Timepieces.)

**2.** The Select a Timepiece dialog box, shown in Figure 8.4, appears. This dialog box offers 18 graphic timepiece designs. There are no other graphics available even though Other Libraries is an option.

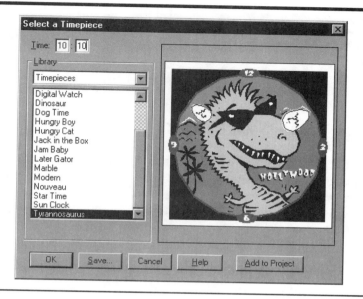

**Figure 8.4:** The Select a Timepiece dialog box lets you choose from 18 custom timepieces.

You can create a Timepiece only with one of the 18 graphics offered in the Timepiece library.

 You can select No Graphic in the Select a Timepiece dialog box, but it's not a real option. If you select No Graphic and click OK, you are sent back to the Smart Graphics menu or to the main project window, depending on which method you used to get here. Selecting No Graphic is the same thing as clicking on Cancel.

**3.** To create a timepiece, select one of the graphics and set the time in the upper-left corner of the dialog box.

Some of the graphic designs in the Timepieces Library are analog and some are digital, as shown here.

 There is no A.M. or P.M. indication on either analog or digital clocks. If you use a 24-hour clock and enter 19:00 as the time, it will be displayed as 7:00 on a analog clock and as 19:00 on a digital clock.

## Naming Smart Graphics

All Smart Graphics are saved as square graphics in a custom library of your choice before they are added to a project. Since Smart Graphics are stored as square graphics, they can be placed in any project. Your custom library becomes another library offered when you browse for graphics. So among the list of available square graphics libraries, you should now find our new custom libraries we called Letters New and Numbers.

It's a good idea to give your custom libraries descriptive names, as we did above. Descriptive names make it easier to find a specific graphic (which is a good reason to give the graphics themselves descriptive names as well), whether you're just browsing or using the Search options.

## ◆ Customizing Borders

Adding a custom border to a project can give your piece a distinctive look. To get into this part of PS Ensemble III, from the main project window select Extras ➤ Smart Graphics ➤ Custom Borders. The Border Type dialog box appears. As shown here, your choices are Border/Mini-Border and Certificate Border.

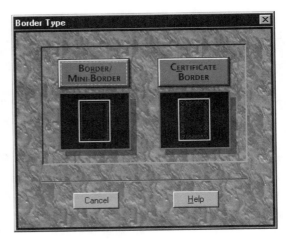

The design process for both types of borders is basically the same. The only difference is that certificate borders are wider and have fewer arrangement choices.

# Arranging a Border

Designing a border is a simple process of arranging square graphics into a design that suits your creative vision. You can choose from the more than 3,700 square graphics in the Print Shop program and arrange them in a variety of ways.

You choose the arrangement in the Border Arrangement area of the Create a Border dialog box, shown in Figure 8.5. A sample illustration of the border appears in the preview area to the right. Figure 8.5 illustrates the Single Piece Repeating arrangement. The other three arrangement options—Corners and Rails, Alternating Rails, and Rails with Centerpieces—are shown in Figures 8.6 through 8.8.

To change the arrangement, just click on the arrow next to the Border Arrangement box and select the arrangement you want. You will get a prompt giving you the opportunity to save your work before you go on to another border arrangement. Once you get beyond this prompt, the Graphic area just below will change to reflect the different graphic elements that make up the new arrangement. Click on the Graphic button below each element to choose a graphic for that element.

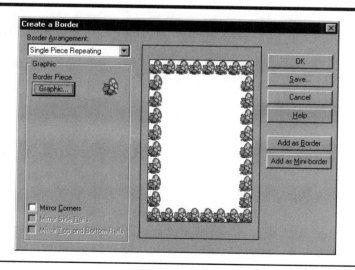

**Figure 8.5:** The Single Piece Repeating arrangement is made up of one square graphic that repeats over and over around the border.

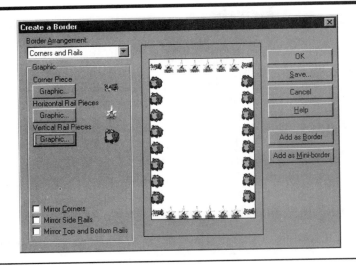

**Figure 8.6:** The Corners and Rails arrangement is composed of three different grpahics, one for the corners, one for the top and bottom rails, and one for the side rails.

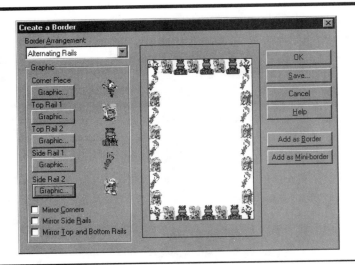

**Figure 8.7:** The Alternating Rails arrangement is composed of five different graphics: one for the corners, two (alternating) for the top and bottom rails, and two (alternating) for the side rails. This arrangement is not available for certificate borders.

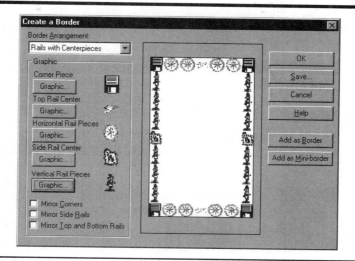

**Figure 8.8:** The Rails with Centerpieces arrangement is made up of five different graphics: one for the corners, one for the top and bottom rails, one for the center of the top and bottom rails, one for the side rails, and one for the center of the side rails. This arrangement is not available for certificate borders.

The Create a Border dialog box also offers three mirroring options. You can mirror corners, side rails, or top and bottom rails by clicking on the appropriate check boxes in the lower-left corner of the dialog box. We'll take a look at some mirror images in the next part of this chapter.

# Choosing Border Graphics

Now that we know about border arrangements, let's try creating a few borders.

1. From the Select a Project screen, select Extras ➤ Smart Graphics ➤ Borders ➤ Border/Mini-Border; the Create a Border dialog box pops up. The default arrangement is Single Piece Repeating, and the preview shows a solid black border.

2. Click on the Graphic button under Border Piece in the Graphic area. You'll see a selection of 334 square graphics in the PS

Squares library. Change your library to Assorted and choose Frog and look at it in the preview area. Note that the frog is facing left.

**3.** Click OK and you return to the Create a Border dialog box with the frog repeated as a border in the preview window. All of the frogs are facing left.

**4.** Click on the Mirror Corners check box. The two right corners become mirror images of the left corners, as shown here.

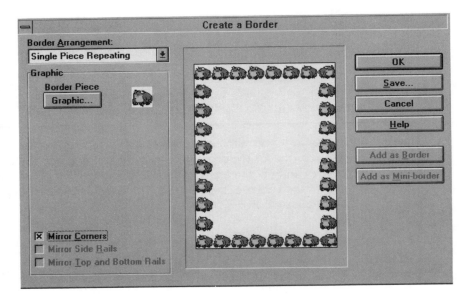

**5.** Now change the border arrangement to Corners and Rails. When the program asks you if you want to save the frog border, click on No. All of the frogs disappear and you have three graphic elements to fill: Corner Piece, Top Rail Piece, and Side Rail Piece.

**6.** Click on the Graphic button below Corner Piece and from the Assorted Library, choose American Flag, and click on OK. A flag appears in each corner of the preview window, with the flagpole on the left side.

**7.** Click on the Graphic button for the top rail piece and from the Assorted Library, choose Cherry Pie. Click on OK. A row of cherry pie slices appears across the top and bottom row of the sample page.

**8.** Click on the Graphic button under Side Rail Piece. You've probably figured out by now that we're making a border that's as American as cherry pie. (Okay, in the saying it's apple pie, but who's checking? We like the way the cherry pie looks.) So what else do we need? Mom, of course. There's an appropriate graphic in the Assorted Library called Woman Icon. Click on it, then click on OK; the side rails in the preview fill with Mom's left profile.

**9.** Check the Mirror Side Rails box; Mom's profile changes from left to right on the right side of the page. Check the Mirror Top and Bottom Rails box; the pies turn upside-down on the bottom row. Check Mirror Corners, and the flagpoles move to the right on the right side of the page. The result looks like Figure 8.9.

As you can see, the graphics can be used in different combinations creating variations almost without limit.

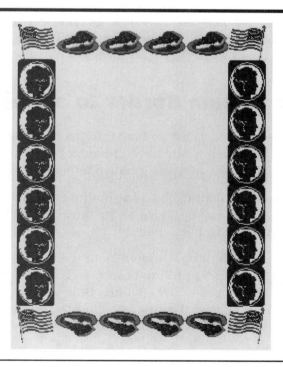

**Figure 8.9:** Checking all the mirroring options produces some interesting and some unacceptable results.

# Saving a Custom Border

As with the other Smart Graphics selections, you must save borders before they can be used in your project. The process for saving a border is exactly like saving an initial cap, number, or timepiece, as discussed above.

You have the option in the Create a Border dialog box to add your border creation to the project as either a border or a mini-border. If you save your creation as a border, it will become a permanent border on the project. Like a PS original border, you will not be able to resize or move it. You will be able to lighten it in the main project window using the Shading Selector on the toolbar. On the other hand, if you save your creation as a mini-border, it will act just like an original Print Shop mini-border, meaning you will be able to resize and move it in a project.

Custom borders are stored in a custom library named by you, just as you named the Letters and Numbers libraries. The Search option in the Borders Browser includes custom borders. Be sure to give your borders descriptive names so you can find them again easily.

# Adding a Custom Border to a Project

To automatically add a custom border to the main project window, click on the Add as Border or Add as Mini-border button in the Create a Border dialog box. After you give your creation a name, it will be added.

If you click on OK instead of Add as Border or Add as Mini-border, the custom border will not be added to the project. It will instead be saved to the library and file you designate.

To add a saved custom border later, go to the main project window, select Object ➤ Add ➤ Border or Mini-border, and double-click on the border placeholder that appears. The Graphics Browser pops up. Select your library from the Graphic Library list, select the border name from the list of graphics, and click OK. The border is added to the project.

# ◆ Designing a Seal

Official-looking seals can give letterhead, envelopes, or almost any piece of printed material a distinctive look. With PS Ensemble III, you can create seals of your own for any project. You can also use the Seal feature to design a creative logo for your business or activity.

Seals are circular and can include a center graphic, an edge graphic, and basic text. You can choose any or all of these design options when you create your seal. Seals are always designed from the main project window, either by adding a seal placeholder or by clicking on a seal placeholder that is already part of a certificate layout. Let's look at adding a seal placeholder and creating a seal.

1. To start, select the Object Menu ➤ Add ➤ Seal or select the Add Object tool ➤ Seal.

2. A seal placeholder appears in the center of your project. Double-click on this placeholder to open the Seal dialog box.

## Adding a Graphic

The Seal dialog box, shown in Figure 8.10, includes two graphic options, Center and Edge. You can choose graphics from either one of these or both of them.

3. Click on Center; the Select a Seal Center dialog box, shown in Figure 8.11, offers 53 different graphics. As usual, you can click through the graphics and see them previewed. When you've made your selection, click on OK to return to the Seal dialog box with the center graphic in place.

4. Click on Edge; the Select a Seal Edge dialog box, shown in Figure 8.12, offers 31 different circle designs for the outside edge of the seal. When you've made your selection, click on OK to return to the Seal dialog box with the edge graphic in place.

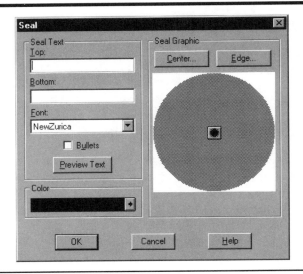

**Figure 8.10:** Seals are designed in the Seal dialog box, which appears when you click on an existing seal or a seal placeholder.

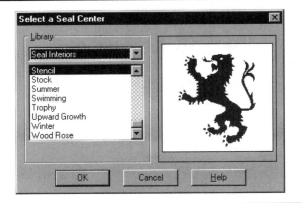

**Figure 8.11:** The Select a Seal Center dialog box offers 53 interior graphics.

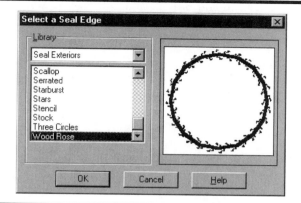

**Figure 8.12:** The Select a Seal Edge dialog box offers 31 exterior designs.

Many of the edge graphics coordinate with center graphics. Coordinated graphics have the same name. For example, Blue Diamond in the Select a Seal Edge dialog box is the coordinating element for Blue Diamond in the Select a Seal Center dialog box. Both are shown here. Other coordinated centers and edges include Florentine, Lace, Link, Oak, Wood Rose, Primary, and Roses.

# Adding Text

Text can be composed in any available font and placed in the upper and lower halves of the seal. Top seal text curves above the center graphic. Bottom seal text curves below the center graphic.

**5.** To enter top text, simply place the cursor in the text box marked Top and begin typing. Do the same in the box marked Bottom for the bottom text. Both top and bottom text can be up to 63 characters long. Seal text is designed to fit into a small area; thus it is small in size and not very readable. Whatever you place here should be succinct.

**6.** Click on the arrow next to the font box to change the font as you please. Text size cannot be changed.

**7.** Place a check in the Bullets box. When you select this box, bullets will be placed on each side of the seal between the top and bottom text.

**8.** Click on the Preview Text button to see all the elements in place in the preview window. The seal previewed here has all the available elements: center graphic, edge graphic, text, and bullets.

You can change the color of monochrome graphics, bullets, and text using the Color area of the Seal dialog box. Whatever color you choose becomes the color for all elements (you cannot color text one color and monochrome graphics another color). If the graphics are already in color, the color you select will apply only to the text and bullets.

You can change the color of monochrome graphics, text, and bullets in the main project window: select the seal, click on the Item Selector, and choose Object, then use the Color Selector to change the color. To change the color behind the seal, select Behind Object from the Item Selector and then select a color.

## Saving a Customized Seal

Unlike smart graphics, seals are not saved to a library. They are saved only as a part of a project. However, you can save one as a graphic file if you like. Here's how.

**1.** Open a new project (a sign or letterhead would be good).

**2.** Select Start From Scratch and then choose either a wide or tall orientation. When you select the orientation, hold down the Ctrl key and you will bypass the backdrop and layout options to go directly to the main project window with a blank page.

**3.** On this blank page, create a seal using the techniques mentioned above.

**4.** Once you have created the seal, resize it to fit the full page or as close to full as you can get.

**5.** Select File ➤ Save As and save the project as a Windows Bitmap file, Windows Metafile, or TIFF Bitmap File. We'd suggest you save this file in the Projects folder or create a brand new folder, called Seals, for example, so you can retrieve it easily when the time comes.

Now you can import this file into any project and resize and move it to the area you want it to cover. You can use this technique to create a logo and import it into letterhead, business cards, labels, or whatever you like.

# ◆ Endnotes

Now you know how to create your own custom graphics. You can:

◆ Design an initial cap and add a graphic to give it style and mood

◆ Create a dramatic number graphic to punctuate an occasion or make a point

◆ Make a timepiece that's set for the exact time you want all your friends to show up for an event

◆ Make a special border with alternating or mirroring graphics, and search from over 3,700 graphics available for the design

◆ Create a seal with coordinating graphics and add color to the design

◆ Design a logo and save it for other projects

You're ready for Chapter 9, "Importing Images."

# Importing Images

## Your mission: to import a graphic and a photo

◆

Importing a graphic or photo into a Print Shop project is easy, provided the graphic's file format is compatible with Print Shop. The import function supports a variety of graphic file formats (graphic types), and it supports a high-resolution file format for importing photos.

# ◆ Importing Graphics

Six types of graphics or photos can be imported into a Print Shop project. The six types and their file extensions are:

| | |
|---|---|
| Bitmap | .bmp |
| Encapsulated Postscript | .eps |
| Joint Photographics Experts Group | .jpg |
| Kodak Photo CD | .pcd |
| Tagged Image File Format | .tif |
| Windows Metafile | .wmf |

 Different programs save graphics as different file types. A graphic from Microsoft Word's Clipart directory, for example, is saved as a Windows Metafile (WMF), while a graphic from Broderbund's Kid Pix for Windows is a Bitmap file (BMP).

To import an image, whether it's a BMP, EPS, JPEG, PCD, TIFF, or WMF file:

**1.** Either click on Object ➤ Add or click on the Add Object tool.

**2.** Select Import.

**3.** Find the graphic you want to add.

**4.** Click on Open to import it.

It's that simple. Give it a try with this new project:

**1.** Select File ➤ New ➤ Signs & Posters ➤ Start From Scratch ➤ Wide ➤ Blank Page ➤ No Layout.

You'll find yourself at the main project window with a blank page, ready to begin importing.

**2.** Pull down the Object menu and select Add. You will be offered a list of objects you can add to your project: Graphic, Square Graphic, Row Graphic, Column Graphic, and so on. You will find Import at the very bottom of the list.

**3.** Click on Import. The Import dialog box pops up.

Search your system for graphics or photos stored outside of Print Shop. If you have Microsoft Office installed on your computer system, take a look at the Clipart folder and you'll find a bunch of them, as seen here in Figure 9.1.

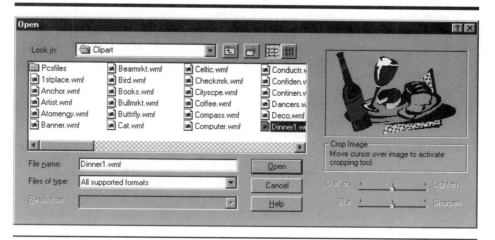

**Figure 9.1:** The Import dialog box allows you to import graphics saved in different file formats.

**4.** Select one of the graphics and click Open to add it to your project.

You can import your graphics or photos from any program in your computer and also from a disc or from a CD.

## Looking at Available Files

You can navigate through your drives and folders by clicking through the drive and folder lists. You could, for example, insert a disk containing a special graphics library and search it for a graphic to import by clicking on the letter for the floppy drive in the Look In box, choosing the file type, and then highlighting available graphics to see them in preview. For example, we scanned in a photograph

taken aboard the aircraft carrier USS Carl Vinson, shown on preceding page, stored it as a TIFF file, and later added it to a thank you note we sent an officer aboard that ship.

BMP, JPEG, TIFF, and PCD files can be cropped before they are imported into the project. WMF, or EPS files cannot be cropped. Refer to the "Cropping Photos" section later in this chapter for more on using this cropping option.

Once you've selected a file, all you have to do is click Open to import it into a project. The graphic will be placed in the center of the project window. You can then move and resize the graphic as desired. Print Shop graphics are scalable graphics, meaning they can be resized without losing shape or clarity. Imported files, on the other hand, may be scaled bitmap files, meaning they are not designed to be resized or reshaped. Scaled bitmap files will not appear smooth if you resize them. If you enlarge an imported scaled bitmap file, the image will begin to break up, or *pixelize*. Thus, imported graphics are best used in their imported size.

Imported color graphics will always display in color if you have a color monitor. Changing the color preference to grayscale in the main project window will not change imported color graphics to grayscale. It may change the color shading of some objects in the graphic but it will not change the entire graphic to grayscale.

## An Importing Tip

A Print Shop project can be saved as a Print Shop Ensemble file, Windows Bitmap file (.bmp), Windows Metafile (.wmf), TIFF Bitmap file (.tif), or JPEG (.jpg). When you save the project, just select TIFF, for example, as your file type rather than the standard Print Shop extension. If you were saving a sign, the standard extension would be .pds (Print Shop sign). Change this to .tif and save.

Now you have a TIFF file that can be imported into another Print Shop project. So you could, for example, start a second sign project and import the first sign project as a graphic, creating an entirely different look and style, as shown in Figure 9.2. Also, saved as a WMF, TIFF, or BMP, the project can be inserted into a compatible program outside Print Shop, such as Microsoft Word.

**Figure 9.2:** You can save a project as a TIFF, BMP, WMF, or JPEG file, then import it as a graphic into another project or another program.

# ◆ Importing Photos

Photos can be imported from any source, such as a prepared disc or CD, a hard drive, or your scanner. To get you started, The PS Ensemble III gives you a great selection of over 100 photos to import into your projects. These photos are stored in the Photo directory on the Print Shop CD as bitmaps. They are not loaded onto your system's hard drive when Print Shop is loaded.

The photos in this directory can be used fairly liberally in your projects. With a few restrictions, they can be copied, modified, and incorporated in materials for personal use, in advertising and promotional materials, and as part of a product for sale. Consult the booklet inserted into the CD-ROM container for specifics.

To look at the Print Shop photos:

**1.** Insert the PS Ensemble III CD into your CD-ROM drive.

**2.** Select Object ➤ Add ➤ Import. The Import dialog box pops up.

**3.** Go to the CD drive, the PSEWIN folder, and then the Photo directory. The program automatically accesses the CD and lists the available photos in the Files box. Highlight the files to preview them.

**4.** Click on the photo named Farmland.bmp. A pasture scene with grazing horses and part of a red-roofed barn is previewed, as shown in Figure 9.3.

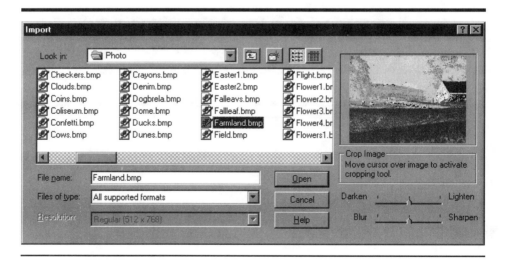

**Figure 9.3:** The Import dialog box displays the photographs provided with the Print Shop program; here it shows the farmland photo in preview.

In the Import dialog box you can also choose a resolution for your imported photo. Photo CD images can be imported in one of five different resolutions:

| | |
|---|---|
| Extra Low | $128 \times 192$ dots per inch |
| Low | $256 \times 384$ dots per inch |
| Regular | $512 \times 768$ dots per inch |
| High | $1,024 \times 1,536$ dots per inch |
| Extra High | $2,048 \times 3,072$ dots per inch |

The more dots per inch, the smoother the image will appear and the less likely it will pixelize if you choose to enlarge it. However, higher-resolution images also take more memory to display, print, and save. The memory requirements for each resolution choice are as follows:

| | |
|---|---|
| Extra Low | 2.5MB |
| Low | 3MB |
| Regular | 7.5MB |
| High | 15MB |
| Extra High | 30MB |

These memory requirements decrease in proportion to how much of the photo you use (we discuss cropping photos next). If you use only a small part of the total image, the memory requirements are considerably less; in this case, it might make sense to use the highest resolution so you can resize as needed and still have a great-looking picture.

# Cropping and Adjusting Photos

Photos can be cropped and adjusted to make them darker or lighter, sharper or blurred before you import them. As you highlight the available photos, you'll notice that the following text appears under the preview box:

**Move cursor over image to activate cropping tool.**

This means exactly what it says. You can crop the photo, choosing to import into your project only that portion of the picture you want. To crop and import a photo:

1. Select the Farmland.bmp photo.

2. Move your cursor over the picture. The cursor arrow changes to crosshairs. Position the crosshairs at the upper-left corner above the horses.

3. Hold down your left mouse button and drag it over the horses, drawing a box around them, as shown here. When you're finished, release your mouse button. If you are not satisfied, just click anywhere on the screen and the box will disappear. Then draw it again.

4. Use the slider bars *Darken - Lighten* and *Blur - Sharp* to change the brightness level or sharpness of your photo.

5. When it's just right, click on Open. The cropped image will be imported into the center of the main project window, as shown here. You can then resize and move the image.

# Resizing and Adding Accessories

Photos in the main project window can be resized or moved to match your creative vision for the project. Be aware that photos will pixelize as you enlarge them; while this may be OK if it's an effect you're aiming for, it won't be OK if you don't want the effect.

Photos in the project window behave the same as Print Shop graphics. To resize a photo keeping the same aspect ratio, select it, then drag one of its handles. To resize the image without maintaining the aspect ratio, hold down the Ctrl key while you drag a handle.

The Print Shop program also includes many things like hats, frames, and glasses to enhance your photos. These graphics are stored in a graphics library called Photo Accessories, accessible by adding a Square Graphic and searching the Photo Accessories library. You can add an accessory and then position it over the photo, putting a hat on someone or adding a cute frame. For more on this file, check out the section on Photo Projects in Chapter 5, "Understanding Print Shop Projects."

# ◆ Endnotes

While the graphics offered by the Print Shop program are considerable, you are not restricted to them. You can import more graphics from other programs or from a disk or CD, and you can do it quite easily. You know how to:

- ◆ Choose a graphic type to import
- ◆ Find a graphic by searching drives and folders
- ◆ Store a Print Shop project as a BMP, WMF, TIFF, or JPEG file and then import it into another project or program
- ◆ Access photos from the Photo images on the Print Shop CD
- ◆ Select a resolution for a photo import
- ◆ Crop a photo before importing it
- ◆ Move and resize an imported image
- ◆ Add a cute accessory to your photograph

You're ready for Chapter 10, "Exporting Graphics."

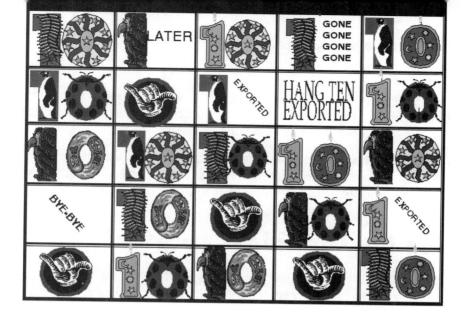

# Exporting Graphics

## Your mission: to export graphics and graphics libraries for use outside of Print Shop

◆

The Graphics Exporter in PS Ensemble III is a handy tool for exporting Print Shop graphics so that they can be used in other graphics or desktop publishing programs. This export option gives you access to Print Shop graphics in any program you choose. In addition to exporting to a file, you can also export to the printer, printing all or a portion of a library.

Exporting a graphic using the Graphics Exporter is so quick and easy that it's hard to believe you're actually doing it. You can export one graphic or a series of graphics—even a whole library—with a single export command. Simply choose the graphic or graphics you want, select a destination file or printer, and you're ready to export.

You can export graphics from any of Print Shop's graphic libraries as well as any user libraries you create. The Graphics Exporter even allows you to preview a graphic before you export it to make sure it's the one you want.

# ◆ Opening the Graphics Exporter

The Graphics Exporter is easily accessed, whether or not you've opened Print Shop. You can enter the Graphics Exporter in three different ways:

- ◆ Before opening Print Shop, click on the Graphics Exporter icon, shown here.
- ◆ Inside Print Shop, choose Extras from the Select a Project dialog box, and the Extra Features dialog box will appear. Click on Graphics Exporter.
- ◆ From Print Shop's main project window, open the Extras menu and choose Export and Print Graphics.

After you have selected the Graphics Exporter using one of these three methods, the Print Shop Graphics Exporter dialog box, shown in Figure 10.1, appears on your screen.

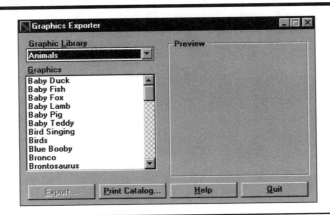

**Figure 10.1:** Whichever method you use to open the Graphics Exporter, this dialog box will appear on your screen.

# ◆ Choosing a Graphic

You can select one graphic to export, or you can select a series of graphics and export all of them with one command. To select a single graphic to export:

1. Open the Graphics Exporter dialog box using one of the methods listed above.

2. In the Graphics Exporter dialog box, click on the Graphic Library drop down list to view the names of all Print Shop libraries and any custom libraries you may have created.

3. Click on a library to view the names of all the graphics in that library. For this example, select PS Squares.

If you need some help finding the right graphic for a particular project, use the advanced Search options in the Graphics Browser to pinpoint the graphic(s) you want. You'll need to do this before you select the Graphics Exporter. The Graphics Browser is discussed in more detail in Chapter 7, "Working with Graphics Libraries."

4. Once you find the graphic you'd like to export, click on it to highlight it. For this example, choose B'day Bear, shown here. The graphic appears in the preview area, and is now ready for export.

Let's say you want to export all of the graphics listed between B'day Bear and Beach Ball in the PS Squares library. It would be tedious to select and export them one at a time. But you can use the Shift key to select a block of graphics to export or the Ctrl key to pick and choose graphics to export. Let's give this a try.

1. Click on the first graphic you want to select—in this case, B'day Bear.

**2.** Hold down the Shift key and click on Beach Ball. All the graphics from B'day Bear to Beach Ball are highlighted. Because you have selected multiple graphics, no graphic appears in the preview window. In fact, in the preview area it says, Cannot Preview with Multiple Graphics Selected.

If you chose to click export now, all the selected graphics would be exported as a group under their Print Shop file names to whatever destination you designated.

**3.** Release the Shift key and click on Beach Ball again. Now only Beach Ball is selected and it appears in the preview window.

**4.** With Beach Ball already selected, hold down the Ctrl key and click on B'day Bear again. Only Beach Ball and B'day Bear are highlighted, and once again no graphic appears in the preview window.

If you chose to export now, you would export only Beach Ball and B'day Bear together under their Print Shop file names to whatever destination you chose.

## ◆ Exporting a Graphic

Before you export a graphic, make sure you know what file format the graphic needs to be in so it is compatible with its destination.

### Designating a File Type

You can export a graphic as one of the following file types:

| | |
|---|---|
| BMP | Windows Bitmap |
| TIFF | Tagged Bitmap (Tagged Image File Format) |
| WMF | Windows Metafile |
| EPS | Encapsulated PostScript |

 The Graphics Exporter's EPS format saves EPS files without preview. This means that when you import these EPS files into a project outside Print Shop, you will not see a preview of the graphic. Rather, you see only a box representing the graphic's location. You can resize and move this box but you will not see the actual graphic until you print the project. Also, keep in mind that it takes a PostScript printer to print an EPS file. If you don't have a PostScript printer, do not export graphics as EPS files.

To assign your graphic a name and file format:

**1.** Highlight Beach Ball and click on Export. A dialog box named *Export 'Beach Ball' as* appears, in which you can name your file, choose a file format, and select a destination, as shown here. When you export multiple graphics, this dialog box will simply be titled *Export Graphics as.*

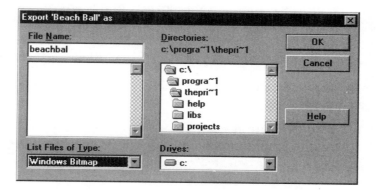

**2.** In the File Name box, the default name is *beachbal* (the first eight letters of the graphic's name in the library list). Type **beach1** as the graphic's new name.

**3.** Click on the List Files of Type drop down list and select Windows Bitmap as the file format for the graphic.

 If you have selected multiple graphics for export, you cannot change any of their names. They will all be exported under the names given to them in Print Shop. You can change their names in Windows Explorer outside Print Shop after they have been exported, if you like.

## Choosing a Destination

You're almost ready to export the beach ball graphic. But first, plan a destination for your Print Shop graphics. It's a good idea to create a special folder on your hard drive or designate a floppy disk for your graphics files so you can access the exported graphics easily. You might even want to create individual folders for the different file formats.

It's a good idea to do this right now, as a matter of fact, so you can actually export the graphics in this chapter into a workable location. Choose a hard drive location or a disc and create a folder called Print Shop Graphics with folders for TIFF, BMP, WMF, and EPS. Once you've done this, you'll be ready to move on with the following exercise.

When your storage location is ready, you're ready to export the beach ball graphic:

**1.** On the Export 'Beach Ball' as dialog box, navigate through the drives and folders to your Print Shop Graphics folder and the BMP folder you just created.

**2.** Click on OK and it's done.

You have now exported the Beach Ball graphic to a file called beach1.bmp in your BMP folder. You are returned to the Print Shop Deluxe Graphics Exporter dialog box, where you can export additional graphics, print libraries, or quit the program.

 Remember that when you export graphics, only copies of the original files are exported. The Print Shop files remain intact and the original libraries are not altered in any way.

# ◆ Exporting a Library

With PS Ensemble III, you have the option of exporting an entire library or a page of a library by using the Print Catalog option in the Print Shop Graphics Exporter dialog box. You can export a library or library page to a file outside of Print Shop or to a printer.

You can print catalogs in color or black and white, depending on the type of printer you have. Complete libraries exported to a file will always be exported in the color of the original Print Shop file—in other words, color graphics will be exported in color, and black and white graphics will be exported in black and white.

When you print exported graphic libraries, 12 to 21 graphics will fit on one page, depending on the graphics' sizes.

## Printing a Catalog

You can select which pages of a library you want to export. For example, you can export only pages 1 and 2 of a library to the printer. However, it is difficult to decide which pages of a library to print, since you don't know which page specific graphics will print on.

To print a page from the PS Squares catalog:

**1.** In the Print Shop Graphics Export dialog box, make sure PS Squares is the current library. If it's not, click on the Graphic Library pull down list and select PS Squares.

**2.** Click on Print Catalog; the Print dialog box, shown here, pops up.

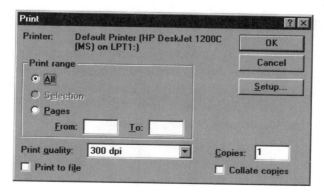

**3.** The default setting for Print Range is All, but for this example we only want to print one page. Click on Pages and type 1 in the From box and 1 in the To box.

**4.** Type the number of copies you'd like to print in the Copies box, in this case 1.

**5.** Click on OK to print page 1 of the PS Squares catalog.

As you've just discovered with this exercise, PS Squares prints 12 graphics per page. You can now calculate which pages to select in order to print a particular series of graphics from this library. For example, if you want to print graphics 20 through 26 from the PS Squares library, you'd print pages 2 and 3. (Graphics 20 through 24 will print on page 2 and graphics 25 and 26 will print on page 3.) Other libraries may print a different number of graphics per page, so it's a good idea to print a sample page as we just did before you do your calculations.

You can only use the Graphics Exporter to print libraries or pages of libraries. To print a single graphic, open a project window, add the graphic you want to print, resize it as needed, then print it from there.

If you are printing more than one copy of a library, you may want to collate the printed pages. To do this, check the Collate Copies box in the lower-right corner of the Print dialog box; the computer will print all of the pages of one copy before printing the next copy. If Collate Copies is not selected, the printer will print all of the copies of page one, followed by all the copies of page two, and so on, and you will have to sort them manually.

## Printing to File

The Print dialog box also offers a Print to file option, which lets you copy an entire library to a disk. This is particularly useful if you do not have a color printer and want to print a graphic library (called a *catalog* here) in color. You can copy the graphic library to a disk, take the disk to a computer that has a color printer, and print.

When you check the Print to file box, and click OK, the Print To File dialog box pops up. Select the specific location including drive, folder, and file name.

When you're printing to a file, you'll see a box that says the catalog is printing on your printer. Actually, it's printing to the disk, not the printer. Print Shop has no prompt that says that it's printing to a file, so it defaults to the one that says it's printing to a printer.

## Exiting the Graphics Exporter

When you're all done exporting, just click on the Quit button in the Print Shop Graphics Exporter dialog box to exit the program.

# ◆ Endnotes

You're ready to export graphics from Print Shop on your own. You can:

- ◆ Open the Graphics Exporter
- ◆ Locate and preview the graphics you want to export
- ◆ Choose a destination for your graphics
- ◆ Export graphics to a printer or to a file
- ◆ Print pages of graphics from a library—or the whole library itself

Now on to some finishing touches in Part Three.

# Part Three:

## Finishing Touches

# CHAPTER ELEVEN

## Broderbund
# TRIBUNE

Issue 1, Volumn 3

Novato, California

## SPELL CHECK, THESAURUS, ATTRIBUTES

| Now, you have it all with Ensemble III | No more speeling mistreaks | Peruse words with Thesaurus (check..arrest) | Punch up headlines by customizing | Use famous signatures as well |
|---|---|---|---|---|
| | | | | A. Lincoln |
| | | | | Carmen Sandiego |

# Working with Text and Headlines

## Your mission: to master all the ways to add text to a project

◆

Text can be added to a project in six different formats:

- ◆ Text blocks
- ◆ Signature blocks
- ◆ Headlines
- ◆ Word balloons
- ◆ Title blocks
- ◆ Quotes and verses

We have already touched on some of these in other chapters, but in this chapter we'll cover them thoroughly and introduce you to the text formats we have not yet explored, such as word balloons and quotes and verses. Examples of these text formats are shown in Figure 11.1. Quotes and verses is not included because it does not have its own text box, but rather is added to a text block or a word balloon using a special button.

**Figure 11.1:** Text can be added to a project in several different ways.

# ◆ Using Spell Check and Thesaurus

The Print Shop Ensemble III gives you invaluable assistance by helping you with the details both of spelling and of choosing just the right word to express yourself. Spell Check and Thesaurus are available on Text blocks, Word Balloons, and Headlines. They are not found on a Title or Signature block. They are simple to use and offer you the opportunity to check your spelling and to choose from a selection of synonyms for the word you have already chosen. Let's take a quick look at these two features.

# Checking Your Spelling

Checking your spelling is as easy as clicking the Spell Check button. When you do this, Print Shop will check all the words in that text box.

1. From the Select a Project dialog box, select Signs & Posters ➤ Start From Scratch and hold down the Ctrl key when you select Wide. You arrive at the Main Project Window with a blank piece of paper.

2. Click on the Add Object Tool ➤ Text to add a text placeholder to your project.

3. Open the text placeholder by double-clicking on it.

4. Type in something—anything will do as long as you misspell a word.

5. Click on Spell Check. The Spell Check dialog box pops up, as shown in Figure 11.2, displaying your misspelled word. Under that word will be alternate spellings offered by the program.

You can accept one of the spellings offered by clicking on Replace or stay with the way you spelled it by clicking on Ignore. If you want to add the word, as you have spelled it, to the dictionary, click on Add.

The Options button on this dialog box lets you fine-tune your spell checking by adjusting the way the spell checker looks at words. You can choose to ignore upper-case words or ignore words with numbers. You can also choose to look for replace-ment words only in the main dictionary. If you do

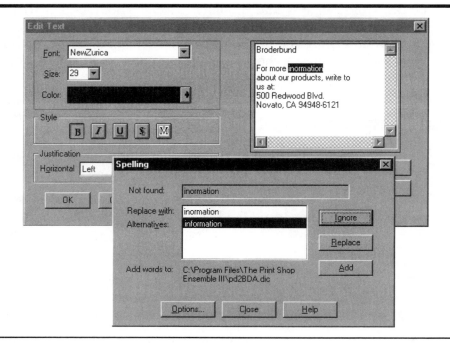

**Figure 11.2:** The Spell Check option offers you the opportunity to check the spelling in your text boxes before you add them to your project.

not select this option, the spell checker will look at all dictionaries, both the main one and your custom dictionary. You create your own custom dictionary by adding words in Spell Check. Every time you add a word it is placed in your custom dictionary. The location of your custom dictionary is indicated at the bottom of the Spelling dialog box after "Add words to." In Figure 11.2, you'll see ours are stored as pd2BDA.dic.

  **6.** Close the Spelling dialog box and return to the Edit Text dialog box. Stay here because we're going to take a look at the Thesaurus next.

## Choosing Your Words

The Thesaurus helps you express yourself by offering you alternate ways to say the same thing. What might otherwise seem like repetition becomes compelling, interesting, even intellectual—well, at least different. This is a great way to enhance your vocabulary and expand your ability to create exciting projects. Let's give it a try.

**1.** Highlight a word and click on the Thesaurus button.

The Thesaurus dialog box pops up, shown here in Figure 11.3. Your word appears in the box called Searched For.

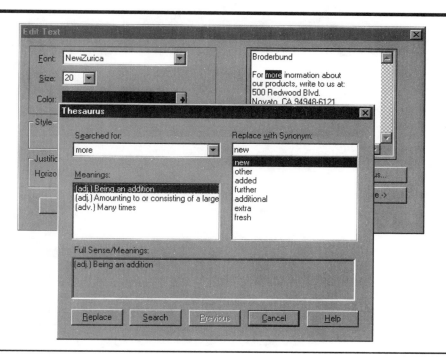

**Figure 11.3:** The Thesaurus offers you alternate words with meanings similar to the word you are currently using.

**2.** In the box called Meanings choose the one closest to your intent. Note that the meaning, in full, appears in the box called Full Sense/Meanings.

You may have more than one meaning listed, as we do. Print Shop offers choices whenever possible, to help you select a meaning closest to your needs.

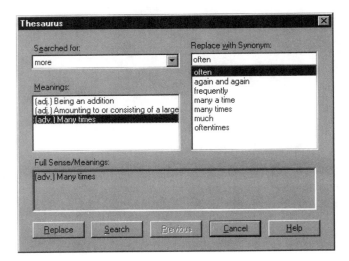

Once you've made a selection, Print Shop offers you a list of synonyms or like words. You can select one of these or stay with your own word. Click on Replace to put your new word selection into your text box.

Other options on this dialog box include:

◆ Search:  Highlight one of the synonyms and click on Search to expand your search for words that have meanings similar to this particular synonym.

◆ Previous:  Click on Previous to return to the last word you selected.

Try out Spell Check and Thesaurus as we work through the text boxes in this chapter.

## ◆ Editing Text Blocks

The Edit Text dialog box, shown in Figure 11.4, pops up when you double-click on a text block or when you select a text block and then select Object ➤ Edit. In this dialog box, you can add text (your own or quotes and verses or choose from the Thesaurus); spell check; select a font and its size, style, and color; justify text; and merge lists. Once you have made your selections, you can preview all the text with its selected attributes before you add it to the project.

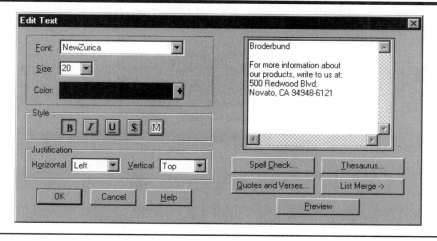

**Figure 11.4:** Double-clicking on a text block opens the Edit Text dialog box.

# Choosing Text Attributes

Changing the text characteristics of your projects is accomplished by changing font, size, color, style, and justification. It's the individual attributes that make up the total look of the presentation, or as it's sometimes referred to, its *style*. Making changes to the text after your project is underway is easy with PS Ensemble III. Let's start a project so you can see exactly what you can do with a text block.

1. If you have an open project, select File ➤ New ➤ Signs & Posters ➤ Customize A Ready Made ➤ Business ➤ Recycle, Save Our Planet, or from the Select a Project dialog box select Signs & Posters ➤ Customize A Ready Made ➤ Business ➤ Recycle, Save Our Planet.

There are two different text blocks on this sign. One begins *Bring your old...* and the second begins *Make Earth...* Let's work with the first text block.

2. Double-click on *Bring your old...* to open the Edit Text dialog box.

All of the text in the text box is highlighted. When text is highlighted like this, any change that you make to the text attributes will change all of the highlighted text. If you want to change attributes for only a part of the text, highlight just that text.

When text is highlighted, any numeric or alphabetic key you hit erases all the highlighted text. This is especially important to remember when you first enter the Edit Text dialog box, because all existing text is highlighted. If you erase text accidentally, click on Cancel to exit the Edit Text dialog box. This cancels anything you did and restores the text. You can then reopen the dialog box and begin editing again.

For now, let's leave all the text highlighted and change its attributes.

3. The current font on this project is Moderne. Click on the Preview button to see what it looks like. To see other available fonts, click on the arrow next to the Font box. As you highlight each font, it will be previewed (as long as you're still in the preview mode). Select Cornerstone as the new font.

You cannot type in the preview area when you are in preview mode. When you are in preview mode, the Preview button changes to an Edit button. Click on the Edit button to return to the text box where you can type any changes to the text.

**4.** Click on the arrow next to the Size box and choose a font size of 24 to replace 30. This size change is also previewed when you're in preview mode.

The text preview box is not the same size as the actual text block on the sign, so you may not be able to see the entire text if the font size is large or there is a lot of text. The preview area does, however, display the text as it will appear in the text block based on the current size, font, and style. You can, of course, change the size of the text block when you return to the main project window if you need to make room for more text.

**5.** Click on the arrow next to the Color box and select another color.

If you're working in color on-screen, you'll note that the current color is yellow. Since our page color is a dark blue, as we can see in the preview area, let's select red as our new text color. The color does not change the style of the letter, but it does have an impact on the overall look of the sign. You can see the color change against the page color in the preview area.

You can change the style of the text, making it bold or italic or adding a shadow or a mask. A mask places a white outline around the text. This is useful for making the text stand out when it's a dark color on a dark background. Underlining, another style option, adds emphasis to a word without having an impact on the basic letter design. Experiment with these styles to see how they affect the text.

**6.** When you've finished looking at style options, select I (for italics).

Here's another option. You can justify the text within the text block, choosing between aligning the text to the left margin of the block, to the right margin, or to the center horizontally. Or you can choose full to stretch the text so that it touches both the left and right margins. You can also justify the text vertically, to the top edge, to the bottom, or to the center.

**7.** Select Center for both the horizontal and the vertical justification. Note that both Spell Check and Thesaurus are available on this text box.

**8.** Click OK when you're happy with your text to return to the main project window, where we'll try making further attribute changes using the text toolbar.

 There are two other important options in the Edit Text dialog box: List Merge and Quotes and Verses. We'll cover list merge commands extensively in Chapter 12, "Creating and Merging Lists," and we'll talk about Quotes and Verses later in this chapter.

# Using the Text Toolbar

A great way to change text attributes in the main project window is to use the Text Toolbar, shown below. When the Text Toolbar is open, its default location is just below the Standard Toolbar, which appears just below the menu. Like the Standard Toolbar, you can move the Text Toolbar around on the page by dragging it. You can also hide it by choosing View ➤ Toolbars ➤ Hide Text Toolbar or, if it's hidden, choose Show Text Toolbar. The Text Toolbar is a great place to do the final tweaking of the text attributes since you can see your changes on the project itself. The one thing you cannot do from the Text Toolbar is type in new text or alter what you've already typed. You must click on the Text box and use the Edit Text dialog box to change text.

The text toolbar gives you access to all the text attributes and layout options you'd find on the Edit Text dialog box. Any changes you make using the text toolbar will be applied to the entire text in the selected text block. If you change the text color, for example, the entire text will be changed to the new color. If you want to change the color of just some of the text, you will have to go back to the Edit Text dialog box.

The text toolbar is available only when you select a text block or a word balloon. It cannot be used for headlines, title blocks, or signature blocks. To edit these, you'll need to go into their separate dialog boxes, covered later in this chapter.

Let's change our text just a bit using the text toolbar.

1. If it's not still selected from before, select the text block that begins *Bring your old...* by clicking on it once. Notice that all options on the text toolbar become dark in color, indicating that they are available.

2. Click on the arrow beside the font box on the text toolbar and change Cornerstone to Boulder. All the text in the block changes to the new font.

3. Click on each one of the eight alignment buttons on the text bar to see the effect each has on the text:

| Button | Aligns text |
| --- | --- |
| | To the left |
| | Centered horizontally |
| | To the right |
| | Justified horizontally |
| | To the top |
| | Centered vertically |
| | To the bottom |
| | Justified vertically |

4. Change the size of the type to 40 and see how it becomes too big to fit in the text box. If you wanted to keep it this size, you'd need to resize the text box so you could see all the text.

5. Click on the bold, italic, and underline buttons to see how your text changes.

6. Click on shadow to add a drop shadow, then click on mask to put a mask around the letters.

As you have now discovered, the text toolbar is great for making changes that you want to see against the entire project, so you can fine-tune your text selections.

Now let's take a look at what we can do with headlines.

# ◆ Working with Headlines

The Print Shop Ensemble III gives you powerful tools to make great headlines. You can access these tools in the Headline dialog box, which is reached by double-clicking on a headline placeholder or by selecting the headline, then selecting Object ➤ Edit.

Let's make some improvements to the headline in the ready-made sign titled Jazz Festival, shown here. Open the Jazz Festival sign.

1. Select File ➤ New (do not save changes) ➤ Signs & Posters ➤ Customize A Ready Made ➤ Community ➤ Event, Jazz Festival.

The Jazz Festival sign opens in the main project window. Take a look at this sign. You'll note that three graphics on this sign actually extend beyond the page. These include a square graphic called Fall Leaf that has been enlarged to fill most of the page; and a row graphic called grapes that has been duplicated and positioned so that its two copies stretch across the sign. Any part of these graphics that goes beyond the page edge, indicated by dotted lines, will not be printed as part of the project. This is a good example of how you can arrange and size graphics to use only parts of them in your project.

**2.** Double-click on the headline *Fall Jazz Festival* to open the Head-line dialog box, shown in Figure 11.5. You can also get to this dialog box by clicking once to select the headline, then selecting Object ➤ Edit. Here you can change the font, style, and color of the type, add various customized effects to the type, and select from a variety of headline designs.

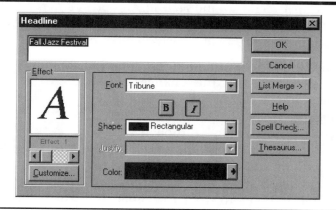

**Figure 11.5:** The Headline dialog box opens with all the existing text selected.

When it is first opened, the Headline dialog box defaults to highlighting all of the copy in the text box. As in the Edit Text dialog box, all the highlighted text will be affected by any changes you make. If you want to change only a part of the text, select just that text. Remember that when text is selected, it can be erased by hitting any numeric or alphabetic key.

You cannot change the size of the type in a headline. The type expands or contracts to fill the headline box. If you want smaller type, make the headline box smaller. If you want larger type, make the box larger.

# Changing Headline Text Attributes

Let's try a few changes to make the Jazz Festival headline more exciting.

**1.** With the headline selected, make the type bold by clicking on the B button. The large *A* in the Effect box will change to reflect your selection. If you want to see the effect on the actual headline, you need to click OK and return to the main project window. We'll do that in a moment.

**2.** Click on I to deselect italicize.

**3.** We think the headline would be more effective if it were on two lines. Place your cursor at the end of the word *Jazz,* delete the space between *Jazz* and *Festival,* and press Enter. The headline splits into two lines and the Justify box now says Left, meaning that both Jazz and Festival are left-aligned. (Left is the default.)

**4.** Click on OK to return to the main project window and see the changes you've made so far. Shown here is the headline both as it was when we opened the project and as it is now. Although we have not changed the font, the type looks different. In addition to making the text bold, we changed the headline to two lines instead of one; this caused the type to stretch in order to fit the headline box. It now looks thicker and bolder.

**5.** The left justification of the headline is making the second line of text seem off somehow, so let's change this. Again, double-click on the headline to return to the Headline dialog box. In the Justify box, note your choices: Left, Center, and Right, all shown here. Change the justification to Center, so that both lines are centered in the headline box.

Your headline should now be split into two lines, fully justified, and bold. Now that we have the text attributes chosen, let's take a look at headline shapes.

## Choosing a Headline Shape

The Shape option in the Headline dialog box offers you 21 different headline shapes. Let's take a look.

**1.** The headline in Jazz Festival is currently rectangular. Click on the Shape box to access the full list available. Each time you select a new shape, you'll have to click OK to return to the project window in order to see the new shape. All 21 possibilities are shown in Figure 11.6. As you can see, each of these shapes gives the project a totally different look.

**2.** When you're done experimenting with shapes, choose Round Top for the headline shape.

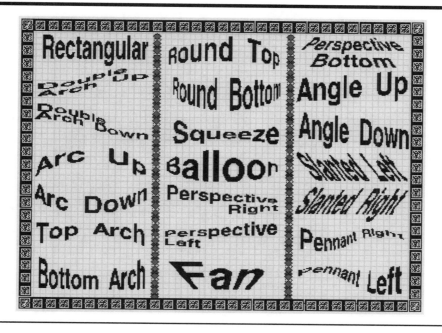

**Figure 11.6:** Choose your headline shape from these 21 different options.

3. Click on OK and take a look at the new headline shape in the project, shown here.

4. Double-click on the headline once again to access the Headline dialog box. Next we'll take a look at the text inside the headline.

# Customizing Headline Text

On the left side of the Headline dialog box is a capital letter *A* with a sliding bar and a Customize button under it. If you slide the bar, you can choose from 25 preset text effects, labeled Effect 1, Effect 2, and so on. The last effect says only *Custom Effect*. This is always the current effect you are using. It could be one you created, the default effect, or, in this case, the ready-made effect for the headline. As you slide to each effect, the *A* changes to show that effect. You can click on the Customize button at any time and change the text effect and color, designing your own effect in the Custom Effect dialog box, shown in Figure 11.7.

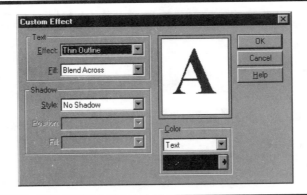

**Figure 11.7:** You can customize your text with outlines, shadows, and color blends using the Custom Effect dialog box.

Let's add an outline around all the text in the Jazz Festival headline.

**1.** Click on the Customize button to open the Custom Effect dialog box.

**2.** In the Text area of the Custom Effect dialog box, you can designate a text effect of plain, thin outline, thick outline, or highlighted. Look for an illustration of all of these in "Designing an Initial Cap" in Chapter 8. You can also select a text fill of solid, blend across, blend down, radiant, or double blend, as shown here. Select these options one by one to see what effect they have on the letter *A* in the preview window. When you're done experimenting, select a thick outline and a solid fill.

You can also add a shadow to your headline text, choosing its style, position, fill, and color. In the Style box you can choose to have no shadow, or a drop shadow, block shadow, or silhouette (these were also illustrated in Chapter 8). If you select a shadow, you can choose its position relative to the letter—upper-right, upper-left, lower-right, or lower-left—from the Position list. If you select a silhouette as your shadow style, you can blend two colors with blend across, blend down, radiant, and double blend options in the Fill box. Keep in mind that this is a silhouette option, not a text option—the silhouette is the area immediately behind the text, not the text itself.

**3.** Experiment with the shadow options to see what effect they have on the letter *A* in the preview window. When you're done, select No Shadow.

**4.** The Color area lets you select the item you want to color and then designate a color. You can choose the color for the text, and the text blend (if you select one of the fill options), outline (if you select thin or thick outline), shadow (if you select a shadow), and shadow blend (if you choose to blend two colors into the shadow). Again, experiment as you will, and when you're done choose green for the text and blue for the outline.

**5.** Click on OK to return to the Headline dialog box, then click OK again to apply the changes to the headline in the main project window. Take a look at the final creation, shown here.

As with all creative pursuits, whether the sign is actually improved by our headline changes is a matter of personal taste. Feel free to make whatever changes you think look best.

 Like the Edit Text dialog box, the Headline dialog box has a List Merge button. We'll cover the list merge options in Chapter 12, "Creating and Merging Lists."

# ◆ Working with Title Blocks

A title block is a combination of a headline and one to two lines of regular text. These blocks can add a great deal of interest to your design, drawing attention to a sign, award, or banner. Title blocks are often used in documents where you need more than one line but want one of the lines to be dominant.

## Choosing Type Styles for Title Blocks

There are only four available headline shapes in title blocks, compared to the 21 available for regular headlines. In title blocks, you can choose rectangular, arch up, squeeze, or top arch.

The second line in a title block is sized in relationship to the headline: small headline over large second line, medium over medium, or large over small. Headlines must be one line of up to 39 characters. Secondary lines can be one or two lines of up to 59 characters total (a return counts as a character).

The Title Block dialog box, shown in Figure 11.8, is divided into two parts, the Title Line (or headline) area and the Secondary Lines area. Both areas have font and text color options. Each area has type style options: bold or italic for the title line and bold, italic, underline, mask, and shadow for secondary lines.

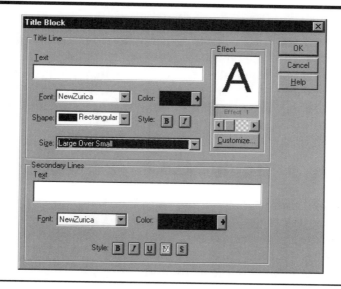

**Figure 11.8:** The Title Block dialog box is divided into two separate areas, one for the title line and one for the secondary lines.

Neither section of the Title Block dialog box offers specific text size options. As you remember, a headline will size to fit its box, and the secondary line is sized in relation to the headline.

## Customizing a Title

The Title Block dialog box also has a Customize button that opens the Custom Effect dialog box for the headline only. This dialog box has all the same options as the one for headlines and all the results look the same.

# ◆ Adding a Signature Block

If you want to have an official signature on projects such as a certificate or an official note, you can add a signature block. Signature blocks come in seven different sizes and configurations that include from one to four signatures. You can even combine blocks if necessary to make larger blocks of signatures.

Signature blocks are designed so that you enter text to appear under a signature line, with the area above the line left blank for a signature when you print it out. If you like, you can spice up a project by adding special Print Shop autographs of famous people such as George Washington. Only PS autographs will appear above the signature line. A line with no chosen PS autograph will remain blank.

## Selecting a Block Type

The seven sizes and configurations for signature blocks are available in the Signature Type dialog box, shown here. You can access this dialog box by clicking on the Object menu and selecting Add ➤ Signature Block or by clicking on the Add Object tool ➤ Signature Block.

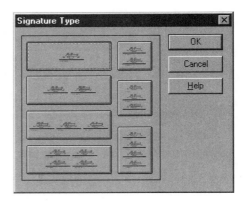

Let's select a style and create a signature block of our own.

**1.** Select File ➤ New ➤ No ➤ Signs & Posters ➤ Start From Scratch, and then hold down Ctrl while you click on Wide as your orientation. You arrive at a blank page in the main project window.

**2.** From the menu select Object ➤ Add ➤ Signature Block. The Signature Type dialog box opens.

**3.** Select the block with two signatures side by side and click on OK.

**4.** The selected signature lines are placed on the center of the page.

You can change to another signature block at any time if you decide you need more or fewer signatures: just double-click on the signature lines to open the Edit Signature Block dialog box (we'll see this next), then click on the Change button. The Signature Type dialog box will reopen and you can select another style. If you choose fewer signatures than you had in your first choice, the lines will be deleted from the bottom up as listed in the Edit Signature Block dialog box. This is important to remember if you've already entered text into any of the signature blocks.

Now let's look at text options for signature lines.

## Choosing Text Attributes for Signature Lines

The Edit Signature Block dialog box, shown in Figure 11.9, lets you designate what will appear in the signature block, as well as what it will look like. You can access it by double-clicking on the signature block or by selecting the signature block and choosing Object ➤ Edit. This dialog box has three sections, one part for PS autographs (which we'll explain below), another where you can type the text to appear under the signature lines, and a third for attributes of the text under the lines.

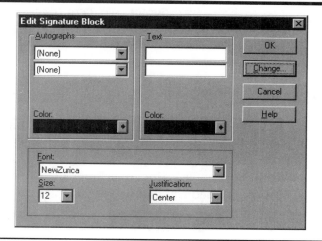

**Figure 11.9:** The Edit Signature Block dialog box lets you insert a famous autograph, add text below signature lines, and designate text attributes.

Note that Figure 11.9 shows two boxes in both the Autographs section and the Text section of the dialog box; this is because we selected a signature block with two signature lines. If we had selected one signature line, one box would appear in each section; three lines would produce three boxes in each section; and so on.

The Justification box gives you various options for justifying the text below the signature lines. These options change based on the configuration of your signature block. For stacked signatures, you can choose Left, Right, Center, or Full. For side-by-side signatures, your choices will be Left, Center, Right, Full, or Left/Right. (Left/Right left-aligns text under the left signature line and right-aligns text under the right signature line.)

## Adding Text to Signature Blocks

Signature blocks are designed for a line of text below the signature line where you can insert a name, title, or any other kind of text. To enter the text, simply place your cursor in one of the text boxes in the Text section of the Edit Signature Block dialog box and start typing. The signature text lines can accommodate up to 30 characters.

You cannot enter text above the signature line except through the autographs provided with the PS program. We'll cover these in the next section. If you don't use a PS autograph, the line is automatically left blank for a signature.

## Inserting Autographs

The PS Ensemble III program provides you with 38 autographs that you can add to lend authority to your documents. You can insert them into any signature block by selecting them from the drop down lists in the Autographs section of the Edit Signature Block dialog box. Print Shop Ensemble III has persuaded the following VIPs to allow you to use their autographs in your projects.

| A. Lincoln | F. Nightingale | R. Bonheur |
|---|---|---|
| B. Franklin | G. Washington | Rembrandt |
| Bear Paw | Geronimo | S. Anthony |
| C. Darwin | H.C. Anderson | Santa Claus |
| C. Dickens | Isaac Newton | Sitting Bull |
| Carmen Sandiego | J. Hancock | The Chief |
| Cat Paw | J. Muir | The President |
| Charlemagne | Joan of Arc | Thumbprint |
| D. Boone | L. Pasteur | Tooth Fairy |
| Dog Paw | L.V. Beethoven | W. Clark |
| Easter Bunny | Leonardo | W. Shakespeare |
| Elizabeth I | Mark Twain | W.A. Mozart |
| Emily Dickinson | Michelangelo | |

Let's change the signature block type, add some text, insert an autograph, and make some changes to the text attributes. You should still be in the main project window with two signature lines side by side on the page.

1. Double-click on the signature lines to open the Edit Signature Block dialog box.

2. Click on the Change button, select the signature block with four signatures in two rows of two, and click on OK.

3. Double-click on the signature lines to open the Edit Signature Block dialog box again.

4. In the Autographs section, click on the arrow next to the first text box and select A. Lincoln from the drop down list that appears. The name *A. Lincoln* now appears in the first box in both the Autographs section and the Text section of the dialog box.

5. Type your name into the second text box under Text, right under A. Lincoln's.

**6.** Select dark gray as the color of the autograph from the Color box under Autographs.

**7.** Leave the default color black as the color of the text. Note that the color of the signature lines will be the same color as the text that appears under them. In this case, both lines will be black.

**8.** In the Size box at the bottom, change the type size to 26. Leave the font as it is.

**9.** Click on OK to return to the main project window. The signature block now contains A. Lincoln's autograph in dark gray. The typed A. Lincoln and your name, as well as the sig-nature lines, are black, as shown here. The line above your name is blank, awaiting your signature.

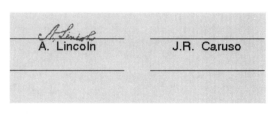

Looks good, but we still have two blank lines. We could go to the dialog box again and add more signatures, but let's delete those two extra signa-ture lines instead.

**10.** Double-click on the signature lines to access the Edit Signature Block dialog box.

**11.** Click on Change. The Signature Type box pops up. Select the block with two signatures, one on top of the other, and click OK. We're back to two signature lines but now they are stacked instead of being side by side.

**12.** Select the signature block and click on the Delete tool or hit the Delete key on your keyboard. The signature block disappears and you once again have a blank page.

Now let's take a look at text in a word balloon.

## ◆ Adding a Word Balloon

Word balloons are an interesting way to add text to your projects. There are 15 word balloon shapes available, as shown in the Word Balloon Type dialog box in Figure 11.10.

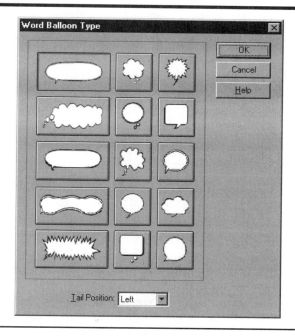

**Figure 11.10:** Word balloons come in many different shapes.

Let's add a word balloon to our blank page.

1. From the menu, select Object ➤ Add ➤ Word Balloon or click on the Add Object tool and select Word Balloon. The Word Balloon Type dialog box pops up.

2. Click on the balloon in the lower-right corner.

3. You can choose to have the tail of the word balloon pointing to the left, centered, or pointing to the right, as shown here, by clicking on your choice in the Tail Position drop down list at the bottom of the dialog box. Select Right and click on OK to return to the main project window.

 The tail position of a word balloon varies depending on its original design in the Word Balloon Type dialog box. For example, if the tail starts in the center position in this dialog box, the tail will shift only slightly left and right. If the tail points far left in the dialog box, it will point far right when you select Right as the tail position and will be centered when you select Center.

Once you've added a word balloon to your project, you'll want to add text to it.

**1.** Double-click on the word balloon or select it and click on Object ➤ Edit. The Edit Word Balloon Text dialog box, shown in Figure 11.11, opens. This dialog box works just like the Edit Text dialog box, with one exception: it has a Change Shape button. If you click on this button, you return to the Word Balloon Type dialog box, where you can change to an entirely different balloon.

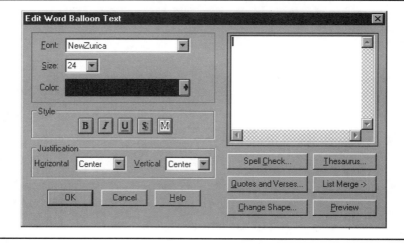

**Figure 11.11:** The Edit Word Balloon Text dialog box offers you the same options as the Edit Text box, with the addition of the Change Shape button.

**2.** Try adding some text to your word balloon. Type **I love PS Ensemble III. It's great stuff!** Note that word balloons, like text blocks, have no limit to the amount of text that can be entered. As long as it fits on the page, you can add text. Also like text blocks, if the text is bigger than the area of the word balloon, the text that doesn't fit will be hidden from sight.

3. When you're finished entering text, click on OK to return to the main project window.

4. Resize the balloon until you can see all the text.

5. Since a word balloon implies a speaker, insert an appropriate graphic. We've chosen Carmen 1 from the Carmen Squares library, as shown here.

 The Edit Word Balloon Text dialog box includes a List Merge button and a Quotes and Verses button, making both of these options available to insert into your word balloon. See Chapter 12 for information about merging lists, and see "Exploring Quotes and Verses" later in this chapter for information about those elements.

Keep this document open; we'll use it again to try out our next type of text block.

## ◆ Exploring Quotes and Verses

PS Ensemble III offers over 1,169 quotes and verses in 13 different libraries for customizing your projects. Quotes and Verses are available in text blocks (T placeholder only) and in word balloons. Some quotes and verses are divided into two separate locations, designated as (1) and (2). These divided quotes and verses are designed to be inserted on different pages of a project or in different areas of the project. For example, the first part is an opening line for the front of a greeting card. The second part completes the thought and is designed for the inside of a greeting card.

Let's try adding a quote to the word balloon we created above.

1. Click on the word balloon to open the Edit Word Balloon Text dialog box. Delete the text you have there now.

2. Click on the Quotes and Verses button.

The Quotes and Verses Browser, shown in Figure 11.12, pops up. This browser works like the Graphics Browser, the Backdrops Browser, and the Borders Browser; it shows the verse names on the left and the full text of the verses in the preview window.

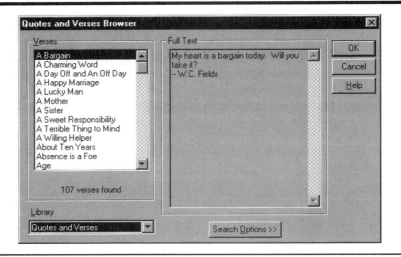

**Figure 11.12:** The Quotes and Verses Browser dialog box shows verse names on the left and the full text on the right.

The 13 different libraries divide the quotes and verses into special occasions and include:

◆ Birthday

◆ On Your Birthday—Jan-Mar

◆ On Your Birthday—Apr-Jun

◆ On Your Birthday—Jul-Sept

◆ On Your Birthday—Oct-Dec

◆ Graduation and Inspiration

- Happiness and Life
- Holidays
- Humor
- Love and Friendship
- Famous Poets
- Proverbs
- Quotes and Verses

Select All Libraries to see all libraries at once.

**3.** As with the other browsers, you can use the search options to conduct a search for the right verse. Click on the Search Options button, then on the Category Keywords button to bring up the Category Keywords dialog box, shown here. The selections are more limited than on the 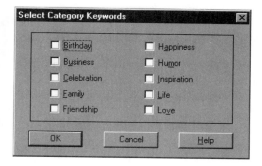 other browser dialog boxes, since you are dealing here with a concept rather than a tangible graphic. In other words, you want a special message rather than a burger-eating dinosaur.

**4.** In the Category Keywords box, check the Humor box and click on OK.

**5.** Click on the Search button to search the library for humor-related quotes and verses. This search produces 273 choices.

**6.** Click on Forget a Face, then click on OK to return to the Edit Word Balloon Text dialog box. Here you can make changes to the type, including style and color. You can also edit the text of the quote or verse.

**7.** Highlight the quote and change the font to Scribble.

**8.** Delete *Groucho Marx*.

**9.** When you're satisfied with your work, click on OK; the text is added to your project. If necessary, resize the word balloon so that all the text fits properly, as shown here. (We've chosen another Carmen Sandiego graphic to accompany the balloon.)

As already mentioned, some quotes and verses are divided into two parts that go together, designated (1) and (2). For example, Boat for Christmas (1) and Boat for Christmas (2) go together, as shown here.

And that's the end of word balloons and this chapter. Select File ➤ New and do not save your changes.

## ◆ Endnotes

That's everything you need to know about text and headlines. You know how to:

- ◆ Spell check and look for new words similar to your own
- ◆ Edit a text block, choose text attributes, and preview the text
- ◆ Use the text bar to change existing text in the main project window
- ◆ Turn text into outlined, shadowed, or silhouetted specialty text
- ◆ Add a signature block and get Mozart to sign it for you
- ◆ Animate a project with a word balloon and add a quote that you wish you'd said yourself

It's a lot to absorb, but as you work on projects, you will become accustomed to all these options and eventually they'll seem simple. You're a text whiz and now you're ready to tackle Chapter 12, "Creating and Merging Lists."

# Creating and Merging Lists

## Your mission: to create and merge name lists

◆

You can use Print Shop's Name List feature to create and merge all kinds of lists. PS Ensemble III name lists come in two different types: address lists and custom lists.

Address lists, as the name implies, are specifically for names and addresses. This is where you'd create a mailing list of your best customers or a Christmas card list of friends and family. Custom lists can be virtually anything, from a list of your favorite CDs to a list of movies you'd like to rent.

Merging information from lists into projects is a great way to add a personal touch. You can merge lists into any project through a word balloon, a text block, or a headline block, all shown here.

Let's take a look at how lists are created.

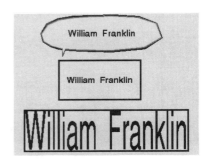

# ◆ Creating Lists

Creating a list is as simple as typing in the information. Once the information has been created and stored, you can access it at any time and bring it into a project.

Address lists are created in the Address List dialog box, and custom lists are created in the Custom List dialog box. You can access these dialog boxes in either of the following ways:

◆ From the Select a Project dialog box, choose Extras ➤ Name Lists ➤ Address List or Custom List.

◆ From the main project window, choose Extras ➤ Edit Address List or Edit Custom List.

The Address List or Custom List dialog box will open. To start a new list, click on File ➤ New. If you want to make changes or additions to an existing list, click on File ➤ Open and select the file you want to work on.

## Making an Address List

To create an address list, just fill in the blanks in the Address List dialog box, shown in Figure 12.1. The Filename section at the top of the dialog box says Untitled.DAT, meaning that this is a brand new address list that has not yet been given a name.

The Name List Entry box near the top of the dialog box shows the first entry in the current address list. Since we haven't created any entries yet, this box is empty in Figure 12.1. Once you have created a list, you can click on the arrow to the right of the box to access an alphabetical drop down list of entries in that particular address list.

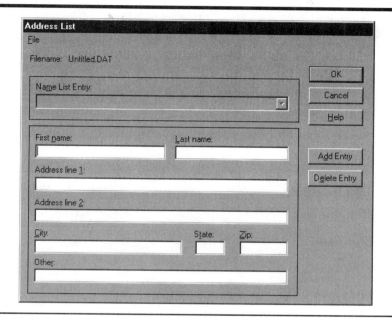

**Figure 12.1:** The Address List dialog box is designed to store a complete address.

The Address List dialog box provides eight information boxes for each entry. Type the relevant information into each text box. The maximum number of characters per text box is as follows:

| Text box | Number of characters |
| --- | --- |
| Last Name | 20 |
| First Name | 20 |
| Address line 1 | 60 |
| Address line 2 | 60 |
| City | 20 |
| State | 2 |
| Zip | 10 |
| Other | 60 |

Use Tab to move down the dialog box from one text box to the next. Use Shift+Tab to move up through the boxes. You can also use your mouse to move from box to box.

You do not have to fill in all the boxes for every entry, but you must fill in the Last Name box because Address Lists are stored alphabetically by the last name. If you fail to put a name in the Last Name line and try to move on, the pop-up prompt, shown here, reminds you that you must enter a name or lose the entry.

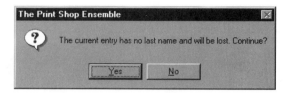

 If you are creating an address list of company names rather than individuals, type the name of the company in the Last Name line and nothing in the First Name line, or, if you need more space, split the company name to fill both the First Name and Last Name lines. If you split the name, remember that the list will be arranged alphabetically based on what is entered in the Last Name line.

Let's create an address list with several entries.

1. From the Select a Project dialog box, select Extras ➤ Name Lists ➤ Address List; the Address List dialog box appears.

2. Type the name and address of a friend in the appropriate boxes. Put your friend's nickname in the Other box.

3. When you've completed the address record, click on Add Entry. The entry disappears and a new, blank Address List dialog box appears.

4. The arrow next to the Name List Entry box is now dark, indicating that there is something hidden from view. Click on this arrow and your friend's name appears, last name first.

The title of an address list entry is always whatever you entered in the last name box followed by what you entered in the first name box. Click on the name and the complete entry for your friend is again on-screen. You can edit or delete it altogether.

**5.** Click on Add Entry again. Your friend's name is again stored and the blank entry form appears again.

**6.** Type a new entry for another friend. When you're finished, click on Add Entry again.

**7.** Repeat the process for a third friend.

Every address list or custom list file can include up to 200 entries, and you can create an unlimited number of address or custom lists.

**8.** Click on OK, and a prompt asks if you want to save your work.

**9.** Click Yes and the Save a List File dialog box appears, as shown here. There are no Files listed because this is our first Address List file.

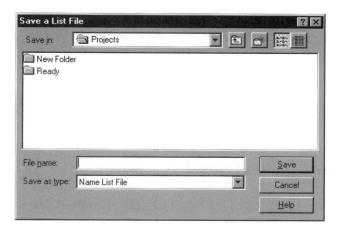

**10.** Type *red* in the Filename box (the extension DAT will be added automatically) and click on Save. You return to the Select a Project dialog box.

A list is saved to the Projects folder unless you designate a different folder when you save it. We would suggest that you create a Lists folder and save all your lists to it. This will make it easier to find them.

Now that you've saved the list, you can open it at any time in either of the following ways:

◆ From the Select a Project dialog box, choose Extras ➤ Name Lists ➤ Address List. The last list you worked on may open automatically when you reach the Address List dialog box. In the Address List dialog box, select File ➤ Open and choose red.dat from the list that appears.

◆ From the main project window, select Extras ➤ Edit Address List. In the Address List dialog box, select File ➤ Open and choose red.dat from the list that appears.

**11.** Create another address list of at least two entries. Follow the same steps you followed to create the red file. Call this second list *green*. We'll use both of these lists when we merge a list into a document later in this chapter.

If you want to create an address or custom list that includes many entries from another list, open the existing list file, as noted above, and use the Save As command from the File menu to save it under a different name. Then open the second file and customize it to your liking.

When you've finished creating your green address list, you should be at the Select a Project dialog box, ready to make a custom list.

## Making a Custom List

As with address lists, all you have to do to create an entry in a custom list is fill in the blanks in the Custom List dialog box, shown in Figure 12.2. The information boxes in this dialog box are labeled simply Line 1, 2, 3, 4, and 5. The maximum number of characters per line is 60.

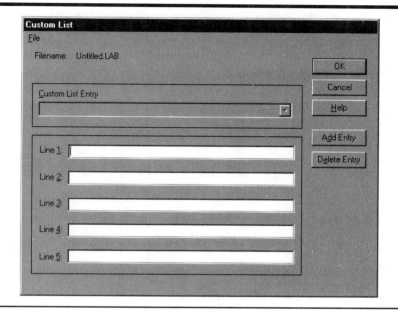

**Figure 12.2:** The Custom List dialog box offers five lines in which to enter what-ever information you wish.

Let's start a custom list of our favorite movies. We can use this list to print labels, among other things.

1. From the Select a Project dialog box, select Extras ➤ Name Lists ➤ Custom List. The Custom List dialog box pops up. (You could also reach this dialog box from the main project window by clicking on the Extras menu and selecting Edit Custom List.)

2. In the Line 1 box, type **Casablanca**. You must always have an entry in Line 1. You do not need to have an entry in any other box to save.

3. Fill in the rest of the boxes as follows:

    Line 2      **102 minutes, black and white**

    Line 3      **Humphrey Bogart, Ingrid Bergman**

    Line 4      **Sydney Greenstreet, Peter Lorre**

    Line 5      **Rick's Café Americain, "As Time Goes By"**

**4.** Click on Add Entry. As before, the entry disappears and the arrow next to the Custom List Entry box turns dark, indicating that there is an entry hidden from view.

**5.** Click on the arrow and a drop down list shows a Casablanca entry. The title of a custom list entry is always whatever you entered in the Line 1 box.

**6.** Add a second Custom List entry as follows:

| | |
|---|---|
| Line 1 | **Dr. No** |
| Line 2 | **112 minutes, color** |
| Line 3 | **Sean Connery, Ursula Andress** |
| Line 4 | **Joseph Wiseman, Jack Lord** |
| Line 5 | **007, Miss Moneypenny, Honey, M, Puss Feller** |

**7.** Click on Add Entry.

**8.** Add a third Custom List entry:

| | |
|---|---|
| Line 1 | **Sleepless in Seattle** |
| Line 2 | **105 minutes, color** |
| Line 3 | **Tom Hanks, Meg Ryan** |
| Line 4 | **Rosie O'Donnell, Rob Reiner** |
| Line 5 | **"Make Someone Happy," "A Kiss to Build a Dream On"** |

**9.** Click on Add Entry to add the entry.

**10.** Before storing this list of movies under a file name, click on Custom List Entry. You'll see all the movies listed in alphabetical order. Select one and its information appears.

**11.** Click on OK, and a prompt asks if you want to save your changes. Click on OK, and the Save a List File dialog box appears. Type **movies** and click Save. The program will automatically add the extension *LAB*. Once you've saved the file, you will be back at the Name List Type dialog box again.

You have created a custom list with three entries. You can open it at any time in either of the following ways:

◆ From the main project window, select Extras ➤ Edit Custom List. In the Custom List dialog box, select File ➤ Open ➤ movies.lab.

◆ From the Select a Project dialog box, select Extras ➤ Name Lists ➤ Custom List. In the Custom List dialog box, select File ➤ Open ➤ movies.lab.

# ◆ Modifying Lists

Name lists are easy to modify. All you need to do is open a list, select the entry you want to modify, and type the changes.

Let's open the *green* address list we created earlier in the chapter.

**1.** From the Select a Project dialog box, select Extras ➤ Name Lists ➤ Address List.

You may discover that the Address List dialog box has an entry in it. If it does, look at the Filename area at the top of the dialog box. You'll probably discover that the entry you see is the first alphabetical entry in the last address file you created.

**2.** Click on the File menu and select Open. The Open a List File dialog box pops up.

**3.** Select green.dat and click on Open. The arrow next to the Name List Entry box becomes dark, and the first name on your list is displayed.

**4.** Click on the arrow and select one of your friends' names from the drop down list of entries. This entry opens. Add another nickname to the Other text box and click on Add Entry.

If you want to delete an entry, select it from the Name List Entry box and click on the Delete Entry button. A prompt appears asking you, "Do you really want to delete this record?" This gives you the opportunity to change your mind, sometimes a good option to have.

# ◆ Merging Lists

You create Print Shop name lists so that you can merge them into your projects using the Merge List command; you can also address envelopes, make labels, or personalize a project message. You can use the Merge List command with a text block, a word balloon, or a headline block.

You can merge only one entry into a project at a time. In other words, you cannot merge Line 1 from the Casablanca entry and Line 1 from the Dr. No entry into the same project. If you try to do this by putting in two Line 1 merge commands, Print Shop will just repeat the entry selected first. In this case, the merge would read *Casablanca, Casablanca*, not *Casablanca, Dr. No*.

## Merging a List into a Project

To merge a list into a project, you need to open a list file so you can see a preview of how the merged text will look in the project.

**1.** From the Select a Project dialog box, select Stationery ➤ Start From Scratch ➤ Envelopes ➤ Quarter Page Card Size ➤ Bay Cruise Backdrop.

Before you select a layout, take a look at your options. Note that some of the choices are preceded by USPS. This stands for United States Postal Service, indicating that the layout meets post office specifications. USPS layouts are only available in postcard and envelope projects.

**2.** Select USPS Bay Cruise 1 Layout.

Instead of going immediately to the main project window, a Return Address dialog box pops up, shown here in Figure 12.3, asking you to type in your return address. The return address you enter will appear in return address boxes automatically. You will not see this prompt again when you work on a postcard or envelope project. If you want to change your return address at some point in the future, you can edit your return address in the Main Project Window. We'll take a look at that in a minute. For now, let's type in an address.

**3.** Type your return address in the appropriate text boxes.

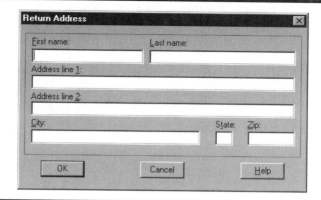

**Figure 12.3:** The address you type into this Return Address dialog box will be placed automatically into all USPS envelope and postcard projects.

**4.** Click on OK and you return to the Select a Layout dialog box with the return address now appearing in the box in the upper-left corner, as shown here.

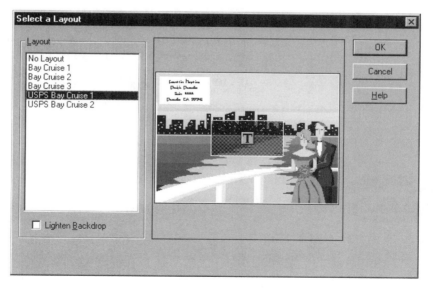

**5.** Click OK to go to the main project window with the return address already appearing on your envelope project.

To change the return address:

1. Click on the Extras menu and select Edit Return Address. The Return Address dialog box pops up, showing the return address currently entered.

2. Edit the entry as you wish.

3. Click OK; you return to the main project window. Your new return address is now inside the white box.

This will remain your return address until you change it. Print Shop can store only one return address at a time.

## Choosing a List to Merge

Let's select a list to merge into this project.

1. Click on the Extras menu again and select Edit Address List from the options offered. The Address List dialog box pops up.

2. Click on the File menu and select Open. The Open a List File dialog box pops up, listing all the address list files available.

3. Select red.dat and click Open. The red address list opens and the first alphabetical entry appears in the Address List dialog box.

4. Click on OK to return to the main project window.

5. Click on the Extras menu once again, then click on Select List Type. You'll see a check mark next to Address List, indicating that it has been selected.

 If you prefer, you can wait until after you have selected your merge fields (see the next section) to select the file to merge into.

## Selecting Merge Fields

Now we're ready to merge the *red* file into the project.

1. Double-click on the text placeholder. As usual, the Edit Text box appears.

**2.** Click on the List Merge button in the lower-right corner. A list of options that correspond to the information boxes in the Address List dialog box pops up, as shown here. If you select an option, the corresponding merge field will appear in the text preview area of the Edit Text dialog box.

**First Name**
**Last Name**
**Line 1 - Full Name**
**Line 2 - Address 1**
**Line 3 - Address 2**
**Line 4 - City, State, Zip**
**Line 5 - Other**
**All Lines**

**3.** Choose the fields you want to include on the envelope: Full Name, Address 1, Address 2 (if you entered additional information in this box), City, State, and Zip. As you select each field, it is recorded as a separate line in the edit box.

**4.** Combine <line 2> and <line 3> (Address 1 and Address 2), as shown here, by typing a comma after <line 2> and then pressing the Delete key to delete the return.

<line 1>
<line 2><line 3>
<line 4>

 You can choose a font and its size, style, and color for a merge field in the Edit Text dialog box just as you would for any other text.

**5.** To see what will actually print on the envelope, click on the Preview button. The merge fields will be replaced by the name and address from the first entry in the selected address list, as shown here.

 Do not be concerned if you do not want the first person on the list to get this envelope. You will have the opportunity to select exactly who on this address list gets the mailing when you actually print the project.

**6.** Once all your merge commands are set in the edit box, click OK to return to the main project window. The envelope is now addressed to the first person on the address list and has your return address on it, as shown in Figure 12.4.

Now we just have to print the project.

**Figure 12.4:** The envelope, complete with addressee and return address.

# ◆ Printing a List

Print Shop knows that you have performed a list merge in this project because you have inserted merge fields. When you print the project, it will use entries from the active list unless you tell it differently. The Print command allows you to designate which entries from the active list you want to merge. You can even change the active list.

Let's give it a try. The envelope should still be open in the main project window.

**1.** Click on the File menu and select Print.

The Print dialog box, shown here, pops up. (Actually there are more options than shown here, but you don't need to worry about them for now. See "Printing Envelopes" in Chapter 14 for a complete explanation of envelope printing options.) Below the List Entries button on the right side of the dialog box is the name of the list we selected earlier, red.dat.

The Number of Copies box defaults to 3 because this is the number of entries in the red.dat file. The 3 is light gray, meaning that you cannot change it, at least not in this box.

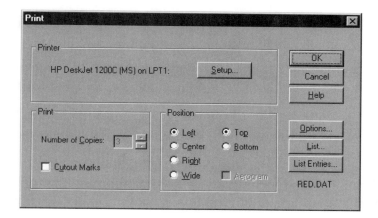

If you want to print a copy of the project for every name in red.dat, you can just click on OK. If you want to select names from the list or change to another list, click on the List button. Let's take a look at how we could change to another list.

**2.** Click on the List button. The Open dialog box pops up. Navigate to the Projects folder or a special List folder you created and find and highlight another list file (with the extension DAT). Look for the green.dat file you created.

If we wanted to change our list, we could, for example, highlight the green.dat file and click Open. We would return to the Print dialog box with our new list opened. For now, cancel and return to the Print dialog box with the red file still open.

**3.** Now click on List Entries to see the list of names in your red file.

**4.** The Select List Entries dialog box, shown in Figure 12.5, pops up, listing all the entries in the *red* file. You can select the entries you want to include in this printing by clicking on them. If you want to deselect an entry, click on it again. If you decide to print all the entries after all, you can click on the All List Entries button at the bottom of the dialog box. For this example, select only one of the entries.

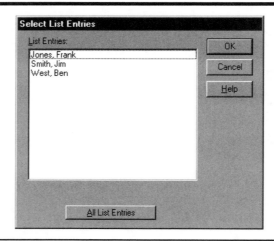

**Figure 12.5:** The Select List Entries dialog box shows all the entries in a file.

**5.** Click on OK. In the Open a List File dialog box, click on OK again. The Print dialog box returns and now the Number of Copies says 1 because you have elected to print a copy of the project to only one name.

**6.** Click on OK to print the envelope.

It's that easy: create a list, open the project you want to merge it into, add merge fields to a text block, headline block, or word balloon, and select which entries you want printed.

 See "Printing a Name List" in Chapter 14 for more information on dealing with problems you might encounter when you print using a list merge.

## ◆ Importing Lists

PS Ensemble III lets you open lists created in other programs and merge them into Print Shop projects, provided these lists meet certain requirements. They must be saved as ASCII files, the fields within each entry must be separated by a tab, and every entry must be separated by a hard carriage return.

In addition, the entries in the files must meet all the specifications listed above relating to the number of characters per line, the number of lines included, and the order of the lines.

You can open outside lists that meet these requirements from the Open a List File dialog box, then merge and print them as you would a Print Shop list.

# ◆ Exporting Lists

You can export Print Shop name lists for use by outside programs that use the same type of file format. PS lists are tab-delimited ASCII files, with a tab character separating every field and a hard carriage return separating every entry.

Let's try exporting a file. We're going to bring the file into Word for Windows but you could also do it in another program. The list file is fine the way it is. You do not need to change it or resave it at all.

1. Open Word.

2. Select File ➤ New and from the General tab, choose Blank Document, and click on OK to open a blank document.

3. Click on Insert ➤ File.

4. Navigate to The Print Shop Ensemble III Projects file and select red.dat.

5. Click on OK and the entire list is imported into the Word document.

If you find searching for the file in this way too time consuming, save the list to a different directory, for example, word\ps\red.dat. This way when you insert the list into the word file, you can get it from the Word directory.

## ◆ Endnotes

That's everything you need to know about name lists. Now you know:

◆ How to create an address list or a custom list

◆ How to open, start, and save a list

◆ How to modify or delete an entry in a list

◆ How to merge a list into a project and how to select and choose which entries from the list get printed on the project

◆ What a USPS format is and why you need it

Most important, you know how easy it is to create and merge lists. Now on to Chapter 13, "Using The Idea Guide."

# Using the Idea Guide

## Your mission: to discover new ways to create great print shop projects

◆

The Idea Guide included as part of The Print Shop Ensemble III program is a vast resource of information for getting more out of your projects, taking them one step further. The Idea Guide is a unique quick-time CD demonstration that will put you 'one step up' on creating your own unique and original projects with Print Shop. You'll find these ideas inspiring and thought-provoking, motivating you to seek out more creative ways to push the program to its limits and beyond. In this chapter, we'll go through the projects featured in the Idea Guide and we'll offer a few ideas of our own.

The Idea Guide is not loaded into your computer on setup. You'll need the Print Shop program CD to open it. Insert the CD, and open The Idea Guide by selecting Start ➤ Programs ➤ The Print Shop ➤ Ensemble Idea Guide. Your computer will automatically look for the Idea Guide on your CD-ROM drive.

The program begins with an opening screen, seen here in Figure 13.1.

**Figure 13.1:** This is the beginning of some great ideas on how to make exciting and innovative projects using The Print Shop Ensemble III.

Start with any one of three project ideas including: Party Ideas, Gift Ideas, or Holiday Ideas.

# ◆ Party Ideas

Using Party Ideas in the Idea Guide, you'll discover how to create and carry-through a theme for your next party by using coordinating graphics for the invitations, for table runners, for place cards, and even for game posters. Also, we'll suggest a few more projects you might create for the party and hopefully inspire you to think of a few yourself.

## Start with the Invitation

First, create a pop-up party invitation with some ingenuity, a pair of scissors, and a little tape. Find a demonstration of how to make this project in the Idea Guide ➤ Party Ideas ➤ Invitation.

You can create the 3-D card, shown in Figure 13.2, by starting with a ready-made half-page greeting card project. From the Select a Project screen, select Greeting Cards ➤ Customize a Ready Made ➤ Invitation ➤ Child Party Invite, Idea Guide. Or from the Open dialog box, select the file Prtyinvt.grm. Customize this ready-made greeting card to make the birthday bear inside pop out. You'll find help in making the pop-up effect in the How To section of the Idea Guide, as noted below.

You can also start from scratch using the step-by-step instructions in the How To section of the Idea Guide to create this project or another similar one with the graphics and text of your own choice.

To reach the How To section, select Idea Guide (make sure The Print Shop CD-ROM is inserted) ➤ Party Ideas ➤ Invitation. The demonstration will begin. Here you'll visually be given instructions on creating the card. When the demonstration is completed, select How To to go to the Idea Guide Help screens. Here you'll be given detailed written instructions that you can print out.

**Figure 13.2:** Create a party invitation with a pop-up effect with some ingenuity, a pair of scissors, and a little tape.

At the main Idea Guide help screen, select Party Ideas ➤ Invitation. Then select Print to print out the detailed instructions.

## Make a Table Runner

You can take the festivities right to the tabletop by using a banner to create a table runner, like the one shown here in Figure 13.3. Find a demonstration of how to create this project in Idea Guide ➤ Party Ideas ➤ Table Runner.

Start from scratch using the step-by-step instructions in the How To section of the Idea Guide to create this project or another similar one with the graphics and text of your choice.

To reach the How To section, select Idea Guide ➤ Party Ideas ➤ Table Runner. When the demonstration is completed, select How To ➤ Party Ideas ➤ Table Runner to get detailed instructions. Select Print to print out these instructions.

**Figure 13.3:** It's simple to make a table runner that'll take the festivities right to the tabletop.

## Create a Place Card

Use a business card project to create place cards for your party guests that'll get everyone in the party mood and give them all a little personal attention. Find a demonstration of how to make this project in Idea Guide ➤ Party Ideas ➤ Place Card.

The place card, shown here in Figure 13.4, is already created for you as a ready-made business card. From the Select a Project screen, select Stationery ➤ Customize a Ready Made ➤ Business Card ➤ Child Placecard. Or from the Open dialog box, select the file prtyname.bcr. Using List and/or List Entries at the Print command, merge the first names from your invitation list right into this project. You can find instructions on how to merge your names in the How To section of the Idea Guide.

Or start from scratch using the step-by-step instructions in the How To section of the Idea Guide to create this project or another similar one with the graphics and text of your choice.

To reach the How To section, select Idea Guide ➤ Party Ideas ➤ Place Card. When the demonstration is completed, select How To ➤ Party Ideas ➤ Place Card to get detailed instructions. Select Print to print out these instructions.

**Figure 13.4:** Use a business card project to create place cards for everyone at your party.

## Play a Game

Start with a sign project to create a variation on the game pin the tail on the donkey. The Idea Guide starts with a cat graphic and uses an eraser to create a pin the tail on the cat game. There are many graphics that lend themselves to this type of creative game so you might want to choose something other than a cat. Find a demonstration of how to make this project in Idea Guide ➤ Party Ideas ➤ Game Poster. You can choose to print this poster 200% or even 400% of original size, taping the pages together to make a giant poster.

This game poster has already been created for you as a ready-made poster. From the Select a Project screen, select Signs & Posters ➤ Customize a Ready Made ➤ Celebrations ➤ Child Game Poster 1 (the cat) and Child Game Poster 2 (the tails), both shown here in Figure 13.5. Or from the Open dialog box, select the files prtypost.srm and prtypast.srm. Print out the poster, put it on the wall, cut out the tails and pin the tail on the cat. It's that easy.

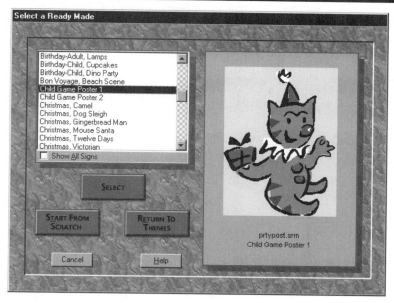

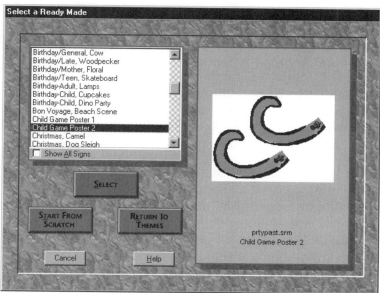

**Figure 13.5:** The Idea Guide starts with a cat graphic and uses an eraser to create a pin the tail on the cat game.

You can also start from scratch using the step-by-step instructions in the How To section of the Idea Guide to create this project or another similar one with the graphic of your choice.

To reach the How To section, select Idea Guide ➤ Party Ideas ➤ Game Poster. When the demonstration is completed, select How To ➤ Party Ideas ➤ Game Poster to get detailed instructions. Select Print to print out these instructions.

# More Party Ideas

Use your imagination to come up with more ways to use Print Shop to make your party special. We'd like to suggest a few to get you started thinking.

## Making a Party Mask

Create a mask, like the one shown here, that everyone can wear at the party. Start with a blank page in Print Shop and add a square graphic that follows the theme of your party. We've used B'day Clown. Now resize the graphic to make the face of your graphic fill the screen. Print your mask and cut it out. Finally, you can cut a rubber band and attach it to both sides of the mask (you can use hair pins) to hold it on the children's heads.

The tricky part of creating this project is resizing and adjusting the graphic to make the face large enough to fill the page. You'll have to resize, make it large, then move the face onto the page and resize again. You'll need to do this several times to finally center the face on the page. Also, if you'd like to make your mask bigger than the size of a regular sheet of paper, print it at 200% or even 400% of its original size. You can then use a little tape to join the pages together before you cut out the face.

## Making Personalized Bracelets

Create party bracelets fashioned from links created using Print Shop. Start from scratch with a Label project. Select a label size, preferably a thin one that will be conducive to creating links. Your bracelet links will be created by folding the label in half, so you'll need to design your graphics or text with the idea that they will wrap around the link or be on one side, as shown here.

Once you've created one label, create different links with other graphics or text by starting from scratch again and creating a second label, then maybe a third and fourth until you have a variety of links. Print on sticky label paper, remove the links, and fold them in half lengthwise from the center out. When you reach the edges, interlink the two ends so one fits inside the other. The sticky underside of the label will create a strong link for your bracelet.

Save the last link for the day of the party, using it to put the bracelet around your partygoer's wrist. Add a name to one or all of your labels and you've created a very special party favor.

## ◆ Gift ideas

Using Gift Ideas in the Idea Guide, you'll discover how to create special gift surprises that are uniquely your own. Create a professional-

looking label for your own homemade goodies, make a great gift certificate, personalize a money envelope, or share your secret recipe. Also, we'll suggest a few more projects you might create for gift giving and hopefully inspire you to think of a few yourself.

# Making a Gift Label

Start with a label project to create a special label for your own homemade specialty. The Idea Guide creates a label for the Tucker family's famous barbecue sauce using a label that prints six to a page. There are 14 different labels in Print Shop, so the size of your label is purely personal. Find a demonstration of how to make the Tucker family label in Idea Guide ➤ Gift Ideas ➤ Gift Label.

This gift label has already been created for you as a ready-made label. From the Select a Project screen, select Labels ➤ Customize a Ready Made ➤ Gift Label, shown here in Figure 13.6. Or from the Open dialog box, select the file gftlabel.lbr.

You can also start from scratch using the step-by-step instructions in the How To section of the Idea Guide to create this project or another similar one with the graphic of your choice.

To reach the How To section, select Idea Guide ➤ Gift Ideas ➤ Gift Label. When the demonstration is completed, select How To ➤ Gift Ideas ➤ Gift Label to get detailed instructions. Select Print to print out these instructions.

# Giving a Gift Certificate

Turn a simple piece of paper into a special gift certificate of your own design, to create a special gift only you can give. Tell someone how great they are or give them 'a night on the town' to be redeemed whenever they choose. Find a demonstration of how to make a special gift for Dad in Idea Guide ➤ Gift Ideas ➤ Gift Certificate.

This gift certificate has already been created for you as a ready-made certificate. From the Select a Project screen, select Certificates ➤ Customize a

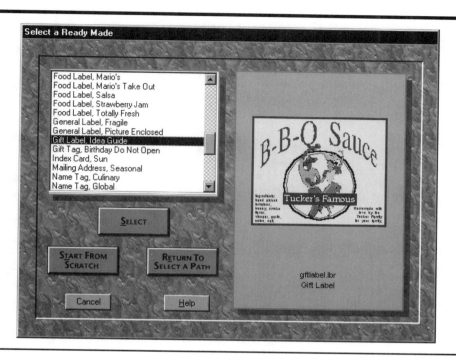

**Figure 13.6:** Start with a label project to create a special label for your home-made specialty.

Ready Made ➤ Achievement ➤ Gift Certificate, shown here in Figure 13.7. Or from the Open dialog box, select the file gftcert.prm. If you have a laser printer, think about adding a little glitz to your gift by adding foil to the certificate. Also, consider a watermarked text background to make it look even more valuable.

You can also start from scratch using the step-by-step instructions in the How To section of the Idea Guide to create this project or another one with the graphic of your choice.

To reach the How To section, select Idea Guide ➤ Gift Ideas ➤ Gift Certificate. When the demonstration is completed, select How To ➤ Gift Ideas ➤ Gift Certificate to get detailed instructions. Select Print to print out these instructions.

**Figure 13.7:** Turn a simple piece of paper into a special gift certificate of your own making.

## Creating Money Envelopes

You can create an attractive envelope that is a gift itself and a beautiful way to give money as a gift. Find a demonstration of how to make a money envelope of your own design in Idea Guide ➤ Gift Ideas ➤ Money Envelopes.

This money envelope has already been created for you as a ready-made envelope. From the Select a Project screen, select Stationery ➤ Customize a Ready Made ➤ Envelope ➤ Gift Envelope, shown here in Figure 13.8. Or from the Open dialog box, select the file gftenvel.erm. Customize it with the name of your special person, changing graphics to reflect their personality and your relationship.

**Figure 13.8:** Create an attractive envelope that is a gift itself and a beautiful way to give money as a gift.

Another possibility is to start from scratch using the step-by-step instructions in the How To section of the Idea Guide to create this project or a similar one with the graphic of your choice.

To reach the How To section, select Idea Guide ➤ Gift Ideas ➤ Money Envelopes. When the demonstration is completed, select How To ➤ Gift Ideas ➤ Money Envelopes to get detailed instructions. Select Print to print out these instructions.

## Sharing a Recipe

Next time you want to share one of your delicious dishes, you can share your recipe at the same time. Make a recipe card worthy of your recipe in Print Shop using the two-sided capability of a postcard project. You will find a demonstration of how to make a special recipe card in Idea Guide ➤ Gift Ideas ➤ Recipe Card. Create a recipe logo for your kitchen on one side and put the recipe on the other, or put the ingredients on one side and the recipe on the other.

This recipe card has already been created for you as a ready-made postcard. From the Select a Project screen, select Stationery ➤ Customize a Ready Made ➤ Post Cards ➤ Gift Recipe, Idea Guide, shown here in Figure 13.9. Or from the Open dialog box, select the file gftrecip.pcr. Customize it with your own favorite recipe.

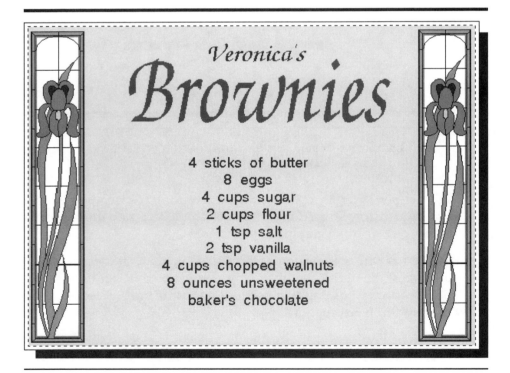

**Figure 13.9:** Make a recipe card worthy of your recipe in Print Shop using the two-sided capability of a postcard project.

You could start from scratch using the step-by-step instructions in the How To section of the Idea Guide to create this project or another similar one with the graphic of your choice.

To reach the How To section, select Idea Guide ➤ Gift Ideas ➤ Recipe Card. When the demonstration is completed, select How To ➤ Gift Ideas ➤ Recipe Card to get detailed instructions. Select Print to print out these instructions.

# More Gift Ideas

Here are a few more ideas to get your creative juices flowing on how to use Print Shop for your gift giving.

## Making it Personal

Create a label, like the one shown here, that puts your name or anyone else's on books, equipment, glasses or cups, briefcases, suitcases, or anything else you'd like to brand with a name to make sure everyone knows exactly whose it is. It's quite simple to do. Just think of the Gift Label project in a different way, using those steps to create a whole new project.

## Creating Your Own Calendar

Use the Calendar project to create a series of personalized monthly calendars that cover the entire year. Use your best photographs or your funniest and add a few of your favorite thoughts or sayings. Or personalize your calendar using the many photographs that are provided on the CD that comes with The Print Shop Ensemble III.

Make one month a single great photograph or a series of photographs in postage stamp size, perhaps a rogue gallery of your family or your coworkers. Use the Photo Accessories library to add art to the shots, including special frames or hats or glasses or mustaches.

By thinking creatively you can make this personal crafts project one that will ensure you're remembered every day of the year. Or make one for yourself that will remind you of those special memories you don't want to forget, like we did in the calendar shown here.

# ◆ Holiday Ideas

In Print Shop you can choose from over 1,000 graphics designed to express a variety of holiday sentiments. In the Holiday Ideas section of the Idea Guide, Print Shop has chosen to focus on the one that brings out the holiday spirit in everyone, Christmas. The Idea Guide will give

you some great ideas for cards that pop up and stand out, for original tree ornaments that are uniquely your own, for paper chains to decorate the tree or the house, and for a special calendar that counts down the days with a treat for every day. Also, we'll suggest a few more projects you might create for the holidays and hopefully inspire you to think of a few yourself.

## Creating a 3-D Card

Make your holiday greetings come alive with a 3-D effect that'll have their eyes popping. All it takes is Print Shop, paper, and a small utility knife to create this memorable note, shown here in Figure 13.10. Find a demonstration of how to make this special holiday card in Idea Guide ➤ Holiday Ideas ➤ Greeting Card.

This 3-D card has already been created for you as a ready-made greeting card. From the Select a Project screen, select Greeting Cards ➤ Customize a Ready Made ➤ Quarter Page ➤ Holiday ➤ Christmas Card, Idea Guide. Or from the Open dialog box, select the file xmascard.grm. Customize it by adding your recipient's names or your own sentiments.

You can also start from scratch using the step-by-step instructions in the How To section of the Idea Guide to create this project or a similar one using the graphic of your choice.

To reach the How To section, select Idea Guide ➤ Holiday Ideas ➤ Greeting Card. When the demonstration is completed, select How To ➤ Holiday Ideas ➤ Greeting Card to get detailed instructions. Select Print to print out these instructions.

**Figure 13.10:** Make your holiday come alive with a 3-D card that'll have their eyes popping.

# Creating Personalized Ornaments

Make picture-perfect tree ornaments of your very own using your favorite photograph and the postcard project. Add a sentiment to the project and it becomes a very special greeting you can send to a friend or relative, as shown here in Figure 13.11. Find a demonstration of how to make this distinctive ornament in Idea Guide ➤ Holiday Ideas ➤ Ornament.

You can start with a ready-made ornament. From the Select a Project screen, select Stationery ➤ Customize a Ready Made ➤ Post Cards ➤ Ornament, Idea Guide. Or from the Open dialog box, select the file xma-sorna.pcr. Add your own photograph or use one of the many offered on the photographs stored on your Print Shop CD. Print your project on postcard stock to give it more stability.

You can also start from scratch using the step-by-step instructions in the How To section of the Idea Guide to create this project or another similar one with the graphic of your choice.

To reach the How To section, select Idea Guide ➤ Holiday Ideas ➤ Ornament. When the demonstration is completed, select How To ➤ Holiday Ideas ➤ Ornament to get detailed instructions. Select Print to print out these instructions.

**Figure 13.11:**  Make picture-perfect tree ornaments of your very own using your favorite photograph and the postcard project. Flip the graphic to make the opposite side.

# Choosing Paper Chains

Here's a project that's fun and easy and one the whole family will want to make together. Gather the family and make it one of those magical holiday nights by creating your own family-designed holiday paper chain, seen here in Figure 13.12. Find a demonstration of how to make this unique project in Idea Guide ➤ Holiday Ideas ➤ Paper Chain.

**Figure 13.12:** Start with a sign project to create a unique paper chain for your tree.

You can start with a ready-made sign. From the Select a Project screen, select Signs & Posters ➤ Customize a Ready Made ➤ Celebration ➤ Paper Chain, Idea Guide. Or from the Open dialog box, select the file xmaschn.srm. Create paper chains using row and column graphics, choosing graphics that complement each other and your own style. Add everyone's name to the chain and print on both sides of the paper to make the effect complete.

You can also start from scratch using the step-by-step instructions in the How To section of the Idea Guide to create this project or another similar one with the graphic of your choice.

To reach the How To section, select Idea Guide ➤ Holiday Ideas ➤ Paper Chain. When the demonstration is completed, select How To ➤ Holiday Ideas ➤ Paper Chain to get detailed instructions. Select Print to print out these instructions.

## Counting Down the Days

You can also design your own unique calendar to count down to a special occasion. Create daily windows that can be opened to reveal a message or graphic (see Figure 13.13) to heighten the expectations. Find a demonstration of how to make this unique project in Idea Guide ➤ Holiday Ideas ➤ Count Down. This project was created as a sign, not a calendar, demonstrating how a little creativity can lead to a totally new way to use a project.

From the Select a Project screen, select Signs & Posters ➤ Customize a Ready Made ➤ Celebration ➤ Advent Sign 1, Idea Guide and Advent Sign 2, Idea Guide. Or from the Open dialog box, select the files xmasign1.srm and xmasign2.srm.

Think of using this same idea for an upcoming wedding, graduation, or vacation, providing a visual surprise for every day leading up to the event. This project uses a grid graphic from the Initial Caps library, Square Graphics to create a grid to guide the positioning of your daily graphics or text. Once your graphics are positioned, you can delete the grid or you can keep it as a design element. This project prints on two separate pieces of paper, with windows created from one page to the next.

You can also start from scratch using the step-by-step instructions in the How To section of the Idea Guide to create this project or a similar one with the graphic of your choice.

To reach the How To section, select Idea Guide ➤ Holiday Ideas ➤ Count Down. When the demonstration is completed, select How To ➤ Holiday Ideas ➤ Count Down to get detailed instructions. Select Print to print out these instructions.

**Figure 13.13:** Count down to a special occasion with a uniquely designed calendar that reveals a new surprise every day.

# More Holiday Ideas

Print Shop can help you celebrate holidays other than Christmas, too. Here are some more Holiday Ideas to help you create special holiday moments.

## Making a String of Scary Things

Here's a great idea for decorating windows at Halloween: make a string of scary things to hang across your window.

Start from scratch in a sign project, holding down the Ctrl key as you select Wide as your orientation. You go immediately to a blank page in the Main Project Window.

Now add a square graphic and go to the graphics browser. Search for Halloween in All Libraries. You're presented with some interesting choices for your scary things, from Dracula to witches to bats.

Choose one you like or choose several different graphics to create rows of scary things, side by side in two rows, top to bottom, as shown on the next page. Print your project, cut the page so you end up with two rows of scary things on two separate pieces of paper.

Cut out your scary things, leaving about an inch at the center between them so they are joined together. Paste the two rows together so you have one long row of scary things. Print your project two times or more to make your string as long as you like.

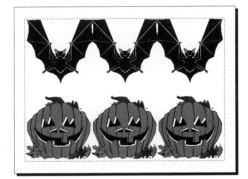

There you have it, a long line of scary things to put you in the mood for a dark Halloween night.

## Creating Holiday Stickers

Make your own stickers for Valentine's Day, Halloween, or any other holiday. It's simple to do and you can personalize them with the name of a special person if you want.

Start with a label project. Choose a label size that best suits the graphics you intend to use. If none of the 14 different labels fit the size you want, create the stickers as a sign project and use a single piece of sticky label paper when you print, then cut out your stickers.

Use one graphic or combine several graphics to make one sticker. You might want to add a word balloon to say something like, 'Will you be my Valentine Jim?'

Use your stickers on gifts, on cards or just as a fun message, anytime.

# ◆ Building on an Idea

To give you an idea of how you can continue to build on an idea, we'd like to go back for a moment to the very first project we did in this book, the Wind Song invitation created in Chapter 1, "Creating Your First Project." You'll remember that we wanted to create an invitation for a special party aboard the computerized sailing cruise ship, the Wind Song. We used graphics and text to convey our message. Take a look at this card at the very end of Chapter 1, "Creating Your First Project" and at our new card, shown here in Figure 13.14.

Given what we now know about Print Shop, let's add a little creativity to that card.

1. Open the Wind Song greeting card and take a look at it again. You should have it stored as a greeting card.

Let's add a window to our card with a pop-up effect and a photograph of the ship itself.

2. On the front of the card, add a square graphic.

3. Now search for a window (a porthole would be great but you won't find one). Take a look at the options available in the Photo Accessories library. There are several there that might work for our nautical theme, including one called Island and one called Tropical. We don't really think these work with the card concept so we've chosen a graphic called Thought Bubble B.

4. Position this new graphic above the woman so she appears to be thinking of the adventure to come. After we print this card, we will cut out this thought bubble so you can see inside the card. Add some text to the bubble, something like "dreaming of blue skies and warm seas."

5. Now go to the inside of the card and import a photograph. We've actually scanned in a photograph of the Wind Song sailing ship for our card. For this exercise, you can select a photograph from those on the CD.

6. Reposition your text boxes so you can place the photo in the upper-right corner of the second inside page so it's just behind the thought bubble. Keep in mind that we want to be able to see the ship when we open the bubble.

7. Print out your new card. Using a small utility knife, cut out the thought bubble leaving one side hinged so it can be opened to see inside.

That's it! We've designed a whole new Wind Song invitation. Pretty neat.

**Figure 13.14:** The addition of a 3-D effect and a photograph of the ship breathes new life into our Wind Song invitation. Here you see the front of the card as it would appear with the thought bubble opened so you can see inside the card.

# ◆ Endnotes

You are ready to think creatively about Print Shop, to expand your ideas beyond the obvious projects, and to devise ways to create new and exciting projects of your own. You have learned:

- ◆ How to use erasers to change existing graphics
- ◆ How to make graphics pop up and out
- ◆ How to make paper chains of scary things
- ◆ How to make your ideas stick with stickers
- ◆ How to create a window to see what's beyond the beginning
- ◆ And a whole lot more

Hopefully, above all, you have learned to push The Print Shop Ensemble III to its limits so you can be more creative than ever. Now, in the final chapter of this book, we'll take a look at troubleshooting printing problems in Chapter 14, "Printing Made Easy."

# Printing Made Easy

## Your mission: to learn tips for printing specific projects and solving printing problems

◆

Throughout the course of this book we've printed various projects and gotten a good idea of the basics of printing. This chapter will give you some tips for printing specific projects. If you need a review of all the print options Print Shop offers, see the "Choosing Preferences" and "Printing a Project" sections of Chapter 3.

There's nothing more frustrating than discovering that one of your great projects just does not print the way it should. PS Ensemble III works with most printers that are supported by Microsoft Windows 95 and NT. Print Shop recommends that you use a 24-pin dot matrix, laser, or ink jet printer for the best print quality.

Many of the print problems you encounter will probably be due to the limitations of your printer. Maybe you're asking it to do something it just cannot do. For example, a monochrome printer cannot print color and only a PostScript printer will print EPS graphics. Aside from these obvious problems, there are other print problems you may encounter that can be solved. The latter part of this chapter will deal with troubleshooting printing to make it easier for you to take that great on-screen project and turn it into a hard copy you can post on the wall or pop in the mail.

# ◆ Printing Specific Projects

Some projects print differently than others because they're a unique size or a distinct orientation. These projects include banners, which print on multiple pages, name lists, which are imported into projects piece by piece, labels, which repeat over and over on a specific area of a page, and business cards, which print eight to ten per page.

## Printing Banners

Banners are multipage, from a minimum of 2 pages to as many as 35. They can be printed on a tractor-fed (continuous) printer or a cut-sheet (one page at a time) printer.

If you're printing on a cut-sheet printer, you will need to glue or tape the pages together. To put the pages together seamlessly, carefully trim one side, then use glue on the edge of the exposed side and transparent tape on the underside. PS Ensemble III suggests that you glue the pages together first and apply the tape to the underside after all the pieces are assembled to your liking.

If you're printing on a dot matrix printer, you may experience some problems with overheating, especially if you're printing a particularly long banner. Overheating can damage the print head, so be careful.

Some printers will shut down automatically if they become overheated, but don't count on this. It's a good idea to stop printing after several minutes to give the printer a breather, just to be on the safe side. You can start again after the printer cools.

If you're having difficulties using a tractor-fed printer, use the Cut sheet banner printing option in the Preferences dialog box to tell the program to treat the printer like a cut-sheet printer, as discussed in Chapter 3.

Banners can be printed in a coloring book format. This option prints the banner in outline form, a good way to check the layout before final printing. You might also want to use this option and then color in your banner just for fun.

## Printing Name Lists

Merge printing with name lists is generally a breeze. The one problem you might confront is cutoff of some of the merged text. This is generally due to the size of the box in which the text is placed. To solve the problem, make sure that the text block, headline block, or word balloon where the merged text will be placed is large enough to accommodate the largest of the merged text.

For example, if you're merging names and addresses, the third name on the list may be longer than the first, so what initially appeared to be a big enough space really isn't. Just resize the text box to make it large enough for this longer name to fit, or reduce the font size of the text in the block, and you won't have any more problems with cutoff.

## Printing Labels

When you select File ➤ Print, the number of labels to be printed on a page is indicated in the Print dialog box. The number of labels printed on a page is determined by the type of label you select. Label size is the very first thing you select when you begin a Label project.

When designing a label, be sure to leave a safe area of white space around the design and text areas. The program automatically scales the label to fit to the printable area of your selected printer. If scaling is being done, the percentage of scaling will be shown in the Print dialog box.

Before you print on pressure-sensitive labels or card stock, *print one page of your labels on plain white paper.* Then hold this paper up to the labels to see if they fit properly. If they don't, use the alignment options in the Print Options dialog box to try to solve the problem. If this doesn't work, try scaling the labels down to make them smaller than 99% so they will fit into their designated areas properly.

When you print labels, you are offered an additional option in the Print dialog box: the Starting Place button. Click on this button to reach a dialog box, shown in Figure 14.1, that allows you to select where you want to start printing on a sheet of labels. This is particularly useful if you're not using a complete sheet of labels.

**Figure 14.1:**  The Starting Place dialog box lets you choose where on the label sheet you want to begin printing.

## Printing Business Cards

Business cards print ten to a page on most printers. Some printers that require a large *grab area* to feed in the paper print cards eight to a page. Cards can be printed on regular paper then photocopied onto card stock or, on some printers, you can print directly onto card stock.

If you're printing onto card stock, make sure your cards line up properly. Print a first page on plain paper, then check this against the card stock to make sure the cards are aligned properly.

## Printing Envelopes

Envelope printing is tricky because it's not a full-page size project and envelopes do not feed into the printer like regular pieces of paper do. When you select File ➤ Print for an envelope, the Print dialog box offers special Position options, which refer to how the envelopes are fed into your printer. The options are Left, Center, Right, Wide, and Aerogram for printer feed and Top and Bottom for the position of the printed text, as shown in Figure 14.2.

If you choose to create a quarter-page size envelope, you will have one other option available when you go to File ➤ Print, a check box called Cutout Marks. This option prints your envelope on a regular size piece of paper with an outline showing you where to cut out the flaps so you can create your own envelope. This envelope size fits a quarter-page greeting card and is useful if your printer is not able to print on a quarter-page envelope.

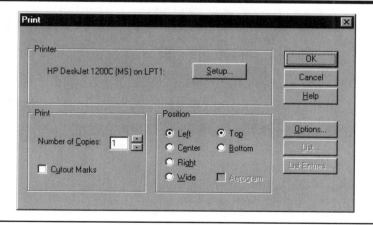

**Figure 14.2:** Position options for envelopes include Left, Center, Right, Wide, and Aerogram.

An aerogram is a type of envelope used mainly for international letters. To create an aerogram, select Aerogram to print the envelope's address in the center of a regular sheet of paper. Turn the page over, feed it back into the printer, and print the message on the opposite side. Then fold the page in thirds so that the address side is out. Put a stamp on it and mail it.

Most printers that feed envelopes left, center, or right print better with the position choice set to Bottom. Most printers that feed envelopes wide print better with the position choice set to Top.

Printers that feed wide may not be able to print all the way to the right edge and thus may not look centered. You cannot eliminate this problem but you can make it less obvious by not putting borders around your envelope design.

If you're still having problems printing, try using the Rotate envelope option in the Preferences dialog box, as discussed in the "Choosing Preferences" section of Chapter 3.

## Printing Transfer Designs

You can flip a sign project so you can print it onto special transfer paper for creating a t-shirt. The Flip printout for transfer design is an option available in the Print Options dialog box. This option is available for sign projects only, text blocks and word balloons will *not* print with this option.

# ◆ Troubleshooting Print Problems

PS Ensemble III provides some help on troubleshooting print problems in its extensive Help library (see Chapter 4, "Getting Help"). If you don't find your particular problem discussed here, check out Help for more information. In the meantime, here are three common problems you might encounter.

# Dealing with Partial Printouts

If your printer is printing only part of your project, it may be that the printer does not have enough memory to store the entire project. Printer memory is separate from your computer's memory. If you don't know how much memory your printer has, check the printer manual to find out.

The higher the resolution at which you elect to print a project, the more memory you will need. For example, with a laser printer, you'll generally need 512K of printer memory to print at 150 dpi (dots per inch). At 300 dpi, you'll need 1MB. If you're having trouble printing, lower the resolution.

If lowering the dpi does not work, the printer may be *timing out* or it may have a third-party print spooler with a time out feature. When a printer times out, it begins to print what it has stored if it doesn't receive any new information within a certain number of seconds. This may prevent part of the project from being stored for printout. This problem can usually be resolved by turning off the time out feature or increasing its value to 90 seconds (see the printer manual for instructions).

# Printing Imported Bitmaps

If you've imported a bitmap and rotated it in the project, you may have trouble printing the bitmap. This may mean that your printer driver does not support the rotation of bitmaps. There's an easy fix that might work. Click on File Preferences and deselect Fast Bitmap Printing. This will slightly increase the printing time but it will probably solve your bitmap printing problem.

# Slow Printing

If printing is taking a lot of time, try turning off your memory resident programs such as screen savers or Microsoft Office. If you're printing on a laserjet-compatible printer, try lowering the printer driver's resolution to 150 dpi. On a dot matrix printer, lower the quality to draft. While these changes will speed up the printing, they will also reduce the quality of the printed output.

# ◆ Endnotes

In this last chapter, you've learned about some print problems you might encounter and how to solve them. You now know:

◆ How to print a banner on a cut-sheet printer

◆ How to align labels and how to choose a starting place on the sheet of labels

◆ How to position envelopes for printing

◆ What to do if you're getting only a partial printout of a project

And best of all, you know everything you ever wanted to know about The Print Shop Ensemble III. You can create great things; we'll leave you now to do just that.

# Appendices

Appendix

A

# Installing and Uninstalling The Print Shop Ensemble III

Installing Print Shop Ensemble III is easy. The installation procedure outlined below lets you install the entire contents in just a few simple steps. Instructions for uninstalling the program are at the end of this appendix.

## ◆ Requirements

What You Need:

- ◆ 33Mhz 486DX or greater microprocessor recommended
- ◆ 8MB of RAM or more recommended
- ◆ Hard disk requirements will range from 9MB to 51MB depending on choice of installation options
- ◆ Microsoft Windows 95

- ◆ SVGA (640x480) display adapter and monitor supporting 256-colors or higher
- ◆ Windows-compatible mouse
- ◆ Windows-compatible printer (24-pin, ink jet, or laser printer recommended)
- ◆ CD-ROM Drive
- ◆ Windows-compatible sound card (for the Ensemble Idea Guide).

System Configuration: May require minor adjustments to the configuration of your operating system and/or updates to the hardware component drivers.

Nice to Have:

- ◆ Modem 14400 or higher
- ◆ Color printer ribbons or cartridges
- ◆ Special paper (textures, or glossy paper, if your printer/manufacturer distributes these)
- ◆ Ink Jet Greeting Cards and Envelopes (5 1/2" x 8 1/2")
- ◆ Heat transfer paper for iron-on projects to make T-shirts, bags, etc.

# ◆ Installation Options

Installing the Print Shop Ensemble III is easy. The installation procedures outlined below let you choose from several installation options.

## Options for Typical Installation

A typical install only copies the minimum required files from The Print Shop Ensemble III to your hard drive. Every time you use the Print Shop Ensemble III you will need to put the program CD-ROM in your CD-ROM drive. This installation needs 15 Megabytes of available hard drive space.

**1.** Place the Print Shop Ensemble III CD in your CD-ROM drive.

**2.** The Broderbund startup dialog box will automatically appear. If your system is not able to automatically display this dialog, click on the Start button on the Windows 95 Taskbar, and select Run....

Type D:\SETUP.EXE in the "Open" field, and then click on OK. (Where "D" is the letter of your CD-ROM drive.)

**3.** Click on Install to begin the installation. Carefully follow the on-screen instructions to install the program.

**4.** The Print Shop Ensemble III will be installed onto your C drive under the directory named Program Files and under a subdirectory named the Print Shop Ensemble III. If you would like to change the destination of this installation click on the Browse button in the Installation Configuration dialog and navigate to the desired installation path.

**5.** While installing, the Print Shop Ensemble III searches your hard drive for previous versions of Print Shop. When it finds a previous version, a prompt asks whether or not you would like to copy your project files from the previous version of Print Shop into the Print Shop Ensemble III projects file. If you answer Yes, the program will copy those over for you.

**6.** After the Print Shop Ensemble III installation is completed you will be given the option of electronically registering your copy of the Print Shop Ensemble III. Please take a few moments to register the Print Shop Ensemble III. Registering your product qualifies you for free technical support and notification of future upgrades and special discounts.

**7.** To use the Print Shop Ensemble III, click Start on the Taskbar, move the cursor to Programs, then the Print Shop. Click on The Print Shop Ensemble III icon.

# Options for Full Installation

Before proceeding with a full installation of the Print Shop Ensemble III, please verify that your computer has at least 51 megabytes of free hard disk space.

**1.** Place the Print Shop Ensemble III CD in your CD-ROM drive.

**2.** Start button on the Windows 95 Taskbar, and select Run... Type D:\SETUP.EXE in the "Open" field, and then click on OK. (Where "D" is the letter of your CD-ROM drive.)

3. Click on Install to begin the installation. Carefully follow the on-screen instructions to install the program.

4. Once you reach the Installation Configuration dialog box, click on the Full button and then click on the Next button.

5. The Print Shop Ensemble III will be installed onto your C drive under the directory named Program Files and under a subdirectory named the Print Shop Ensemble III. If you would like to change the designation of this installation, click on the Browse button in the Installation Configuration dialog box and navigate to the desired installation path.

6. While installing, the Print Shop Ensemble III searches your hard drive for previous versions of Print Shop. When it finds a previous version, a prompt asks whether or not you would like to copy your project files from the previous version of Print Shop into the new version of Print Shop projects file. If you answer yes, the program will copy those over for you. If you answer no, the Print Shop Ensemble III does not copy them over.

7. After the Print Shop Ensemble III installation is completed you will be given the option of electronically registering your copy of the Print Shop Ensemble III. Please take a few moments to register the Print Shop Ensemble III. Registering your product qualifies you for free technical support and notification of future upgrades and special discounts.

## Options for Custom Installation

The Print Shop Ensemble III allows you to select the files and features to install on your hard drive with a Custom Installation. To select this installation option, click on the Custom button within the Installation Configuration dialog box.

1. To reach the Installation Configuration dialog box, insert the Print Shop Ensemble III CD-ROM in the CD-ROM drive.

2. Click on the Install button and follow the directions within in the Welcome dialog box. Once you reach the Installation Configuration dialog box, click on the Custom button and than click on Next. Click Yes on the directory confirmation box.

3. The Components to Install dialog box allows you to select or dese-lect those items you would like installed onto your hard drive. You may select or deselect any of the five files that show up in this screen. These five compnents are the Program Files, Ready Made Projects, Help Files, Graphics Libraries, and Fonts.

4. Once you have chosen the files you would like installed onto your hard drive, click on the Next button and continue to follow the installation instructions on the screen.

5. The Print Shop Ensemble III searches your hard drive for previous versions of Print Shop. When it finds a previous version, a prompt asks whether or not you would like to copy your project files from the previous version of the Print Shop Ensemble III project files into the new version of the Print Shop project files. If you answer Yes, the program will copy those over for you. If you answer No, the Print Shop Ensemble III does not copy them over.

6. After The Print Shop Ensemble III installation is completed, you will be given the option of electronically registering your copy of the Print Shop Ensemble III. Please take a few moments to regis-ter the Print Shop Ensemble III. Registering your product qualifies you for free technical support and notification of future upgrades and special discounts.

# ◆ Electronic Registration

The Print Shop Ensemble III lets you register by modem. To electronically register your copy of the program, click the button that indicates Register By Modem, and follow the instructions. Some business phone systems require a prefix number to be dialed to reach an outside line. If yours is one of those systems, click the Dial Out Prefix button and enter the num-ber in the space provided. Once you have entered your information, you can send it toll-free via modem (in the US and Canada only).

If you have a modem and want to register electronically, but you don't want to do so now, click the Cancel button. To electronically register later, right-click on the CD-ROM drive icon in the My Computer window while The Print Shop Ensemble III disc is in the CD-ROM drive, then select Electronic Registration from the menu.

If you do not have a modem, or do not wish to register by modem, click the Register by Mail button and register using the enclosed registration card.

As a registered user, you'll get:

◆ Notification of new versions of Print Shop
◆ Discounts on new versions of Print Shop
◆ Special offers on new products related to Print Shop
◆ Free technical support
◆ Special offers on other Brøderbund products

We recommend that you register your product in order to take advantage of the offers listed above.

# ◆ Uninstalling the Program

To completely remove the Print Shop Ensemble III from your Windows 95 system you must uninstall. To uninstall follow these simple directions:

1. Click on the Start button at the left side of the Windows 95 taskbar.

2. Navigate to Settings and click on the Control Panel.

3. From the Control Panel double-click on the Add/Remove Programs icon.

4. At the Install/Uninstall tab, click to highlight the Print Shop Ensemble III.

5. Click on the Add/Remove button.

6. From the Confirm File Deletion dialog box click on the Yes button if you want to uninstall the Print Shop Ensemble III. If you do not wish to uninstall the Print Shop Ensemble III click on the No button. By clicking on No, you will be sent back to the Install/Uninstall tab dialog box.

If you click Yes in the Confirm File Deletion dialog box, the uninstall program will activate and remove the Print Shop Ensemble III from your system. When it is finished removing your program click the OK button.

# Appendix B

# Specialized Paper Sources

Projects look great printed on specialty paper. Here are our favorite paper companies. You can call them to receive copies of their catalogs.

## Avery®

A complete line of laser labels and card products, ink jet labels, index products, and Communique specialty papers.

| | | |
|---|---|---|
| Phone | 800-252-8379 | Mon–Fri 6 a.m.– 4 p.m. PST |
| Fax | 800-862-8379 | 7 days a week, 24 hours a day |

# Beaver Prints™

Innovative laser papers including preprinted photography. Great prices on hundreds of designs and formats. Unique products, brochures, letterhead, envelopes, and specialty products.

| | | |
|---|---|---|
| Phone | 800-742-6070 | Mon–Fri 8 a.m.–8 p.m. EST |
| Fax | 814-742-6063 | 7 days a week, 24 hours a day |

# Idea Art

Over a thousand choices of high-quality, environmentally friendly designs for brochures, flyers, newsletters, invitations, and more. All papers are recycled and printed with natural soy inks.

| | | |
|---|---|---|
| Phone | 800-433-2278 | Mon–Fri 7:30 a.m.–6 p.m. CST |
| Fax | 800-435-2278 | 7 days a week, 24 hours a day |

# Paper Access

Over 500 unique preprinted and unprinted papers in a full range of items and sizes.

| | | |
|---|---|---|
| Phone | 212-463-7035 | Mon–Fri 9 a.m.–7 p.m. EST |
| | | Sat 11 a.m.–6 p.m. EST |
| Fax | 212-924-7318 | 7 days a week, 24 hours a day |

# Paper Direct®

Thousands of specialty preprinted and unprinted papers, envelopes, labels, and presentation products.

| | | |
|---|---|---|
| Phone | 800-272-7377 | Mon–Fri 8 a.m.–9 p.m. EST |
| | | Sat 10 a.m.–4 p.m. EST |
| Fax | 201-271-9601 | 7 days a week, 24 hours a day |

# Queblo®

Elegant embossed and foil-stamped papers; designs for brochures, newsletters, and business cards; full-color labels; and much more. Money-back guarantee and fast delivery.

| Phone | 800-523-9080 | Mon–Fri 7:30 a.m.–7:30 p.m. EST |
| Fax | 800-554-8779 | 7 days a week, 24 hours a day |

# Index

**Note to the Reader:** First level entries are in **bold**. Page numbers in **bold** indicate the principal discussion of a topic or the definition of a term. Page numbers in *italic* indicate illustrations.

## Numbers

**3-D greeting cards**, 278–279, *279*

## A

**accessing**. *See also* opening
  lists, 92
  Print Shop Connection Web page, 144
**Add command**, Object menu, 75–76, 77–79
**Add Objects tool**, **41–46**. *See also* Standard Toolbar
  adding objects with placeholders, 44, *45*
  Ctrl key + Add Objects tool, 45–46
  customizing placeholders, 45–46
  placeholders defined, **42–44**
  selecting type of, 41–42
**adding**. *See also* entering; installing
  autographs to signature blocks, 236–238
  borders, 186
  graphics
    to greeting cards, 20–22, *21*
    to seals, 187–189, *188*, *189*
  headlines, 77–79
  objects, 75–76
  objects with placeholders, 44, *45*
  shadows to objects, 79–80

  text
    to greeting cards, 24–25, *25*
    to seals, 189–190
    to signature blocks, 236
    to word balloons, 240–241, *240*
**address lists**, 246–250, *247*. *See also* lists
**Advent calendars**, 282, *283*
**aligning objects**, **83–84**
**aspect ratio**
  changing for graphics, 36–37
  changing for headlines and text blocks, 37–38
**attachments**, sending online greetings as, 142–143
**autographs in signature blocks**, 236–238
**Avery labels and specialty papers**, 305

## B

**backdrops**. *See also* graphics
  backdrop libraries, 150, 151
  Backdrops Browser, 8–10, *10*, 20–21, *21*
  changing, **85**
  displaying and hiding, 91
  for greeting cards, **8–11**, **22–23**
    finding, 9–10, *10*
    previewing, 10–11
    selecting for front, 8–9, *8*

selecting for inside, 22–23
Page Blend options, 89–90
project layers and, 81
searching backdrop libraries, 8–10,
*10*, 20–21, *21*
selecting, 111, *112*
**banners**
changing banner length, 86–88
creating, **118–120**
editing banner headlines, 77
printing, 290–291
**Beaver Prints specialty papers**, 306
**bitmap files**. *See also* graphics
importing, 194, 196
printing problems, 295
**blends**
for headlines, 15–16, *16*, 78,
**230–232**, *230*
Page Blend command, 88–90
**.bmp files**. *See bitmap files*
**Bookmark menu**, in Help, 103–104
**bookmarks**, 118
**borders**, **180–186**. *See also* graphics;
Smart Graphics
adding custom borders to projects,
186
creating, **181–183**, *181*, *182*, *183*
mini-borders versus certificate borders, 180
saving custom borders, 186
selecting border graphics, 183–185,
*185*
**bracelets for parties**, 271
**brightness settings**, for imported
photos, 200
**Bring Forward and Bring to Front
commands**, Object menu, 80–81
**browsers**. *See also* Graphics Browser
Backdrops Browser, 8–10, *10*,
20–21, *21*

Browsers tab in Preferences dialog
box, 66
setting up Web browsers, 138–140,
*139*
**business cards**, 292–293

**C**

**calendars**
count-down calendars, 282, *283*
creating, **123–127**, *124*, *126*
for gifts, 277–278
**cards**. *See also* greeting cards
business cards, 292–293
place cards, 267, *268*
postcards, 122–123
recipe cards, 276–277, *276*
**categories**, searching graphics libraries
by, 157
**certificate borders**, 180
**certificates**
creating, **120–121**
gift certificates, 272–273, *274*
**chains of paper**, 280–282, *281*
**changing**. *See also* editing
aspect ratio
for graphics, 36–37
for headlines and text blocks,
37–38
backdrops, 85
banner length, 86–88
color or shading of objects, 51–54
fonts, 14–15
graphics' size, 35–37
layouts, 86
text attributes of headlines, 228–229
text color in greeting cards, 18–19
**chapters in Help**, 98
**checking spelling**, **216–218**, *218*
**choosing**. *See selecting*
**clearing**. *See deleting*

**clocks**, **178–180**, *179*
**Color Selector tool**, 51–54
**coloring books**, 116
**colors**
  changing color or shading of objects,
    51–54
  changing text color in greeting cards,
    18–19
  coloring objects, 51–54
  of imported graphics, 196
  Page Blend options, 88–90
**common project design elements**,
  **108–113**
  customizing ready-made projects,
    108–110
  selecting backdrops, 111, *112*
  selecting layouts, 111–113, *113*
  selecting orientation, 110–111
  selecting paths, 108–110
  starting from scratch, 110
**configuring.** *See* **setting up**
**connecting to the Internet**, 92,
  **138–140**, *139*
**Contents button**, in Help, 96, 99
**converting.** *See also* changing
**copying and pasting objects**, 71–73
**count-down calendars**, 282, *283*
**covering parts of projects**, **131–132**
**Create a Number dialog box**, 177–178,
  *177*
**creating**
  borders, 181–183, *181*, *182*, *183*
  greeting cards, 5
  headlines in greeting cards, 14
  initial caps, 171–176, *171*
  lists, **246–253**
    address lists, 246–250, *247*
    custom lists, 246, 250–253, *251*

  outlines, shadows, and blends for
    headlines, 15–16, *16*, 78,
    **230–232**, *230*
  projects, **113–131**, **136**
    banners, 118–120
    calendars, 123–127, *124*, *126*
    certificates, 120–121
    greeting cards, 113–116
    labels, 127–129
    online greetings, 136, *137*
    Photo Projects, 129–131
    signs and posters, 30–31, 68,
      116–118, 294
    stationery, 121–123
  Smart Graphics numbers, 176–178,
    *177*
  text effects, 15–16, *16*, 78
  timepieces, 178–180, *179*
  word balloons, 239–240
**cropping photos**, 196, 199–200
**Ctrl key.** *See also* Shift key; shortcut
  keys
  + Add Object tool, 45–46
  + Add Objects tool, 45–46
  + Pointer tool, 36–37
  resizing photos, 200
**custom installation options**, 302–303
**Custom Libraries command**, Extras
  menu, 92
**custom lists**, 246, 250–253, *251*. *See
  also* lists
**customizing**
  greeting cards, 5
  Idea Guide projects, 285–286, *286*
  placeholders, 45–46
  ready-made projects, 5, 108–110
  title blocks, 233
**cutting and pasting objects**, 71–73

**D**

**defining.** *See* **creating**
**Delete command**, Edit menu, 73
**Delete tool**, 46–47
**deleting**
 graphics from graphics libraries, 161, 166
 graphics libraries, 167
 objects, 46–47, 73
**designing.** *See* **creating**
**dialog boxes**, Help in, 105
**displaying.** *See also* hiding
 backdrops, 91
 Navigation Toolbar, 91
 online greetings, 143
 placeholders, 91
 toolbars, 91
**documents**, moving in windows, 40, *41*
**drag and drop**, printing with, 67
**duplicating objects**, 73–74

**E**

**Edit Address List command**, Extras menu, 92
**Edit command**, Object menu, 76–77
**Edit Custom List command**, Extras menu, 92
**Edit menu**, **70–75**, **102–103**. *See also* menus
 Copy command, 72
 Cut command, 71
 Delete command, 73
 Duplicate command, 73–75
 in Help, **102–103**
 Paste command, 72–73
 Redo command, 71
 Select All command, 74–75
 Undo command, 70–71

**Edit Return Address command**, Extras menu, 92
**Edit Text dialog box**, 221, *221*
**editing.** *See also* changing
 banner headlines, 77
 graphics, 76
 graphics libraries, **164–167**
  deleting graphics, 161, 166
  deleting libraries, 167
  preparing to edit, 164–165, *165*
  renaming graphics, 166
 lists, 253
 text blocks, **37–38**, **221–226**
  opening Edit Text dialog box, 221, *221*
  resizing, 37–38
  selecting text attributes, 222–224
  with Text Toolbar, 224–226
 text in greeting cards, 17
**effects for headlines**, 15–16, *16*, 78, **230–232**, *230*
**electronic registration**, **303–304**
**e-mail attachments**, sending online greetings as, 142–143
**encapsulated PostScript (EPS) files**, 194, 196
**entering.** *See also* adding
 text in greeting cards, 18
**envelopes**
 for money gifts, 274–275, *275*
 printing, 293–294, *293*
**erasing.** *See* **deleting**
**exiting Print Shop Ensemble**, 70
**Export and Print Graphics command**, Extras menu, 92
**exporting**, **92**, **203–211**
 graphics, **92**, **205–208**
  naming, 207–208
  overview of, 92, 203, 211
  selecting export destination, 208

selecting file type, 206–207
selecting graphics to export, 205–206
Graphics Exporter
  exiting, 211
  opening, 204, *204*
  overview of, 203–204
graphics libraries, **209–211**
  to files, 210–211
  to printer, 209–210
lists, **261**
**extensions for imported graphics**, 194
**Extra Features dialog box**, 161, *161*
**Extras menu**, **91–92**, 138

**F**

**File menu**, **56–70**, **102**. *See also* menus
  Exit command, 70
  in Help, 102
  New command, 57
  Open command, 57–61, *58*, *59*, *60*
  overview of, 56–57
  Preferences command, 64–66
  Preview command, 69
  Print command, 66–68
  Printer Setup command, 69
  Revert to Saved command, 63
  Save As command, 63
  Save command, 61–62, *61*
  Send command, 140
**file name extensions**, for imported graphics, 194
**files**. *See also* projects
  exporting graphics libraries to, 210–211
**Find Options dialog box**, in Help, 101
**Find Setup Wizard dialog box**, in Help, 99, *99*
**finding**. *See also* searching

backdrops for greeting cards, 9–10, *10*
files for importing, 195–196
Help topics, 100–102
**Flip tool**, 48
**flipping**
  objects, **48**, **83**
  printouts for transfer designs, 68, 294
**fonts**, changing, 14–15
**framing**
  objects, **48–49**, *49*, 80
  text boxes, 26–27
**full installation options**, 301–302

**G**

**games**, 268–270, *269*
**General tab**, Preferences dialog box, 64–65
**gift ideas**, **118**, **271–278**. *See also* Idea Guide
  bookmarks, 118
  calendars, 277–278
  gift certificates, 272–273, *274*
  labels, 272, *273*, 277
  money envelopes, 274–275, *275*
  recipe cards, 276–277, *276*
  wrapping paper, 118
**graphics**, **169–191**. *See also* backdrops; placeholders
  adding
    to greeting cards, **20–22**, *21*, 26
    to seals, 187–189, *188*, *189*
  bitmap files
    importing, 194, 196
    printing problems, 295
  borders, **180–186**. *See also* Smart Graphics
    adding custom borders to projects, 186
    creating, 181–183, *181*, *182*, *183*

mini-borders versus certificate borders, 180
saving custom borders, 186
selecting border graphics, 183–185, *185*
deleting from graphics libraries, 161, 166
editing, 76
exporting, **92**, 92, **205–208**
naming, 207–208
overview of, 92, 203, 211
selecting export destination, 208
selecting file type, 206–207
selecting graphics to export, 205–206
importing, **194–197**
color graphics, 196
file types and file extensions, 194
finding available files, 195–196
importing graphics, 194–195, *195*
saving projects and importing into other projects, 196–197, *197*
importing photos, **130**, **197–201**
brightness and sharpness settings, 200
cropping, 196, 199–200
file types and file extensions, 194
overview of, 130
Photo Accessories library, 201
previewing, 198, *198*
Print Shop photos, 197–198, *198*
resizing, 200
resolution settings, 199
overview of, 169, 191
renaming, 166
resizing with Pointer tool, 35–37
seals, **187–191**
adding graphics, 187–189, *188*, *189*
adding text, 189–190

saving custom seals, 190–191
starting, 187, *188*
Smart Graphics, **91**, **169–180**. *See also* borders
initial caps, 171–176, *171*
naming, 180
numbers, 176–178, *177*
opening Smart Graphics dialog box, 91, 170–171, *170*
overview of, 91, 169
timepieces, 178–180, *179*
types of, **150–151**
**Graphics Browser, 151, 153–160**
opening, 151
overview of, 20–21, *21*
searching libraries, **153–160**
by category keywords, 157
with multiple keywords, 157–159, *158*
with project text, 159–160
starting searches, 153–156, *154*, *156*
**Graphics Exporter**
exiting, 211
opening, 204, *204*
overview of, 203–204
**graphics libraries, 149–167**
backdrop libraries, 150, 151
Custom Libraries command in Extras menu, 92
editing, **164–167**
deleting graphics, 161, 166
deleting libraries, 167
editing libraries, 165–167
preparing to edit, 164–165, *165*
renaming graphics, 166
exporting, **209–211**
to files, 210–211
to printer, 209–210
layout libraries, 150

merging, **160–164**
  merging libraries, 163–164
  overview of, 160–161
  preparing to merge, 161–163, *161, 162*
overview of, 149–150, 167
Photo Accessories library, 201
searching, **8–10, 20–21, 151, 153–160**
  for backdrops, 8–10, *10*
  by category keywords, 157
  with multiple keywords, 157–159, *158*
  opening Graphics Browser, 151
  overview of, 20–21, *21*
  with project text, 159–160
  starting searches, 153–156, *154, 156*
types of, 150–153
**greeting cards**, **3–28**. *See also* online greetings
3-D greeting cards, **278–279**, *279*
back of card, **25–28**
  framing text boxes, 26–27
  selecting graphics, 26
  selecting layouts, 25
backdrops, **8–11**, 22–23. *See also* graphics
  finding, 9–10, *10*
  previewing, 10–11
  selecting for front, 8–9, *8*
  selecting for inside, 22–23
creating, **113–116**
customizing ready-made cards versus creating from scratch, 5
graphics
  adding to front, **20–22**, *21*, 26
  selecting for back, 26
headlines, **14–16, 24–25**
  changing fonts, 14–15
  creating, 14

creating text effects, 15–16, *16*
for inside of card, 24–25
inside contents, **22–25**
  adding text, 24–25, *25*
  previewing layouts, 24
  selecting backdrops, 22–23
  selecting layouts, 23–24
layouts
  previewing inside layout, 24
  selecting for back, 25
  selecting for front, 7, 12–13, *12, 13*
  selecting for inside, 23–24
moving objects, **19–20**
overview of, 3, 27, *28*
searching backdrop libraries, 8–10, *10*, 20–21, *21*
selecting
  layouts, 7, 12–13, *12, 13*, 23–24, 25
  orientation, 6–7, *7*
  project type, 4
  size, 6, *6*
starting, 4–5, *5*
text, **17–19, 24–27**. *See also* headlines
  adding to inside, 24–25, *25*
  changing text color, 18–19
  creating text effects for headlines, 15–16, *16*
  editing, 17
  entering, 18
  framing text boxes, 26–27

## H

**Halloween decorations**, 283–284
**Hand tool**, 40, *41*
**hardware requirements**, **299–300**
**headlines**, **226–232**. *See also* text
  adding, 14, 77–79
  changing text attributes, **228–229**

creating outlines, shadows, and
blends, 15–16, *16*, 78, **230–232**,
*230*
editing banner headlines, 77
in greeting cards, **14–16**, **24–25**
changing fonts, 14–15
creating, 14
creating text effects, 15–16, *16*
for inside of card, 24–25
opening Headline dialog box,
226–227, *227*
selecting headline shape, **229–230**,
*229*
sizing, 37–38, 227
title blocks, **232–233**, *233*
**Help**, **92–93**, **95–106**
Contents button, 96, 99
in dialog boxes, 105
Find Options dialog box, 101
Find Setup Wizard dialog box, 99, *99*
Index dialog box, 101
main Help screen, **96–98**
overview of, 96–97, *96*
using Help chapters, 98
using Help screen links, 97–98
menus, **92–93**, **102–105**
Bookmark menu, 103–104
Edit menu, 102–103
File menu, 102
Help menu, 92–93, 105
Options menu, 104–105
overview of, 95–96, 105–106
searching, 100–102
setting up, 99, *99*
**hiding**. *See also* displaying
backdrops, 91
Navigation Toolbar, 91
placeholders, 91
toolbars, 91

**holiday ideas**, **278–284**. *See also* Idea
Guide
3-D greeting cards, 278–279, *279*
count-down calendars, 282, *283*
Halloween decorations, 283–284
paper chains, 280–282, *281*
stickers, 284
tree ornaments, 279–280, *280*

## I

**Idea Art specialty papers**, 306
**Idea Guide**, **263–287**
customizing ideas, **285–286**, *286*
gift ideas, **118**, **271–278**
bookmarks, 118
calendars, 277–278
gift certificates, 272–273, *274*
labels, 272, *273*, 277
money envelopes, 274–275, *275*
recipe cards, 276–277, *276*
wrapping paper, 118
holiday ideas, **278–284**
3-D greeting cards, 278–279, *279*
count-down calendars, 282, *283*
Halloween decorations, 283–284
paper chains, 280–282, *281*
stickers, 284
tree ornaments, 279–280, *280*
overview of, 263–264, *264*, 287
party ideas, **265–271**
bracelets, 271
games, 268–270, *269*
invitations, 265–266, *266*
masks, 270
place cards, 267, *268*
table runners, 266, *267*
starting, 264, *264*
**importing**, **130**, **193–201**
graphics, **194–197**

color graphics, 196
file types and file extensions, 194
finding available files, 195–196
importing graphics, 194–195, *195*
saving projects and importing into
other projects, 196–197, *197*
imported bitmap printing problems,
295
lists, **260–261**
photos, **130, 197–201**
brightness and sharpness settings,
200
cropping, 196, 199–200
file types and file extensions, 194
overview of, 130
Photo Accessories library, 201
previewing, 198, *198*
Print Shop photos, 197–198, *198*
resizing, 200
resolution settings, 199
**Index dialog box**, in Help, 101
**initial caps, 171–176**, *171*
**inserting.** *See* **adding; entering**
**installing Print Shop Ensemble,**
**300–303.** *See also* adding
custom installation options, 302–303
full installation options, 301–302
typical installation options, 300–301
**Internet**
accessing Print Shop Connection
Web page, 144
connecting to, 92, **138–140,** *139*
setting up Internet connections,
**137–140,** *139,* 141–142
**invitations,** 265–266, *266*
**Item Selector tool,** 51–54

**J**

**JPEG files,** 194, 196

**K**

**keyboard shortcuts,** 56. *See also* Ctrl
key; Shift key
**keywords,** searching graphics libraries
by, 157
**Kodak Photo CD files,** 194

**L**

**labels**
Avery labels and specialty papers, 305
creating, **127–129**
gift labels, 272, *273,* 277
printing, 291–292, *292*
**layouts**
changing, **86**
for greeting cards
previewing inside layout, 24
selecting for back, 25
selecting for front, 7, 12–13, *12, 13*
selecting for inside, 23–24
layout libraries, 150
orientation
selecting, 110–111
selecting for greeting cards, 6–7, *7*
selecting, 111–113, *113*
**letterhead,** 121–122
**linking objects,** 38
**links,** in Help, 97–98
**lists, 92, 245–262, 291**
accessing, 92
creating, **246–253**
address lists, 246–250, *247*
custom lists, 246, 250–253, *251*
editing, **253**
exporting, **261**
importing, **260–261**
merging into projects, **254–258**
overview of, 254–256, *255*
selecting lists to merge, 256

selecting merge fields, 256–257,
    *258*
overview of, 245–246, 262
printing, **258–260**, *260*, 291
**locking objects**, **83**

## M

**masks for parties**, 270
**memory**
    photo resolution and, 199
    printing problems and, 295
**menus**, **55–93**, **102–105**
    Edit menu, **70–75**, **102–103**
        Copy command, 72
        Cut command, 71
        Delete command, 73
        Duplicate command, 73–75
        in Help, 102–103
        Paste command, 72–73
        Select All command, 74–75
        Undo command, 70–71
    Extras menu, **91–92**, 138
    File menu, **56–70**, **102**
        Exit command, 70
        in Help, 102
        New command, 57
        Open command, 57–61, *58, 59, 60*
        overview of, 56–57
        Preferences command, 64–66
        Preview command, 69
        Print command, 66–68
        Printer Setup command, 69
        Revert to Saved command, 63
        Save As command, 63
        Save command, 61–62, *61*
    in Help, **92–93**, **102–105**
        Bookmark menu, 103–104
        Edit menu, 102–103
        File menu, 102

Help menu, 92–93, 105
        Options menu, 104–105
    keyboard shortcuts, 56
    Object menu, **75–84**
        Add command, 75–76
        Align commands, 83–84
        Edit command, 76–77
        Flip command, 83
        Frame command, 80
        Lock and Unlock commands, 83
        Order commands, 80–81
        Rotate command, 82
        Scale command, 81–82
        Shadow command, 79–80
    overview of, 55–56, 93
    Project menu, **84–90**
        Banner Length command, 86–88
        Change Backdrop command, 85
        Change Layout command, 86
        Page Blend command, 88–90
        project-specific commands, 90
    View menu, **90–91**
**merge printing lists**, 258–260, *260*,
    291
**merging**
    graphics libraries, **160–164**
        merging libraries, 163–164
        overview of, 160–161
        preparing to merge, 161–163, *161,
        162*
    lists into projects, **254–258**
        overview of, 254–256, *255*
        selecting lists to merge, 256
        selecting merge fields, 256–257,
        *258*
**mini-borders**, 180
**modems**, 137–138
**modifying.** *See* **changing; editing**
**money envelopes**, 274–275, *275*

moving. *See also* cutting and pasting
   documents in windows, 40, *41*
   objects
      on greeting cards, 19–20
      multiple objects, 35
      overview of, 34
      with Pointer tool, 19, 34–35
   Standard Toolbar, 32–33

**N**

name lists. *See* lists
**naming**
   exported graphics, 207–208
   renaming graphics, 166
   renaming projects, 63
   Smart Graphics, 180
**Navigation Toolbar**, displaying or |
   hiding, 91
**New command**, File menu, 57
**notepads**, 121–122
**numbers**, Smart Graphics for, **176–178**,
   *177*

**O**

**Object menu**, **75–84**. *See also* menus
   Add command, 75–76, 77–79
   Align commands, 83–84
   Edit command, 76–77
   Flip command, 83
   Frame command, 80
   Lock and Unlock commands, 83
   Order commands, 80–81
   Rotate command, 82
   Scale command, 81–82
   Shadow command, 79–80
**objects**. *See also* placeholders
   adding, 75–76, 77–79
   adding with placeholders, 44, *45*
   adding shadows, 79–80

   aligning, **83–84**
   changing color or shading, 51–54
   coloring, 51–54
   cutting, copying, and pasting, **71–73**
   deleting, **46–47**, 73
   duplicating, **73–74**
   editing, **76–79**
      adding headlines, 77–79
      editing banner headlines, 77
      editing graphics, 76
   flipping, **48**, **83**
   framing, **48–49**, *49*, 80
   linking, 38
   locking and unlocking, **83**
   moving
      on greeting cards, 19–20
      multiple objects, 35
      with Pointer tool, 19, 34–35
      single objects, 34
   rotating, **38–39**, **82**
   scaling, **81–82**
   selecting
      all objects, 74–75
      for color changes, 51–52
   shading, 51–54
**online greetings**, **135–145**. *See also*
   greeting cards
   accessing Print Shop Connection
      Web page, 144
   creating, **136**, *137*
   overview of, 135–136, 144–145
   sending
      as attachments, 142–143
      overview of, 136–138, **140–142**,
      *141*
   setting up Internet connections,
      137–140, *139*, 141–142
   viewing, **143**

**Open dialog box, 57–61**
Description box, 60–61, *60*
finding files, 58–60
opening projects, 57–58
previewing projects, 57–58, *58*, *59*
**opening**
Edit Text dialog box, 221, *221*
existing projects, 57–61, *58*, *59*, *60*
Graphics Browser, 151
Headline dialog box, 226–227, *227*
Print Shop Ensemble, 4
Smart Graphics dialog box, 91, 170–171, *170*
**Options menu**, in Help, 104–105
**Order commands**, Object menu, 80–81
**orientation**
selecting, 110–111
selecting for greeting cards, 6–7, *7*
**ornaments for Christmas trees**, 279–282, *280*, *281*
**outlines for headlines**, 15–16, *16*, 78, **230–232**, *230*

**P**

**Page Blend option**, Item Selector tool, 54
**Page option**, Item Selector tool, 54
**page orientation**
selecting, 110–111
selecting for greeting cards, 6–7, *7*
**paper chains**, 280–282, *281*
**paper sources, 305–307**
**partial printouts**, 295
**party ideas, 265–271.** *See also* Idea Guide
bracelets, 271
games, 268–270, *269*
invitations, 265–266, *266*
masks, 270
place cards, 267, *268*

table runners, 266, *267*
**pasting.** *See* **copying and pasting; cutting and pasting**
**PCD files**, 194, 196
**Photo CD files**, 194
**Photo Projects**, creating, **129–131**
**photos, importing, 130, 197–201.** *See also* graphics
brightness and sharpness settings, 200
cropping, 196, 199–200
file types and file extensions, 194
overview of, 130
Photo Accessories library, 201
previewing, 198, *198*
Print Shop photos, 197–198, *198*
resizing, 200
resolution settings, 199
**place cards**, 267, *268*
**placeholders, 42–46**
adding objects with, 44, *45*
customizing, 45–46
defined, **42–44**
displaying and hiding, 91
**Pointer tool, 19, 34–38.** *See also* Standard Toolbar
Ctrl key + Pointer tool, 36–37
linking objects, 38
moving objects, 19, 34–35
resizing graphics, 35–37
resizing headlines or text blocks, 37–38
Shift key + Pointer tool, 35
**postcards**, 122–123
**posters**, creating, **116–118**
**Preferences dialog box**, overview of, 64–66
**Prepare Your Message dialog box**, 140–141, *141*

**previewing**
  backdrops, 10–11
  layouts, 24
  photos for importing, 198, *198*
  projects, 69
  ready-made projects, 58
**Print command**, File menu, 66–68
**Print Shop Ensemble III**
  electronic registration, **303–304**
  exiting, 70
  hardware and software requirements,
    299–300
  installing, **300–303**
    custom installation options,
      302–303
    full installation options, 301–302
    typical installation options,
      300–301
  opening, 4
  Print Shop photos, 197–198, *198*
  uninstalling, **304**
**Print tab**, Preferences dialog box, 65
**printers**
  exporting graphics libraries to,
    209–210
  setting up, 69
**printing**, **289–296**
  banners, 290–291
  business cards, 292–293
  with drag and drop, 67
  envelopes, 293–294, *293*
  graphics libraries, 209–210
  labels, 291–292, *292*
  lists, 258–260, *260*, 291
  overview of, 289–290, 296
  transfer designs, 68, 294
  troubleshooting, **294–295**
**Project menu**, **84–90**. *See also* menus
  Banner Length command, 86–88
  Change Backdrop command, 85

Change Layout command, 86
Page Blend command, 88–90
project-specific commands, 90
**projects, 107–133**. *See also* greeting
  cards; Idea Guide; online greetings;
  signs
adding borders, 186
common design elements, **108–113**
  customizing ready-made projects,
    108–110
  selecting backdrops, 111, *112*
  selecting layouts, 111–113, *113*
  selecting orientation, 110–111
  selecting paths, 108–110
  starting from scratch, 110
covering parts of, **131–132**
creating, **113–131**, **136**
  banners, 118–120
  calendars, 123–127, *124, 126*
  certificates, 120–121
  greeting cards, 113–116
  labels, 127–129
  online greetings, 136, *137*
  Photo Projects, 129–131
  signs and posters, 30–31, 68,
    116–118, 294
  stationery, 121–123
merging lists into, **254–258**
  overview of, 254–256, *255*
  selecting lists to merge, 256
  selecting merge fields, 256–257,
    *258*
opening, **57–61**, *58, 59, 60*
overview of, 107–108, 132–133
previewing, **69**
ready-made projects
  customizing, 108–110
  overview of, 5, 31
  previewing, 58
renaming, 63

reverting to last saved version, 63
saving, 61–63
saving and importing into other projects, 196–197, *197*
selecting, 74–75
selecting project type, 4
starting, 57
types of, **107–108**

### Q

**Queblo specialty papers**, 307
**quitting Print Shop Ensemble**, 70
**quotes and verses**, **241–244**, *242*

### R

**ready-made projects**. *See also* projects
customizing, 5, 108–110
overview of, 31
previewing, 58
**recipe cards**, 276–277, *276*
**Redo command**, Edit menu, 71
**Redo tool**, 50
**registering Print Shop Ensemble**, **303–304**
**renaming**. *See also* naming
graphics, 166
projects, 63
**resizing**
graphics with Pointer tool, 35–37
headlines, 37–38, 227
photos, 200
text blocks, 37–38
**resolution settings**
for photos, 199
and printing problems, 295
**Revert to Saved command**, File menu, 63
**rotating objects**, **38–39**, **82**
**runners for party tables**, 266, *267*

### S

**Save As command**, File menu, 63
**Save command**, File menu, 61–62, *61*
**saving**
borders, 186
projects, 61–63
projects and importing into other projects, 196–197, *197*
seals, 190–191
**scaling objects**, 81–82
**screen links**, in Help, 97–98
**scroll bars**, 40
**seals**, **187–191**. *See also* graphics
adding graphics, 187–189, *188*, *189*
adding text, 189–190
saving custom seals, 190–191
starting, 187, *188*
**searching**. *See also* finding
backdrop libraries, 8–10, *10*, 20–21, *21*
graphics libraries, **8–10**, **20–21**, **151**, **153–160**
for backdrops, 8–10, *10*
by category keywords, 157
with multiple keywords, 157–159, *158*
opening Graphics Browser, 151
overview of, 20–21, *21*
with project text, 159–160
starting searches, 153–156, *154*, *156*
Help, **100–102**
**Select All command**, Edit menu, 74–75
**Select List Type command**, Extras menu, 92
**Select a Path dialog box**, 5
**Select a Seal Center dialog box**, 187, *188*
**Select a Seal Edge dialog box**, 187–189, *189*

**Select a Timepiece dialog box**, 178–180, *179*

**selecting**

Add Objects tool type, 41–42

all objects, 74–75

backdrops

for greeting card front, 8–9, *8*

for greeting card inside, 22–23

overview of, 111, *112*

border graphics, 183–185, *185*

destination for exported graphics, 208

file type for exported graphics, 206–207

graphics

to export, 205–206

for greeting cards, 20–22, *21*, 26

layouts

for greeting cards, 25

overview of, 111–113, *113*

objects for color changes, 51–52

orientation

for greeting cards, 6–7, *7*

overview of, 110–111

paths, 108–110

project type, 4

projects, 74–75

ready-made projects versus starting from scratch, 108–110

signature block type, 234–235

size of greeting cards, 6, *6*

text attributes

for headlines, 228–229

for signature blocks, 235–236, *235*

for text blocks, 222–224

**Selection tool**, 33

**Send Backward and Send to Back commands**, Object menu, 80–81

**Send command**, File menu, 140

**sending online greetings**

as attachments, 142–143

overview of, 136–138, **140–142**, *141*

**setting up**

Help, 99, *99*

Internet connections, 137–140, *139*, 141–142

printers, 69

Web browsers, 138–140, *139*

**shading objects**, 51–54

**shadows**

adding to objects, 79–80

for headlines, 15–16, *16*, 78, **230–232**, *230*

**sharpness settings**, for imported photos, 200

**Shift key**. *See also* Ctrl key; shortcut keys

+ Pointer tool, 35

+ Rotate tool, 39

**shortcut keys**, 56. *See also* Ctrl key; Shift key

**showing.** *See* **displaying**

**signature blocks**, **234–238**. *See also* text

adding text, 236

inserting autographs, 236–238

selecting block type, 234–235

selecting text attributes, 235–236, *235*

**signs**

creating, 30–31, **116–118**

Flip Printout for Transfer Design option, 68, 294

**size**, selecting size of greeting cards, 6, *6*

**sizing**

graphics with Pointer tool, 35–37

headlines, 37–38, 227

photos, 200

text blocks, 37–38

**slow printing**, 295

**Smart Graphics, 91, 169–180.** *See also*
   graphics
   borders, **180–186**
      adding custom borders to projects,
         186
      creating, 181–183, *181, 182, 183*
      mini-borders versus certificate
         borders, 180
      saving custom borders, 186
      selecting border graphics, 183–185,
         *185*
   initial caps, **171–176,** *171*
   naming, 180
   numbers, **176–178,** *177*
   opening Smart Graphics dialog box,
      91, 170–171, *170*
   overview of, 91, 169
   timepieces, **178–180,** *179*
**Smart Graphics command,** Extras
   menu, 91
**software requirements, 299–300**
**special effects for headlines,** 15–16,
   *16,* 78, **230–232,** *230*
**specialty papers, 305–307**
**Spell Check, 216–218,** *218*
**Standard Toolbar, 29–54.** *See also*
   toolbars
   Add Objects tool, **41–46**
      adding objects with placeholders,
         44, *45*
      Ctrl key + Add Objects tool, 45–46
      customizing placeholders, 45–46
      placeholders defined, **42–44**
      selecting type of, 41–42
   Color Selector tool, 51–54
   Delete tool, 46–47
   Flip tool, 48
   Frame tool, 48–49, *49*
   Hand tool, 40, *41*
   Item Selector tool, 51–54

   moving, 32–33
   overview of, 29, 33–34, *33*
   placing next to Text Toolbar, 33
   Pointer tool, **19, 34–38**
      Ctrl key + Pointer tool, 36–37
      linking objects, 38
      moving objects, 19, 34–35
      resizing graphics, 35–37
      resizing headlines or text blocks,
         37–38
      Selection tool and, 33
      Shift key + Pointer tool, 35
   Redo tool, 50
   Rotate tool, 38–39
   Shading Selector tool, 51–54
   Undo tool, 47, 50
   Zoom tool, 40–41, *41,* 46, *47*
**Start From Scratch option,** Select a
   Path dialog box, 5
**starting**
   greeting cards, 4–5, *5*
   Idea Guide, 264, *264*
   projects, 57
   seals, 187, *188*
**stationery, 121–123**
**stickers,** 284

**T**

**table runners,** 266, *267*
**text, 215–226.** *See also* headlines
   adding
      to seals, 189–190
      to signature blocks, 236
      to word balloons, 240–241, *240*
   changing fonts, 14–15
   editing text blocks, **37–38, 221–226**
      opening Edit Text dialog box, 221,
         *221*
      resizing, 37–38
      selecting text attributes, 222–224

with Text Toolbar, 224–226
in greeting cards, **17–19**, **24–27**
   adding to inside, 24–25, *25*
   changing text color, 18–19
   creating text effects for headlines,
      15–16, *16*
   editing, 17
   entering, 18
   framing text boxes, 26–27
quotes and verses, **241–244**, *242*
searching graphics libraries with
   project text, 159–160
signature blocks, **234–238**
   adding text, 236
   inserting autographs, 236–238
   selecting block type, 234–235
   selecting text attributes, 235–236,
      *235*
Spell Check, **216–218**, *218*
Thesaurus, **218–221**, *219*
title blocks, **232–233**, *233*
types of, 215–216, *216*
word balloons, **238–241**
   adding text, 240–241, *240*
   creating, 239–240
   types of, 238, *239*
**text effects for headlines**, 15–16, *16*,
   78, **230–232**, *230*
**Text Toolbar**, 33, 224–226
**Thesaurus**, **218–221**, *219*
**3-D greeting cards**, **278–279**, *279*
**TIFF files**, 194, 196
**timepieces**, **178–180**, *179*
**title blocks**, **232–233**, *233*
**toolbars**. *See also* Standard Toolbar
   Text Toolbar, 33, 224–226
   toolbar options, 91
**transfer designs**, printing, 68, 294

**tree ornaments**, 279–280, *280*
**troubleshooting printing**, **294–295**
**typical installation options**, 300–301

## U

**Undo command**, Edit menu, 70–71
**Undo tool**, 47, 50
**uninstalling Print Shop Ensemble**,
   304
**unlocking objects**, 83

## V

**verses**, **241–244**, *242*
**View menu**, **90–91**
**viewing.** *See* **displaying**

## W

**watches**, **178–180**, *179*
**watermarked paper**, 120–121
**Web browsers**, 138–140, *139*
**Windows Metafiles (.wmf)**, 194, 196
**Wizards**, Find Setup Wizard in Help,
   99, *99*
**word balloons**, **238–241**. *See also* text
   adding text, 240–241, *240*
   creating, 239–240
   types of, 238, *239*
**World Wide Web.** *See* **Internet**
**wrapping paper**, 118

## Z

**Zoom commands**, in View menu, 90
**Zoom tool**, 40–41, *41*, 46, *47*